INTERNATIONAL LAW AND THE USE OF
BY NATIONAL LIBERATION MOVEME

International Law
AND THE
Use of Force
BY
National Liberation Movements

HEATHER A. WILSON

CLARENDON PRESS · OXFORD

Oxford University Press, Walton Street, Oxford OX2 6DP
Oxford New York Toronto
Delhi Bombay Calcutta Madras Karachi
Petaling Jaya Singapore Hong Kong Tokyo
Nairobi Dar es Salaam Cape Town
Melbourne Auckland
and associated companies in
Berlin Ibadan

Oxford is a trade mark of Oxford University Press

Published in the United States
by Oxford University Press, New York

First published 1988,
First issued as a paperback 1990

British Library Cataloguing in Publication Data
Wilson, Heather A.
International law and the use of force by
national liberation movements
1. War (International law)
2. National liberation movements
I. Title   341.6'3   JX4511
ISBN 0–19–825662–0

Library of Congress Cataloging in Publication Data
Wilson, Heather A.
International law and the use of force by national
liberation movements.
Rev. version of author's thesis (Ph.D.)—Oxford
University, 1985.
Bibliography: p. Includes index.
1. War (International law)   2. National liberation
movements.   3. Self-determination, National.   4. War
victims—Legal status, laws, etc.   I. Title.
JX4511.W56   1988   341.6   87–31398
ISBN 0–19–825662–0

Printed and bound in
Great Britain by Biddles Ltd
Guildford and King's Lynn

In memory of my grandparents
George and Annie Wilson

Acknowledgements

This study is a revised version of a thesis submitted in 1985 for the degree of Doctor of Philosophy at Oxford University.

I began the project in 1982 under the guidance of Professor Hedley Bull, then Montague Burton Professor of International Relations at Oxford. His premature death in the spring of 1985 was deeply felt by many. I can only hope that the keen insight and rigorous habits of thought which he expected from his students no less than himself are reflected in these pages.

Highest thanks must also go to Professor Adam Roberts, then of St Antony's and now of Balliol College, whose supervision and advice during my last year at Oxford was invaluable.

This project would not have been possible without the generous financial support of the Rhodes Trustees, who have my thanks in return, as does the staff of the Bodleian Law Library and the staff and members of Jesus College, Oxford. I am also indebted to Dr Jiri Toman of the Henry Dunant Institute who helped me to find information in Geneva which I could not have found alone.

H.

Contents

PART III: RIGHT AUTHORITY

PART IV: PROTECTION OF VICTIMS

List of Principal Abbreviations

AFDI	*Annuaire français de droit international*
AJIL	*American Journal of International Law*
Am. Univ. LR	*American University Law Review*
ANC	African National Congress
ANCZ	African National Council of Zimbabwe
ANLF	Afghan National Liberation Front
ASIL	*Proceedings of the American Society of International Law*
BYIL	*British Yearbook of International Law*
CDDH	Diplomatic Conference on the Reaffirmation and Development of International Law Applicable in Armed Conflicts, Geneva 1974–7
ECA	Economic Commission for Africa
EPLF	Eritrean People's Liberation Front
FFI	French Forces of the Interior
FLCS	Front de Libération de la Côte des Somalis (Afars and Issas)
FLN	National Liberation Front of Algeria
FNLA	Frente Naçional de Libertação de Angola
FRELIMO	Mozambique Liberation Front
GAOR	*General Assembly Official Records*
GPRA	Gouvernement Provisoire de la République Algérienne
GRAE	Angolan Revolutionary Government in Exile
ICJ Rep.	International Court of Justice Reports
ICJ Review	*Review of the International Commission of Jurists*
ICLQ	*International and Comparative Law Quarterly*
ICRC	International Committee of the Red Cross
IRRC	*International Review of the Red Cross*
ISA	Islamic Society of Afghanistan
KNP	Polish National Committee (World War I)
LNTS	*League of Nations Treaty Series*
LQR	*Law Quarterly Review*
MNLF	Moro National Liberation Front (Philippines)
MOLINACO	Mouvement de Libération Nationale des Comores
MPLA	Movimento Popular de Libertação de Angola
NYIL	*Netherlands Yearbook of International Law*
OAU	Organization of African Unity
OR	*Official Records of the Diplomatic Conference on the Reaffirmation and Development of International Humanitarian Law Applicable in Armed Conflicts, Geneva (1974–1977)*
PAC	Panafricanist Congress (South Africa)

PAIGC	Partido Africano da Independencia da Guine e Cabo Verde (Guinea-Bissau and Cape Verde)
PFLP	Popular Front for the Liberation of Palestine
PFLP—GC	Popular Front for the Liberation of Palestine—General Command
PLO	Palestine Liberation Organization
Polisario	Frente Popular para la Liberación de Saguia el-Hamra y Rio de Oro (Western Sahara)
SC	Security Council
SCOR	*Security Council Official Records*
SDAR	Saharan Arab Democratic Republic (Western Sahara)
SPUP	Seychelles People's United Party
SR	*Summary Records*
SWAPO	South West Africa People's Organization (Namibia)
UNGA	United Nations General Assembly
UNITA	União Naçional para a Independência Total de Angola
ZANU	Zimbabwe African National Union
ZAPU	Zimbabwe African People's Union

Introduction

When Grotius wrote, 'Public war ought not to be waged except by the authority of him who holds the sovereign power,' he was explaining an idea that was already several hundred years old.[1] By the dawn of the twentieth century it was axiomatic that only States could wage war. There were different words for other forms of violence: insurrection, civil unrest, piracy, or rebellion. At most, there was 'civil war', where the adjective modified the idea and the law which applied.

In the last forty years ideas about what constitutes war and which entities in international politics may wage war have changed. The rapid dissolution of colonial empires and the growing consensus that there is a right of peoples to self-determination has led some to conclude that wars of national liberation are international wars, even though they are not inter-State wars. The purpose of this book is to explore how these changes in ideas have affected the law of war.

For most purposes, the law of war may be divided into two parts: the legitimacy of the resort to force, and the rules governing the conduct of hostilities. In legal texts these two branches are often called *jus ad bellum* and *jus in bello*, respectively. Both branches of the law, as they apply to wars of national liberation, have changed considerably in the last forty years and since 1960 in particular. This book examines these developments. More specifically, I have sought answers to four questions:

(i) What is traditional international law on the authority to use force and the humanitarian law of war?

(ii) How has self-determination developed from a principle of political thought to a right in international law?

(iii) Is the use of force by national liberation movements to secure the right of their peoples to self-determination legitimate?

(iv) To what extent does the humanitarian law of armed conflict apply in wars of national liberation?

The four parts of this book examine these questions in succession.

Defining 'national liberation movement' is a challenging task. The label, as popularly used, is imprecise. In the twentieth century, a war of national liberation may be described as a conflict waged by a non-State community

---

[1] Hugo Grotius, *De Jure Belli Ac Pacis*, i.3.5[7].

against an established government to secure the right of the people of that community to self-determination.[2] This definition begs the very difficult question of exactly who the 'self' is that has this right to self-determination. A large part of Chapter 4 discusses this problem.

The idea that national liberation movements may legitimately use force in world politics has profound implications for our conception of international society. It has long been accepted that international relations is not solely the study of relationships between States. More recently, it has been generally accepted that international law applies to entities other than States. Despite these incursions on the role of States in some aspects of international relations, until recently the use of force remained the exclusive province of the sovereign State. To suggest that entities other than States may legitimately use force, and that international wars need not necessarily be inter-State wars, challenges conventional ideas about the nature of international society.

Since 1945 the movement against colonialism, driven primarily by the newly independent States, has challenged some of our ideas about international law. One part of the law which has been affected by these changes is the law of war. There have been a number of studies on the rise of nationalism in the Third World, self-determination, and decolonization, but none concentrate on the right of self-determination and its effect on the law of war. It is here, in this small and as yet uncharted area, where I hope to make my contribution.

---

[2] See N. Ronzitti, 'Resort to Force in Wars of National Liberation', in *Current Problems of International Law: Essays on UN Law and on the Law of Armed Conflict*, ed. Antonio Cassese (Milan: Dott. A. Guiffre, 1975), 319; N. Ronzitti, 'Wars of National Liberation: A Legal Definition', *Italian Yb. IL*, 1 (1975), 197; Richard A. Falk, 'Intervention and National Liberation', in *Intervention in World Politics*, ed. Hedley Bull (Oxford: Clarendon Press, 1984), 123; Georges Abi-Saab, 'Wars of National Liberation and the Laws of War', *Annales d'Études internationales*, 3 (1972), 93; A. Belkherroubi, 'Essai sur une théorie juridique des mouvements de libération nationale', *Rev. égyptienne de droit international*, 28 (1972), 22; Michel Veuthey, *Guérilla et droit humanitaire* (Geneva: Institut Henry-Dunant, 1976), 11; S. N. MacFarlane, 'The Idea of National Liberation' (D.Phil. Thesis, Oxford, 1982), 364.

PART I

The Law

I

The Concept of Law

1.1 Introductory

This chapter addresses certain fundamental questions about the nature and function of international law without which this book would be incomplete. It is not intended to be an exhaustive examination of the definition, sources, and subjects of international law, as these questions have been amply discussed elsewhere. Rather, its purpose is to state briefly the assumptions on which later arguments are based, and to examine in a general way certain issues which are central to the discussion which follows. More specifically, this chapter addresses three questions:

 (i) What is international law?
 (ii) Who are the subjects of international law?
 (iii) What are the sources of international law?

1.2 Definitions and Subjects

The absence of legislative bodies and clear judicial authority makes international law more difficult to define than municipal law. Yet a book which professes to address an issue of international law must clearly state from the outset what is meant by that term.

In 1876 Lord Russell of Killowen defined international law as 'the sum of the rules or usages which civilized states have agreed shall be binding upon them in their dealings with one another.'[1] Leading scholars in the first half of the twentieth century gave similar definitions,[2] as did the Permanent Court of International Justice in the *Lotus* case in 1927 which held that

[1] Lord Russell of Killowen in his address at Saratoga in 1876, quoted in *West Rand Central Gold Mining Co.* v. *The King* [1905] 2 KB 391.
[2] See T. J. Lawrence, *The Principles of International Law*, 7th edn. (London: Macmillan, 1923), 1; William E. Hall, *A Treatise on International Law*, 8th edn. (Oxford: Clarendon Press, 1924), 1; Henry Wheaton, *Elements of International Law*, reproduction of the edn. of 1866 by Richard Henry Dana, ed. George G. Wilson (Oxford: Clarendon Press, 1936), 20; Green H. Hackworth, *Digest of International Law* (Washington: GPO, 1940), i. 1; L. Oppenheim, *International Law: A Treatise*, 6th edn. (London: Longman, Green and Co., 1940), i. 4–5; Charles C. Hyde, *International Law Chiefly as Interpreted and Applied by the United States*, 2nd rev. edn. (Boston: Little, Brown and Co., 1947), i. 1; J. Hatschek, *An Outline of International Law* (London: Bell and Sons, 1930), 3; J. L. Brierly, *The Law of Nations: An Introduction to the International Law of Peace*, 1st edn. (Oxford: Clarendon

International law governs relations between independent States. The rules of law binding upon States therefore emanate from their own free will as expressed in conventions or by usages generally accepted as expressing principles of law and established in order to regulate the relations between these coexisting independent communities or with a view to the achievement of common aims.[3]

Accepting these definitions would ignore many of the most controversial issues of the post-World War II era by including only States as the actors in the system. There is a growing tendency to acknowledge that the sovereign State is not the only recipient of rights and duties under international law. It is more correct to regard international law as a body of rules which binds States and other agents in world politics in their relations with one another and is considered to have the status of law.[4] That entities other than States can be subjects of international law is not a universally accepted idea, and exactly what entities do have this status is an even more controversial topic.

Hall notes that primarily international law governs the relations of independent States, but 'to a limited extent . . . it may also govern the relations of certain communities of analogous character'.[5] Schwarzenberger, Friedmann, and Lawrence share similar views, the latter noting that the subjects of international law are sovereign States 'and those other political bodies which, though lacking many of the attributes of sovereign states, possess some to such an extent as to make them real, but imperfect, international persons.'[6]

Whereas these scholars tend to define subjects of international law as States and certain unusual exceptions, there are others who go further in opening up the realm of reasonable subjects of the law of nations. Notable among them is Sir Hersch Lauterpacht. In his view,

International practice shows that persons and bodies other than States are often made subjects of international rights and duties; that such developments are not inconsistent with the structure of international law and that in each particular case the question whether a person or a body is a subject of international law must be

Press, 1928), 1; H. W. Bowen, *International Law* (London: G. P. Putnam's Sons, 1896), 1; cf. Georg Schwarzenberger, *A Manual of International Law*, 1st edn. (London: Stevens and Sons, 1947), 1.

[3] *S. S. Lotus* (*France* v. *Turkey*), Permanent Court of International Justice, Judgment 9, 7 Sept. 1927, Ser. A, No. 10, 18.

[4] See Hedley Bull, *The Anarchical Society* (London: Macmillan, 1977), 127; Hersch Lauterpacht, 'The Subjects of the Law of Nations', *LQR*, 63 (1947), 444; Rosalyn Higgins, *The Development of International Law Through the Political Organs of the United Nations* (London: Oxford Univ. Press, 1963), 1; Philip Jessup, *A Modern Law of Nations* (n.p.: Archon Books, 1968), 17; J. G. Castel, *International Law: Chiefly as Interpreted and Applied in Canada*, 3rd edn. (Toronto: Butterworth, 1976), 1.

[5] Hall, 17.

[6] Lawrence, 69; Schwarzenberger, *Manual*, 48; Wolfgang Friedmann, *The Changing Structure of International Law* (London: Stevens and Sons, 1964), 213–15.

answered in a pragmatic manner by reference to actual experience and to the reason of the law as distinguished from the preconceived notion as to who can be the subjects of international law.[7]

The status of organizations in international law is less controversial than the assumption of rights and duties by individuals or groups of individuals. Although it may be argued that some international organizations derive their authority from the sovereignty of their members who have signed agreements creating these organizations, the authority of some organizations goes beyond the consent of the sovereign States participating and the organization can take on a character in international law separate from its members. The International Court in the *Reparation* case held:

The subjects of law in any legal system are not necessarily identical in their nature or in the extent of their rights, and their nature depends upon the needs of the community. Throughout its history, the development of international law has been influenced by the requirements of international life, and the progressive increase in the collective activities of States has already given rise to instances of action upon the international plane by certain entities which are not States.[8]

Referring to the United Nations, the Court concluded that

[T]he Organization is an international person. That is not the same thing as saying that it is a State, which it certainly is not, or that its legal personality and rights and duties are the same as those of a State. . . . [I]t is a subject of international law and capable of possessing international rights and duties, and . . . it has capacity to maintain its rights by bringing international claims.[9]

The list of organizations which have legal personality is extensive and would include, for example, the European Economic Community, the various specialized agencies of the United Nations like the International Labor Organization, the Organization of African Unity, and the Organization of American States.

All of these examples are bodies composed of or created by States. When one moves beyond international organizations to consider individuals and groups not created by States and in some cases not even sanctioned by them, the issue becomes more controversial.

Early examples of individual responsibility like the laws against piracy and the prosecution of war criminals are often disregarded as 'weak samples of special pleading'.[10] But recent developments in human rights

[7] Lauterpacht, *LQR*, 444.

[8] *Reparation for Injuries Suffered in the Service of the United Nations*, Advisory Opinion (1949) 4 ICJ Rep. 178–9.

[9] Ibid. 179.

[10] Georg Schwarzenberger, 'The Protection of Human Rights in British State Practice', in *Current Legal Problems*, vol. i. ed. George W. Keeton and Georg Schwarzenberger (London: Stevens and Sons, 1948), 153; see also Herbert W. Briggs (ed.), *The Law of Nations: Cases, Documents and Notes*, 2nd edn. (London: Stevens and Sons, 1953), 96.

law, particularly as concerns the rights of the individual against his own
State, provide evidence that individuals can be subjects of international
law, at least in some limited sense. Philip Jessup, one of the most
renowned advocates of the individual in international law, wrote:

The place of the individual in international law was recognized by the Rome
Convention of 1950 which established the European Court of Human Rights and
the European Commission of Human Rights. The eleven States which have
submitted declarations under Articles 46 and 25 of that Convention have conferred
jurisdiction on the Court and on the Commission and thereby admit that
individuals have legal rights—'human rights'—which they may invoke in an
appropriate forum even against the States of which they are nationals.[11]

The development of human rights law is delicately intertwined with both
the right of peoples to self-determination and the recent developments in
the humanitarian law of armed conflict which are central to this book.[12]
Here, I raise the issue only to demonstrate that individuals *can* have rights
and duties under international law.

While it is possible for organizations and individuals to be subjects of
international law, States remain the dominant agents in world politics and
the dominant actors in international law. This dominance has led some
theorists to distinguish 'subjects' of the law from 'objects' of the law,
suggesting that although entities other than States may have rights and
duties in international law, these rights are conferred upon them by States
and, presumably, may be taken away by States.[13] Certainly different legal
persons have different rights and duties and it is quite common and often
helpful to compare different types of actors with States—the archetypal
legal person. But the theoretical distinction between 'subjects' and
'objects' of the law is not entirely helpful as it can deflect emphasis from
the objective examination of the facts of international practice.

The concept of international law as a body of rules binding only States is
no longer valid. That it is *possible* for non-State entities to be the recipients
of rights and duties under international law does not explain how a non-
State entity may gain such status, nor how their rights and duties differ
from those of States. No arbitrary definition precludes national liberation
movements from assuming status in international law when the requirements of international life necessitate their inclusion.

1.3 Sources of International Law

In contrast with municipal law, in international society there is no

---

[11.] Jessup, p. vii.
[12] See Chapters 4 and 7.
[13] See Georg Schwarzenberger and E. D. Brown, *A Manual of International Law*, 6th edn.
(Abingdon: Professional Books, 1976), 42.

legislative body capable of making international law. The absence of formal mechanisms for law creation enhances the importance of material sources which are '*evidences* of the existence of consensus among states concerning particular rules or practices'.[14]

Article 38 of the Statute of the International Court of Justice was written for the functional application of the Court, but is generally recognized as an authoritative statement of the sources of the law even though the Article itself does not use the word 'sources'.[15] Article 38 provides:

1. The Court, whose function is to decide in accordance with international law such disputes as are submitted to it, shall apply:

(*a*) international conventions, whether general or particular, establishing rules expressly recognized by the contesting states;

(*b*) international custom, as evidence of a general practice accepted as law;

(*c*) the general principles of law recognized by civilized nations;

(*d*) subject to the provisions of Article 59, judicial decisions and the teachings of the most highly qualified publicists of the various nations, as subsidiary means for the determination of rules of law.

2. This provision shall not prejudice the power of the Court to decide a case *ex aequo et bono*, if the parties agree thereto.[16]

Although the Article does not explicitly list the subparagraphs in descending order of importance beyond stating that judicial decisions and the teachings of publicists are subsidiary, there is some importance attached to the order of the rules to be applied. In one draft of the Statute the word 'successively' appeared, and source (*a*) is based on mutually accepted obligation of the parties which is stronger evidence of the law than general practice accepted as law, source (*b*).[17] It would be wrong to apply this hierarchy strictly, however.[18] For example, a peremptory norm of general international law, or *jus cogens*, voids a conflicting treaty. Such a norm can only be modified by a subsequent norm of general international law.[19]

[14] Ian Brownlie, *Principles of Public International Law*, 3rd edn. (Oxford: Clarendon Press, 1979), 2.

[15] Brownlie, *Principles*, 3; Castel, 10; D. W. Greig, *International Law*, 2nd edn. (London: Butterworth, 1976), 5–6.

[16] Article 59 of the Statute provides that a 'decision of the Court has no binding force except between the parties and in respect of that particular case'.

[17] Brownlie, *Principles*, 3.

[18] Judge Quintana in the *Right of Passage Case*, dissenting opinion (1960) ICJ Rep., 90, stated, '[A]lthough I agree that [Article 38] establishes a legal order of precedence in the application of sources of international law, I consider that the validity of a general principle may take the place of international custom, and the existence of international custom the place of a treaty.'

[19] See Article 53 of the 1969 Vienna Convention on the Law of Treaties; Brownlie, *Principles*, 512; Allan Rosas, *The Legal Status of Prisoners of War: A Study in International Humanitarian Law Applicable in Armed Conflicts* (Helsinki: Suomalainen Tiedeakatemia, 1976), 96–104; cf. Georg Schwarzenberger, 'International Jus cogens?', *Texas LR*, 43 (1965), 476.

1.4 The UN and the Development of Law

The role of the United Nations in the development and interpretation of international law is controversial. Resolutions passed by the United Nations General Assembly are not generally recognized as a source of international law. Article 25 of the UN Charter obligates members 'to accept and carry out decisions of the Security Council', but there is no similar provision for recommendations of the General Assembly. Most writers agree that, except for resolutions relating to the internal functioning of the organization, resolutions of the General Assembly do not create binding obligations in positive law *per se*.[20] Apart from the adherence to Article 25, 'acceptance at San Francisco of the principle of majority decision in the political organs of the United Nations did not also mean acceptance of their decisions as being binding upon individual member States'.[21] This does not mean that resolutions of the General Assembly have no legal effect, although the degree of their effect is disputed.

One of the most generous interpretations of the legal effect of General Assembly resolutions is provided by F. B. Sloan, who points out that the Charter, though not obligating members to abide by Assembly resolutions, does not specifically negate the obligation to accept its recommendations. 'The most that can be said is that there is a presumption against these recommendations possessing binding legal force. But it is not an irrebuttable presumption . . . '[22] Not irrebuttable perhaps, but few would find the rebuttal convincing.

A more moderate comment on the legal effect of Assembly resolutions was presented by Professor Lauterpacht in the *South-west Africa Voting Procedure Case*:

Whatever may be the content of the recommendation and whatever may be the nature and circumstances of the majority by which it has been reached, it is nevertheless a legal act of the principal organ of the United Nations which Members of the United Nations are under a duty to treat with a degree of respect appropriate to a Resolution of the General Assembly.[23]

---

[20] F. B. Sloan, 'The Binding Force of a "Recommendation" of the General Assembly of the United Nations', *BYIL*, 25 (1948), 31; U. O. Umozurike, 'Self-determination in International Law' (D.Phil. Thesis, Oxford, 1969), 120; Michla Pomerance, *Self-determination in Law and Practice: The New Doctrine in the United Nations* (London: Martinus Nijhoff, 1982), 64–5; C. J. R. Dugard, 'The Organisation of African Unity and Colonialism: An Inquiry into the Plea of Self-defence as a Justification for the Use of Force in the Eradication of Colonialism', *ICLQ* , 16 (1967), 174–5; Brownlie, *Principles,* 14–15 and 695–8; Higgins, *Development,* 4–5; G. Arangio-Ruiz, 'The Normative Role of the General Assembly of the United Nations and the Declaration of Principles of Friendly Relations', *Recueil des cours*, 137 (1972-III), 448–9; Francis Vallat, 'The Competence of the UN General Assembly', *Recueil des cours*, 97 (1959-II), 231.

[21] H. Waldock, 'General Course on Public International Law', *Recueil des cours*, 106 (1962-II), 25.

[22] Sloan, 191.

[23] *South-West Africa Voting Procedure Case* (1955) ICJ Rep., 20.

Richard Falk has called this the 'quasi-legislative competence of the General Assembly'.[24]

There is considerable opposition to this interpretation of the legal effect of resolutions of the United Nations. Michla Pomerance argues quite strongly that the 'Charter provisions regarding the Assembly's powers are clear and unequivocal; only a formal amendment can transform the Assembly into more than a deliberative organ adopting resolutions with generally hortatory effect; . . . [C]onsensus has not yet become a recognized process of law-creation.'[25]

Another more generally accepted argument on the legal effect of Assembly resolutions is that while creating no prima facie legal obligation, they are evidence of customary international law.[26] Embattled diplomats have argued that an impotent gesture made more loudly and more often does not a law make. In other words, annual passage of General Assembly resolutions, even by large majorities, does not give those resolutions the force of law. This defence overlooks the fact that international custom is to be deduced from the practice of States, and the United Nations, as a nearly universal organization of States, is an appropriate body to look to for developments in the law. As James Crawford explains:

State practice is just as much State practice when it occurs in the 'parliamentary' context of the General Assembly as in more traditional diplomatic forms. The practice of States in assenting to and acting upon law-declaring resolutions may be of considerable probative importance, in particular where that practice achieves reasonable consistency over a period of time.[27]

Not all resolutions of the General Assembly should be given the same weight, however. Those specifically addressing problems of international law are obviously more indicative of the legal position of States. Similarly, resolutions passed unanimously or with large majorities are stronger evidence of a consensus concerning particular rules than those passed with large segments of dissenting opinion.

If this body of resolutions as a whole provides evidence of customary international law, at what point does this repeated practice harden into a rule of law? Rosalyn Higgins admits there is no easy answer, but suggests

[24] R. A. Falk, 'On the Quasi-legislative Competence of the General Assembly', *AJIL*, 60 (1966), 782.

[25] Pomerance, 64.

[26] Friedmann, 139–40; Arangio-Ruiz, 470; Kenneth Bailey, 'Making International Law in the UN', *ASIL*, 61 (1967), 236; Gabriella Rosner Lande, 'The Changing Effectiveness of General Assembly Resolutions', in *The United Nations*, vol. iii of *The Strategy of World Order*, ed. Richard A. Falk and Saul H. Mendlovitz (New York: World Law Fund, 1966), 230; Castel, 27; Pomerance, 64; Brownlie, *Principles*, 695; Sloan, 18; Higgins, *Development*, 2; James Crawford, *The Creation of States in International Law* (Oxford: Clarendon Press, 1979), 91.

[27] Crawford, 91.

that it is 'at the point at which states regard themselves as legally bound by the practice'.[28] One is ultimately forced to return to the definition of international law: a rule becomes law when it is considered to be obligatory, and to have the status of law. Since the development of customary law often takes considerable time, there may be a period when resolutions of the Assembly have moral force, but no legal force.[29] This period of transition when there is no strong consensus on the status of the law is an inherent difficulty in a primitive legal system like international law which depends upon custom as one of its sources.

In addition to providing evidence of custom, resolutions of the General Assembly may also be the basis of subsequent treaties ratified by States. In this case the legal effect is derived from the treaty, not the resolution.[30]

To summarize the legal effect of resolutions of the General Assembly, the following points may be made:

1. With the exception of resolutions regarding internal organizational matters, resolutions of the General Assembly are not binding *per se*, although those rules of general international law which they may embody are binding on member States, with or without the resolution.

2. Resolutions of the General Assembly may have a quasi-legislative force which requires member States to give them consideration in good faith.

3. Resolutions of the General Assembly are evidence of customary international law subject to the proviso that the extent to which legal matters were considered must be examined before much weight is given to them.

4. Resolutions of the General Assembly can serve as the basis of subsequent treaties acceded to by States.

[28] Higgins, *Development*, 6.
[29] Higgins, *Development*, 7.
[30] Sloan, 18.

2

The Authority to Use Force
in International Law

2.1 Introductory

The purpose of this chapter is to examine who had the authority to use force in international law before the idea that identifiable peoples have a right to self-determination gained much support.

Ideas change slowly and inconsistently. It would be misleading and somewhat simplistic to suggest that there is a clear division between traditional legal principles and some new law or a particular date on which these new rules came into force. Indeed, some scholars maintain that the traditional rules are still the law today, while others claim that the new ideas have always been part of the law. Both views have an element of truth. Changes in ideas about legitimate authority are part of the seamless evolution of ideas. This chapter tries to describe a reference point without minimizing the complexity of international law.

2.2 The Concept of Legitimacy

There is some confusion about the word 'legitimacy' and the related phrases 'legitimate authority' and 'the legitimate use of force'. The words are used for two different but related ideas and the distinction between the two is often intentionally blurred. In its strictest sense 'legitimate' means 'in compliance with the law'. International law accepts the use of force by some agents in world politics in particular circumstances. The agents which have this legal right to decide to resort to the use of force may be called legitimate authorities.

In a broader sense 'legitimate' is not restricted to that which is specifically sanctioned by law. This more common use of the word implies that an action is just or right irrespective of its legality. There are many issues in international relations which international law simply does not regulate. There are also situations in international politics, as in domestic politics, where an act may be 'just' in a moral sense, but not in compliance with the law. In this context 'legitimate' implies moral approval but not necessarily legal approval.

The ambiguity of this word is particularly evident in the United Nations, where ambiguity often hides lack of consensus. At times members are commenting on the status of the law, at others they are supporting the justness of a cause, and often they are doing both. So when members support 'the legitimate right of peoples to self-determination' or 'the legitimate representative of a people' or 'the legitimacy of a struggle for independence' one cannot hastily conclude that this is an unequivocal statement of a country's position on a question of international law.

As might be expected, these two concepts of legitimacy—that an action is in compliance with the law and that it is morally just or right—often overlap. This is particularly important in a system like international law, where obligation is deduced from the will of each individual member of the international community and the collective will may evolve into a customary rule of international law.

Because of this curious interrelationship between these two concepts of legitimacy, one must consider both 'legitimacy' meaning collective if ill-defined moral approbation, and 'legitimacy' meaning compliance with international law, even though the final aim is to determine what the *law* is and how it has changed. The point at which a moral principle supported by States hardens into a rule of law is not easily determined. The difficulty or even impossibility of scientific precision denies neither the existence of the transition nor the importance of its outcome.

2.3 The Authority to Use Force in World Politics

In the thirteenth century Thomas Aquinas wrote, '[I]n order that a war may be just three things are necessary. In the first place, the authority of the prince, by whose order the war is undertaken . . . '[1] His second and third requirements for a just war, like those of his predecessor St Augustine, bishop of Hippo, were a just cause and right intent. Most contemporary analyses of *jus ad bellum* concentrate on the second and, to a lesser degree, the third requirements while presuming compliance with the first. Volumes on the prohibition of the use of force by States fill shelves, but few mention, and still fewer question, 'the authority of the prince' as a prerequisite for the legitimate use of force. This is not surprising given the rise of the sovereign State to a pinnacle of power unknown to Aquinas, yet tacitly assumed by twentieth-century jurists.

The idea that only a sovereign State may legitimately wage war seems a foregone conclusion in the twentieth century. Indeed, this requirement is

[1] St Thomas Aquinas, *Summa theologica*, Secunda secundae, Quaestio XL (de bello), quoted in John Eppstein, *The Catholic Tradition of the Law of Nations* (London: Burns, Oates and Washbourne, 1935), 83.

often included in the definition of war. But it was not always this way. From the middle of the twelfth century with the publication of Gratian's *Decretum* to the late thirteenth century when Thomas Aquinas wrote his *Summa theologica* one can find in the writing of the canonists a particularly contentious debate on right authority in just war theory. The canon lawyers writing in this period were by no means unanimous in their opinions about which agents could legitimately resort to the use of force. At one extreme were those who limited the right to wage war to the emperor and, in some special cases, the pope. At the other extreme, men like William of Rennes suggested that every feudal lord who had no superior within the feudal hierarchy had the authority to use force. There was a third position, propounded by Pope Innocent IV, among others, which limited the waging of a just war to those authorities having no superior over them.[2]

The canonists of this period were particularly occupied with the idea of legitimate authority. They were living in a period of tremendous social and political change. By the middle of the thirteenth century the decentralized system of feudalism was losing ground and the canonists turned their attention to a new world of consolidated city-states and growing kingdoms.[3] The main problem for canon lawyers was to define who among existing political leaders had the authority to initiate war.[4] Similarly, the rebirth of the just war debate in recent years was caused by changes in society: the rapid decolonization of much of the world, the widespread occurrence of civil conflicts, the use of extremes of violence, and the desire of identifiable peoples to join international society as independent sovereign States.

From the sixteenth century sovereigns gradually asserted a monopoly on the use of violence both within their borders and against other sovereigns. By the close of the nineteenth century, sovereignty and the exclusive right to wage war were characteristics of a State so strongly established that to suggest otherwise would have seemed preposterous.[5]

The growth of a system of sovereign nation-states since the sixteenth century makes the contemporary controversy different from that of the thirteenth century. This States system, though often criticized for its apparent inability to control the use of force between States, has been fairly successful in controlling violence within the borders of States. This security and order which the canonists did not have no doubt influences the

---

[2] Frederick H. Russell, *The Just War in the Middle Ages* (Cambridge: Cambridge Univ. Press, 1975), 298–9; James Turner Johnson, *Just War Tradition and the Restraint of War* (Princeton: Princeton Univ. Press, 1981), 163; James Turner Johnson, *Ideology, Reason, and the Limitation of War* (Princeton: Princeton Univ. Press, 1975).

[3] Russell, 258.

[4] Turner Johnson, *Just War*, 151.

[5] See Daoud L. Khairallah, *Insurrection Under International Law* (Beirut: Lebanese University, 1973), 98.

way in which we think about these problems and the degree to which we take social order for granted.

Thus, although it is widely accepted in contemporary society that only sovereign States may wage war, it was not always so, nor is it inevitable that it must be so.

In traditional international law there was a very clear distinction between international armed conflicts and non-international armed conflicts. In the last three decades, with the growth of the idea of an international right of self-determination and the prevalence of 'internationalized' civil wars, the distinction between the two has not been as clear. Nevertheless, in this section the two types of conflict have been separated to explain the two quite separate approaches to what used to be seen as two very different types of conflict.

2.31 Legitimate Authority in International Armed Conflict

Restrictions on the use of force by States are largely a development of the twentieth century.[6] It was at the dawn of this century that William Edward Hall wrote:

As international law is destitute of any judicial or administrative machinery, it leaves states, which think themselves aggrieved, and which have exhausted all peaceable methods of obtaining satisfaction, to exact redress for themselves by force. It thus recognizes war as a permitted mode of giving effect to its decisions.

He continued,

International law has consequently no alternative but to accept war, independently of the justice of its origin, as a relation which the parties to it may set up if they choose, and to busy itself only in regulating the effects of the relation. Hence both parties to every war are regarded as being in an identical legal position, and consequently as being possessed of equal rights.[7]

But parties to the conflict were in an identical legal position and possessed of equal rights only in so far as they were exercising the sovereign rights of States. By the twentieth century the authority to wage war was firmly restricted to sovereign States. Subordinate princes could not legitimately wage war with their own private armies. Pirates were criminals under international law. Even the very powerful trading companies, like the British South Africa Company, which governed large areas of the globe during the period of colonization were

---

[6] See Ian Brownlie, *International Law and the Use of Force by States* (Oxford: Clarendon Press, 1963).

[7] W. E. Hall, *A Treatise on International Law*, 8th edn. (Oxford: Clarendon Press, 1904), 60–1.

ultimately responsible to the sovereign and their authority could be withdrawn by vote of Parliament.[8]

In the first half of the twentieth century the State retained its monopoly of violence although legal limitations on the use of force by States grew. Evidence of this reaffirmation can be found in the late nineteenth- and early twentieth-century codification of the humanitarian law of war.

The laws of armed conflict are firmly rooted in customary law, but in the late nineteenth and early twentieth centuries these customary principles began to be codified. It is important when examining the provisions of these agreements not to confuse the authority to resort to force (*jus ad bellum*) with the rules applicable in armed conflicts (*jus in bello*). The latter are intended to mitigate the horrors of war, not to sanction the use of force by any authority, as is often noted in the preambles of these conventions. However, the entities included in these agreements, particularly the clauses on the qualifications of legitimate combatants, and the field of application provisions, are an indication of who was considered to have the authority to resort to force in the first place.

The 1907 Hague Convention IV and the Regulations attached to it replaced the 1899 Hague Convention II. It did not codify all the laws and customs of war as evidenced by the Martens Clause in the Preamble, but that which it did codify was recognized by the International Military Tribunal at Nuremberg as declaratory of customary international law.[9]

Hague Convention IV regulated the actions of States. Although some contemporary scholars have suggested that Hague Convention IV could be applied to national liberation movements as 'Powers',[10] there is little doubt that the intention of the signatories was to regulate the actions of States or, at most, resistance movements representing an occupied State.

Article 2 of the Convention provides that the Regulations 'do not apply except between contracting Powers, and then only if all the belligerents are parties to the Convention'. Article 6 provides that 'Non-signatory Powers may adhere to the present Convention', and Article 9 that copies of the Convention 'shall be sent, through the diplomatic channel, to the Powers which have been invited to the Second Peace Conference'.[11] These clauses suggest that 'Powers',

---

[8] T.J. Lawrence, *The Principles of International Law*, 7th edn., rev. Percy H. Winfield (London: Macmillan, 1923), 68.

[9] Adam Roberts and Richard Guelff (eds.), *Documents on the Laws of War* (Oxford: Clarendon Press, 1982), 44. On 11 Dec. 1946 the UN General Assembly unanimously adopted Resolution 95 which affirmed 'the principles of international law recognized by the Charter of the Nuremberg Tribunal and the Judgement of the Tribunal'.

[10] Georges Abi-Saab, 'Wars of National Liberation and the Laws of War', *Annales d'Études internationales*, 3 (1972), 93–117.

[11] 1907 Hague Convention IV Respecting the Laws and Customs of War on Land, in Roberts and Guelff, 46–7. Unless otherwise noted, all documents cited on the law of war may be found in this collection.

like those who were invited to the conference, were States complete with diplomatic channels.

The Regulations themselves refer to acts of governments,[12] of States,[13] of countries,[14] and of nations.[15] The Regulations also refer to 'belligerents' or 'belligerent parties' or 'belligerent powers',[16] 'hostile parties' or 'hostile armies',[17] and simply 'parties',[18] all of which are not necessarily States. But the context in which these words are used, often in the same articles which refer explicitly to States or governments, suggests that the intention of the signatories was to regulate wars between States. 'Belligerent parties' or 'hostile parties' were undoubtedly considered to be States even if these phrases opened the door to progressive application to other entities in later years.

The Regulations did include militia and volunteer corps in the category of belligerents if they complied with the conditions of Article 1. The States present agreed that:

The laws, rights, and duties of war apply not only to armies but also to militia and volunteer corps fulfilling the following conditions:

1. To be commanded by a person responsible for his subordinates;
2. To have a fixed distinctive emblem recognizable at a distance;
3. To carry arms openly; and
4. To conduct their operations in accordance with the laws and customs of war.[19]

This Article, and Article 2 which includes participants in a *lévee en masse* as belligerents, were the same as Articles 9 and 10 of the unratified Brussels Declaration of 1874 with the exception of the addition of volunteer corps as well as militia in Article 1.

There was controversy over Articles 1 and 2 because they do not mention resistance in occupied territory. The Belgian delegate asked whether it was wise, 'in advance of war and for the case of war, expressly to legalize rights of a victor over the vanquished, and thus organize a *regime* of defeat'.[20] General Sir John Ardagh of Great Britain was more to the point. He proposed the addition of an Article providing, 'Nothing in this chapter shall be considered as tending to diminish or suppress the right which belongs to the population of an invaded country to patriotically oppose the most energetic resistance to the invaders by every legitimate

[12] Articles 4, 7, 10, 11, 12, 14, and 48.
[13] Articles 6, 8, 14, 16, 37, 39, 48, 53, 55, and 56.
[14] Articles 1, 16, 23, 24, and 43.
[15] Article 23.
[16] Articles 2, 3, 23, 36, 43, and 44.
[17] Articles 23, 29, 37, and 42.
[18] Articles 40 and 41.
[19] Article 1, 1907 Hague Regulations attached to Hague Convention IV.
[20] Mr Beernaert (Belgium), 6 June 1899, Report to the Conference from the Second Commission on the Laws and Customs of War on Land, in *The Reports to the Hague Conferences of 1899 and 1907*, ed. James B. Scott (Oxford: Clarendon Press, 1917), 139.

means'.[21] The German delegate disagreed most strongly with this proposal granting 'an unlimited right of defence'.[22]

To avoid paralysing disagreement on this fundamental point, Mr Martens of Russia proposed a declaration which was eventually included in the Preamble of the 1899 and 1907 Hague Convention IV. The Martens Clause provides,

Until a perfectly complete code of the laws of war is issued, the Conference thinks it right to declare that in cases not included in the present arrangement, populations and belligerents remain under the protection and empire of the principles of international law, as they result from the usages established between civilized nations, from the laws of humanity, and the requirements of the public conscience.

It is in this sense especially that Articles 1 and 2 adopted by the Conference must be understood.

The Belgian delegate then announced that, because of this declaration, his government could vote in favour of Articles 1 and 2, and the British delegate withdrew his motion.[23]

The Martens Clause was included as a compromise on the status of resistance groups in occupied territory. However, the subject of disagreement was only the status of those in the occupied territory of what used to be an independent State who used force against an occupying State. The conference did not concern itself with rebels within an existing State who, quite clearly, remained subject to the penalties of municipal law.

Thus, militia and volunteer corps referred to in Article 1 and resistance movements which might have had certain rights in customary law recognized in the Martens Clause were qualified belligerents only if they belonged to a party to the conflict: a State *de jure* or *de facto*.[24]

The French–Mexican Mixed Claims Commission upheld the inapplicability of the Hague Regulations to anything but inter-State conflicts in the *Jean-Baptiste Caire Case* (1929). In the opinion of the president, the responsibility of belligerents and the duty to make reparations applied only to international wars, and not to internal armed conflicts.[25]

---

[21] Ibid. 141.

[22] Colonel Gross von Schwarzhoff (Germany), ibid. 142.

[23] Ibid. 141–2.

[24] See Lawrence, 493; L. Nurick and R. W. Barrett, 'Legality of Guerrilla Forces Under the Laws of War', *AJIL*, 40 (1946), 567.

[25] *Estate of Jean-Baptiste Caire (France)* v. *United Mexican States* (1929) 5 Reports of International Arbitral Awards 528. In Report II of the *British Claims in the Spanish Zone of Morocco*, Judge Huber said that he was in favour of the *analogous* application of Hague Convention IV, obligating States to be responsible for acts committed by their armed forces, to internal conflicts. 'Sans doute', wrote the judge, 'cette convention [Hague Convention IV, 1907] n'est directement applicable à aucune des situations dont le rapport doit s'occuper, mais le principe qu'elle établit mérite d'être retenu également en ce qui concerne l'éventualité d'une action militaire en dehors de la guerre proprement dite.' 2 Reports of International Arbitral Awards 645.

Experience in World War II, when surviving governments were in exile and replaced by 'puppet' regimes while partisans continued to resist occupation, led governments to agree explicitly that resistance movements may be entitled to prisoner-of-war status even when operating in occupied territory. In the Third Geneva Convention of 1949, Relative to the Treatment of Prisoners of War, Article 4A(2) includes among those entitled to prisoner-of-war status:

Members of other militias and members of other volunteer corps, *including those of organized resistance movements*, belonging to a Party to the conflict and *operating in or outside their own territory, even if this territory is occupied*, provided that such militias or volunteer corps, including such organized resistance movements, fulfill the following conditions:

(a) that of being commanded by a person responsible for his subordinates;
(b) that of having a fixed distinctive sign recognizable at a distance;
(c) that of carrying arms openly;
(d) that of conducting their operations in accordance with the laws and customs of war.[26] (Emphasis supplied.)

The four requirements to be met by these belligerents are the same as those in the Hague Regulations for militia and volunteer corps. However, this Article does not extend the privileges of prisoner-of-war status to any militia which complies with subparagraphs (*a*) to (*d*). Only militias and volunteer corps belonging to a party to the conflict which had or has control of a territory are included in the scope of the Conventions. Article 4A(2) was drafted to remedy a problem of occupation, not national liberation.

There are situations in which belligerent occupation and wars of national liberation overlap. Namibia after the withdrawal of the mandate, Moroccan occupation of the Western Sahara, and Indonesian occupation of East Timor are arguable examples. But the provisions in the Article requiring that resistance movements belong to a party to the conflict and the territorial element suggest that it was not the intention of the drafters specifically to include wars of national liberation in the Convention. Jean Pictet described the motivation for Article 4(2) which confirms this view:

Many countries were occupied, armistices were concluded and alliances reversed. Some Governments ceased to be, others went into exile and yet others were brought to birth. Hence arose an abnormal and chaotic situation in which relations under international law became inextricably confused. In consequence, national groups continued to take an effective part in hostilities although not recognized as belligerents by their enemies, and members of such groups, fighting in more or less disciplined formations in occupied territory or outside their own country, were

[26] Article 4A(2), Geneva Convention Relative to the Treatment of Prisoners of War of 12 August 1949.

denied the status of combatant, regarded as 'francs-tireurs' and subjected to repressive measures.[27]

Article 2 of the same Conventions provides further evidence that, at least until 1949, States were considered to be the only legitimate authorities in international armed conflicts. The Article states:

In addition to the provisions which shall be implemented in peacetime, the present Convention shall apply to all cases of declared war or of any other armed conflict which may arise between two or more of the High Contracting Parties, even if the state of war is not recognized by one of them.[28]

This Article, particularly the clause which provides for the application of the Convention to any other armed conflict 'even if the state of war is not recognized', has been interpreted in more recent years, in conjunction with a liberal interpretation of Article 4A(2), to include wars of national liberation within the scope of the Conventions.[29] Without denying that the authoritative interpretation of treaties is important in the development of international law, there can be little doubt that this Article was included to ensure the application of the Conventions when *States* do not recognize a state of war as existing, and was not intended to include armed conflict with entities which were not States. Rather, this provision also arose from the experience of World War II. G. I. A. D. Draper explained that

The earlier Geneva Conventions were considered to apply only in case of war, either validly declared or recognized by either belligerent as amounting to a state of war in International Law. Thus, in a case where both contestants denied a state of war, the earlier Conventions were not legally applicable, e.g. in the case of the conflict between China and Japan in 1937.[30]

Pictet comments that 'any difference arising between two States and leading to the intervention of members of the armed forces is an armed conflict within the meaning of Article 2'.[31] Similarly, Draper notes that it 'is suggested that this phrase will cover any situation in which a difference between two States leads to the intervention of armed forces within the extended meaning conferred upon the latter term by Article 4 of the Prisoner of War Convention'.[32] Most obviously, Article 2 refers to 'High Contracting Parties', and only States could become parties to the Conventions.

At least until 1949, it appears that only States possessed the requisite

---

[27] Jean S. Pictet (ed.), *The Geneva Conventions of 12 August 1949: Commentary* (Geneva: ICRC, 1952), iii. 52.

[28] Article 2, para. 1 common to the Geneva Conventions of 1949.

[29] See Udo Wolf, 'Prisoner-of-war Status and the National Liberation Struggles', *International Review of Contemporary Law,* 1 (1984), 31–46.

[30] G. I. A. D. Draper, *The Red Cross Conventions* (London: Stevens and Sons, 1958), 10.

[31] Pictet, *Commentary*, iii. 23.

[32] Draper, *Red Cross*, 11.

authority to resort to the use of force against other States. Only their representatives were considered to be legitimate combatants and thereby immune from prosecution for their lawful acts of war. Those who used force, for whatever reason, and were not members of the armed forces, militia, or volunteer corps of a State, resistance movements complying with Article 4A(2) of the Geneva Conventions, or participants in a *levée en masse*, were subject to municipal criminal laws.

Finally, individuals or groups who used force against a State but did not qualify as legitimate combatants were criminals under municipal law but were not criminals in international law. Julius Stone summarized their position:

> While the matter may not even yet be free of doubt, it would seem almost certain that guerrillas, even when they are unprivileged belligerents, are (like spies) merely left by international law to punishment by the enemy States under its own law, or that of the occupied territory, and are not criminals under international law.[33]

Thus, historically, in international law national liberation movements were not authorities in their own right capable of resorting to the use of force in an international war. Only States had this capacity.

2.32 Legitimate Authority in Non-international Armed Conflict

Thus far I have considered only legitimate authority in international armed conflicts. It may seem unusual to devote so much time to explaining the authority to use force in international armed conflicts when wars of national liberation fit quite logically into the category of civil war. The growing consensus that self-determination is a right in international law which it is legitimate to remedy under international law made this necessary. This development, discussed below in Chapters 4 and 5, led to the characterization of wars of national liberation as international wars by definition. On the other hand, wars of national liberation had, and still have, many of the characteristics of civil war.

For the most part, traditional international law is silent on the use of force within the borders of States. Since, by the nineteenth century, international law was a body of rules governing relationships between States, violence within a State was considered beyond the bounds of international legal regulation.[34] Because international law neither condemns nor condones revolution within an established State, some claim

---

[33] Julius Stone, *The Legal Controls of International Conflict*, rev. edn. (Sydney: Maitland, 1959), 567.

[34] Evan Luard, 'Civil Conflicts in Modern International Relations', in *The International Regulation of Civil Wars*, ed. Evan Luard (London: Thames and Hudson, 1972), 19; Morris Greenspan, *The Modern Law of Land Warfare* (Los Angeles: Univ. of California Press, 1959), 619; Abi-Saab, *Annales*, 94; Quincy Wright, 'US Intervention in the Lebanon', *AJIL*, 53 (1959), 121; Erik Castren, *Civil War* (Helsinki: Suomalainen Tiedeakatemia, 1966), 19; Jean Pictet, *Humanitarian Law and the Protection of War Victims* (Leiden: Sijthoff, 1975), 55.

that there is a right of revolution. This idea, at least as old as the French Revolution, is somewhat misleading. There is no rule of international law prohibiting revolution, and, if a revolution succeeds, there is nothing in international law that prohibits the acceptance of the outcome even though it was attained by the use of force. To that extent, international law accepts revolution. Although this is sometimes characterized as a 'right', it can more accurately be described as passive ignorance of actions considered to be beyond the bounds of the law. There is no right of revolution and there is no prohibition of revolution as revolution itself has not been part of international law.

But international law has not been entirely silent on the use of force within the borders of States. Since it does accept the outcome of internal violence, the international community recognized certain levels of conflict at which rights and duties in international law are attained by groups opposed to a government in civil conflict.

These highly theoretical and often ignored series of steps gradually acknowledging the success of a rebellious movement were based on the military and political success of the movement and the degree to which it resembled a sovereign State. These general rules ascribing rights and duties to nascent States or governments took no account of the purpose of the rebellion, but only its outcome. In reality, these rules of international law were often ignored, and any discussion of them is bound to be somewhat artificial. Nevertheless, there were three categories of civil conflict with different legal consequences flowing from each: rebellion, insurgency, and belligerency. Rebellion is a sporadic challenge to the legitimate government. Insurgency and belligerency are higher on the continuum of ascending intensity and 'are intended to apply to situations of sustained conflict, [where there is] a serious challenge carried on through a considerable period of time over a wide space and involving large numbers of people within the society'.[35]

In a rebellion, internal disturbances such as riots, or isolated and sporadic acts of violence, the rebels have no rights or duties in international law. A third State might recognize that a rebellion exists, but under traditional international law a rebellion within the borders of a sovereign State is the exclusive concern of that State. Rebels may be punished under municipal law and there is no obligation to treat them as prisoners of war.[36] Traditional international law prohibits assistance to the rebels from third States on the grounds that this is unlawful intervention in the internal affairs of a State; aid to the recognized government fighting the

---

[35] Richard A. Falk, 'Janus Tormented: The International Law of Internal War', in *International Aspects of Civil Strife*, ed. James N. Rosenau (Princeton: Princeton Univ. Press, 1964), 197.

[36] Herbert W. Briggs (ed.), *The Law of Nations*, 2nd edn. (London: Stevens and Sons, 1953), 791.

rebels is permitted. Because rebels have no legal rights, and may not legitimately be assisted by outside powers, traditional international law clearly favours the established government in the case of rebellion, regardless of the cause for which the rebels are fighting.

The criteria for the recognition of insurgency are not clearly agreed upon.[37] Sir Hersch Lauterpacht asserted that

[A]ny attempt to lay down conditions of recognition of insurgency leads itself to misunderstanding. Recognition of insurgency creates a factual relation in that legal rights and duties as between insurgents and outside states exist only insofar as they are expressly conceded and agreed upon for reasons of convenience, of humanity or of economic interest.[38]

There seems to be general agreement that recognition of insurgency is recognition of a 'factual relation' or acknowledgement of the fact that an internal war exists.[39] Beyond that, there is little explanation of the characteristics of the 'fact'. There are no requirements for the degree of intensity of the violence, the extent of control over territory, the establishment of a quasi-governmental authority, or the conduct of operations in accordance with any humanitarian principles which would indicate recognition of insurgency is appropriate. Indeed, the only criterion for recognition, if one could call it that, is necessity. According to Starke, outside powers may enter into some contact with the insurgents to protect their nationals, their commercial interests, and their sea-borne trade.[40] One must conclude that, although traditional international law does not specify what characteristics rebels must have to be recognized as insurgents, they must have sufficient control over territory and sufficient military might for the interests of foreign States to be affected, giving rise to the necessity of some kind of relations with the insurgents. Yet, at the same time, the insurgents do not have the characteristics or qualifications of a belligerent. This is no more than saying that insurgents have characteristics between those of rebels and belligerents which require that other States have some form of limited relations with them.

There is slightly more agreement on what rights and duties insurgents assume under traditional international law. It is generally agreed that insurgents do not have the right to blockade ports, to visit or search foreign ships on the high seas, or to capture those vessels.[41] Insurgents may

[37] Greenspan, 619; Luard, 21.

[38] Hersch Lauterpacht, *Recognition in International Law* (Cambridge: Cambridge Univ. Press, 1947), 276–7.

[39] C. C. Hyde, *International Law Chiefly as Interpreted and Applied by the United States*, 2nd rev. edn. (Boston: Little, Brown and Co., 1947), 203; Greenspan, 619; Rosalyn Higgins, 'International Law and Civil Conflict', in *The International Regulation of Civil Wars*, ed. Evan Luard (London: Thames and Hudson, 1972), 170; Briggs, 1003.

[40] J. G. Starke, *An Introduction to International Law*, 5th edn. (London: Butterworth, 1963), 145.

[41] Lawrence, 332; Greenspan, 620; Briggs, 1003.

'prevent supplies from abroad destined for the legitimate government from entering the territory where the war is being waged',[42] and they may lawfully requisition property of foreigners and nationals.[43] As far as capacity to conclude agreements and relations with foreign powers is concerned, Briggs contends that the parent State still has 'responsibility for acts of insurgents which by due diligence it might have prevented'.[44] In other words, claims for foreign property destroyed can still be made of the legitimate government if that government could have prevented its loss. However, although the legitimate government ultimately represents the country, insurgents may enter into agreements on 'routine matters' and make arrangements for humanitarian protection through the International Committee of the Red Cross.[45]

There is least agreement among authors about the status of the combatants themselves. Hyde, Higgins, and Greenspan claim that recognition of insurgency means that the insurgents are 'contestants-at-law' and no longer merely law-breakers.[46] Recognition 'constitutes a belief by a foreign power that the insurgents should not be executed as rebels if captured'.[47] Briggs and Castren, on the other hand, maintain that only recognition of belligerency gives combatants the protection of international law and insurgents are still subject to the criminal law of the parent State.[48]

Finally, there is general agreement that the rights insurgents do have are limited ones and do not extend beyond the territorial limits of the State involved in an internal war.[49]

The criteria for recognition of belligerency are more precisely defined than those for insurgency. First, and generally agreed upon, there must be a widely spread armed conflict with the dimensions of a war;[50] second, the insurgents must control a substantial part of national territories;[51] and third, the interests of the recognizing State must be affected such that it is necessary that it take a position.[52] In addition Schwarzenberger, Higgins, and Luard maintain that the insurgents must conduct hostilities in accordance with the laws of war.[53]

---

[42] Greenspan, 620; see also Hyde, i. 203.

[43] Greenspan, 620.

[44] Briggs, 999.

[45] Castren, *Civil War*, 117.

[46] Hyde, i. 203; Higgins, 'Civil Conflict', 170; Greenspan, 620.

[47] Greenspan, 620.

[48] Briggs, 1000; Castren, *Civil War*, 97.

[49] Georg Schwarzenberger, *International Law*, vol. i (London: Stevens and Sons, 1968), 693.

[50] Hyde, i. 19; Lawrence, 329; Hackworth, i. 385; Schwarzenberger, *International Law*, ii. 708; Higgins, 'Civil Conflict', 170.

[51] Werner Levi, *Contemporary International Law: A Concise Introduction* (Boulder, Colo.: Westview Press, 1979), 71; Luard, 20; Higgins, 'Civil Conflict', 170.

[52] Lawrence, 329; Luard, 20; Higgins, 'Civil Conflict', 170; Hyde, i. 198.

[53] Schwarzenberger, *International Law*, ii. 708; Higgins, 'Civil Conflict', 170; Luard, 20.

Although these criteria for recognition of belligerency are much clearer than those for insurgency, there is still substantial room for interpretation. There is no precise meaning of a 'widespread conflict' or a 'substantial part' of national territories. It is not at all clear when recognition has become a 'practical necessity'. Thus, even though recognition of belligerency is sometimes referred to as a duty when the criteria for recognition are fulfilled, in reality, recognition of belligerency under traditional international law was largely discretionary.[54] However, certain judicial decisions have not relied upon recognition by third States to establish the belligerency of the parties to a conflict. In the *Prize Cases*[55] Judge Grier for the U.S. Supreme Court held:

As a civil war is never publicly proclaimed, *eo nomine* against insurgents, its actual existence is a fact in our domestic history which the court is bound to notice and to know.

The true test of its existence, as found in the writings of sages of the common law, may be thus summarily stated: 'When the regular course of justice is interrupted by revolt, rebellion or insurrection, so that the courts of justice cannot be kept open, civil war exists and hostilities may be prosecuted on the same footing as if those opposing the government were foreign enemies invading the land.'

The Court also held that

It is not the less a civil war, with belligerent parties in hostile array, because it may be called an 'insurrection' by one side, and the insurgents be considered as rebels or traitors. It is not necessary that the independence of the revolted province or State be acknowledged in order to constitute it a party belligerent in a war according to the law of nations.

At least with regard to reparation for damages caused, recognition of belligerency by the parent State or a foreign State involved in a dispute is not a prerequisite for application of the law of belligerency if the Court decides that the conditions for belligerent rights were met. This, of course, is cold comfort for insurgents who are denied the rights of belligerents and are considered rebels, traitors, or pirates.

Similarly, the parent State may decide for any number of reasons to extend certain belligerent rights without recognizing a state of belligerency. Such an action, not at all uncommon, avoids the political consequences of actually acknowledging that an armed conflict exists. Governments are usually very careful to state that their actions are purely humanitarian or expedient and do not constitute implicit recognition of belligerency.

Recognition of belligerency gives insurgents rights and duties in inter-

---

[54] Hackworth, i. 319; Luard, 20; J. W. Garner, 'Recognition of Belligerency', *AJIL*, 32 (1938), 111-13; Khairallah, 19; Abi-Saab, *Annales*, 94.
[55] *Prize Cases* (1862) 2 Black 635.

national law analogous to those of States. Harding wrote in a letter to Lord Malmesbury in 1858 on the insurrection in San Domingo that

Each 'de facto' Government engaged in a Civil War is 'prima facie' a regular Government in relation to those Foreign Nations, who remain Neutral, and is entitled, as such, to exercise complete Sovereign authority within the Territory actually in its power . . .[56]

Furthermore, a recognized belligerent has rights on the high seas with respect to foreign ships. In *The Three Friends* (1896) the Court held,

[T]he recognition of belligerency involves the rights of blockade, visitation, search and seizure of contraband articles on the high seas, and abandonment of claims for reparation on account of damages suffered by our citizens from the prevalence of warfare.[57]

The belligerent power is a lawful subject of international law, sufficiently analogous to a State to be given belligerent rights and be accorded the protection of the humanitarian law of war. It does not have all the rights of a State. Lawrence notes,

[O]n the other hand, its government cannot negotiate treaties, nor may it accredit diplomatic ministers. The intercourse it carries on with other powers must be informal and unofficial. It has no rights, no immunities, no claims, beyond those immediately connected with its war.[58]

Recognition of belligerency differs from recognition of a government. In 1937 Mr Anthony Eden, the British Foreign Secretary, noted:

Recognition of belligerency is, of course, quite distinct from recognizing any one to whom you give that right as being the legitimate Government of the Country. It has nothing to do with it. It is a conception simply concerned with granting rights of belligerency which are of convenience to the donor as much as they are to the recipients.[59]

In practice the traditional international law on recognition of insurgency and belligerency is more theoretical than real. Since World War I the recognition of belligerency has scarcely ever occurred, and not at all since World War II.[60] Even in the Spanish Civil War the insurgents were never recognized as belligerents, despite the fact that in 1936 the government of Spain blockaded the ports held by the insurgents, which by some accounts

---

[56] FO 83/2262, 14 Apr. 1858, quoted in H. A. Smith, *Great Britain and the Law of Nations*, vol. i (London: P. S. King and Son, 1932), 329.
[57] *The Three Friends* (1896) 166 US 1, quoted in Hackworth, i. 385.
[58] Lawrence, 64.
[59] Quoted in Starke, 147.
[60] Luard, 20.

could have been considered an implicit recognition of belligerency by the government of Spain.[61]

The important point here is what this international law of internal warfare means for the authority to use force in civil war. Even though the recognition of insurgency and belligerency fell into disuse, the underlying idea that the use of force within a State against the established government was initially a matter for municipal law did not. The use of force by elements opposed to an established government, for whatever cause, was neither condoned nor condemned by customary law. Recognition of belligerency and insurgency were ways for States to acknowledge a change in the factual situation after a rebellion had begun. The resort to the use of force in the first place remained a matter of self-help beyond the purview of international law.

In addition to customary international law relative to internal war, there are a limited number of relevant international conventions, including Article 3 common to the 1949 Geneva Conventions.[62] This Article provides for limited humanitarian protection in armed conflicts not of an international character, for 'persons taking no active part in the hostilities'. Soviet jurists in particular suggest Article 3 is evidence of the 'recognition as subjects of international law not only of States, but also of nations struggling for their independence'.[63] This argument is difficult to accept, particularly since Article 3 does not protect combatants and applies to armed conflicts 'not of an international character'. Furthermore, the parties to the Conventions were particularly wary of such an interpretation and included in the Article an unequivocal reservation that the 'application of the preceding provisions shall not affect the legal status of the Parties to the conflict'. As if this were not clear enough, the intention of the Diplomatic Conference of 1949 was further emphasized in Resolution 10. In its opinion, the existing rules of international law on the recognition by third States of the belligerency of parties to armed conflicts were not modified by the Geneva Conventions.[64] Article 3 does not prevent the established government from punishing rebels under municipal law, nor does it change their status in law.

The following propositions represent an attempt to summarize tra-

---

[61] Dietrich Schindler, 'State of War, Belligerency, Armed Conflict', in vol. i of *The New Humanitarian Law of Armed Conflict*, ed. Antonio Cassese (Naples: Editoriale Scientifica, 1979), 5.

[62] See Habana Convention of 20 Feb. 1928 on the Duties and Rights of States in the Event of Civil Strife and a 1957 Protocol to that Convention; and Article 19 of the 1954 Hague Convention on the Protection of Cultural Property in the Event of Armed Conflict.

[63] K. Krylov, 'K Obsuzhdeniyu Voprosov Teorii Mezhdunarodnogo Prava' (Concerning the Dimensions of Theories of International Law), *Sovetskoe Gosudarstvo I Pravo*, 7 (1954), 76, quoted in George G. Ginsburgs, ' "Wars of National Liberation" and the Modern Law of Nations: The Soviet Thesis', *Law and Contemporary Problems*, 29 (1964), 913.

[64] Jean S. Pictet, *Commentary*, vol. iv (Geneva: ICRC, 1958), 654.

ditional principles of international law on the authority to resort to the use of force.

1. Before the development of the idea that there is a right to self-determination there was a clear distinction in international law between international armed conflicts and non-international armed conflicts.

2. In the case of international armed conflicts the only authority which could legitimately resort to the use of force was a State.

3. Traditional rules of international law neither condemned nor condoned the use of force within national boundaries against an established government.

4. In a rebellion, the rebels were subject to municipal law and had no international rights or duties.

5. In the case of insurgency, the insurgents had limited rights and duties within the territory that they occupied.

6. In the case of belligerency, the belligerents had rights within their territory *and* the rights of belligerents with respect to third States.

7. The status of parties to an internal conflict was determined by their political and military success and not by the perceived righteousness of their efforts.

2.4 Intervention in Internal Conflicts

The growth of the idea that national liberation movements may legitimately use force in world politics encouraged the belief that a State not directly involved may legitimately assist national liberation movements fighting for self-determination. This section explains the law governing relationships between national liberation movements and outside States before this idea gained widespread support.

The rules of international law governing the relationship between outside States and the parties fighting a civil war are of practical importance to the parties involved. These rules are also indicative of the status of each party in international law and the perceived legitimacy of their activities.

In the case of rebellion, the prevailing view in international law has been that assisting the legitimate government is lawful and assisting the rebels is not.[65] According to James Garner, in the case of a rebellion,

---

[65] Briggs, 992; Rosalyn Higgins, *The Development of International Law Through the Political Organs of the United Nations* (London: Oxford Univ. Press, 1963), 173; Rosalyn Higgins, 'Internal War and International Law', in vol. iii of *The Future of the International Legal Order*. ed. C. E, Black and R. A. Falk (Princeton: Princeton Univ. Press, 1971), 94–5; Higgins, 'Civil Conflict', 172; Castren, *Civil War*, 117; Wolfgang Friedmann, 'Intervention, Civil War and the Role of International Law', *ASIL*, 59 (1965), 72.

There is no rule of international law which forbids the government of one state from rendering assistance to the established legitimate government of another state with a view of enabling it to suppress an insurrection against its authority. Whether it shall render such aid is entirely a matter of policy or expediency and raises no question of right or duty under international law. If assistance is rendered to the legitimate government it is not a case of unlawful intervention as is the giving of assistance to rebels who are arrayed against its authority.[66]

State practice seems to support this view when one considers the number of occasions when aid in the form of armed forces or materials of war has been given to governments in order to suppress rebellions. Ian Brownlie notes,

Great Britain sent troops to Portugal in 1826 at the request of the Portuguese government to assist in preventing a successful rebellion by Don Miguel. Russia sent troops to Hungary in 1849 at the request of Austria to assist in the suppression of the Hungarian revolt. American economic aid and arms were supplied to the Chinese National Government in the period 1946 to 1949 for use in the war against the Communist forces. British troops were employed in aid of the Netherlands government forces in Indonesia in 1946 and American military aid was supplied to France for use against the Viet-Minh forces in Indo-China. The Soviet government assumed in its statements on the situation in Hungary in October and November 1956, that armed aid to the existing government was lawful. More recently in 1958, American forces were landed in the Lebanon to aid the Chamoun government against rebels and British forces were flown to Jordan to support the Jordan government in face of imminent civil strife.[67]

In 1930 the US government defended the support of a government against rebels when it prohibited the shipment of weapons to Brazil to anyone except the government. The Department of State explained,

Until belligerency is recognized, and the duty of neutrality arises, all the humane predispositions toward stability of government, the preservation of international amity, and the protection of established intercourse between nations are in favour of the Existing Government.[68]

In the case of rebellion, the established government had a significant advantage.

The obligations of third States when insurgency is recognized is not agreed upon.[69] Rosalyn Higgins argues that, where a status of insurgency is recognized,

[T]here is in effect an international acknowledgement of an internal war, but third parties are left substantially free to determine the consequences. Where country A,

[66] James W. Garner, 'Questions of International Law in the Spanish Civil War', *AJIL*, 31 (1937), 68.
[67] Brownlie, *Force*, 322.
[68] Department of State, Latin America Series, No. 4, 1931, in Higgins, 'Internal War', 98.
[69] Luard, 21.

noting a civil war in country B, acknowledges the rebels as insurgents, it is regarding them as contestants-at-law, and not as mere law-breakers. But it is still free, under traditional international law, to help the legitimate government, but should desist from helping the rebels.[70]

But this is by no means a universally held opinion. Hyde maintains that

[T]he State that recognizes the condition of insurgency is hardly in a position to deny that its own subsequent acts by way of military assistance to either contestant constitute intervention for the justification of which solid and convincing excuses must be given.[71]

Friedmann, Wright, and Hall hold similar views.[72] The argument posed is one of principle. If the insurgents create a significant challenge to the established government with no support from a third party, then the legitimacy of the government in its own municipal law is in question. Accordingly, the principles of sovereignty and independent existence require abstention from interference in internal affairs. The State should remain free to decide the character of its government even by force of arms, so long as insurgents are not supplied by a third party.

Quincy Wright argues against intervention on either side for slightly different reasons. He cautions against internationalizing local disputes where outside States recognize different factions in the conflict, and maintains 'that in respect to military intervention, the critical line is not recognition of belligerency, but the uncertainty of the outcome'.[73]

Of course the situation is changed if the insurgents are supported by an outside power. Should this be the case, aid to the established government is no doubt justified in international law. Since 1945 it has been common for States to justify their intervention this way. Brownlie notes that

British aid to the Athens government against rebels from 1944 to 1946 was justified in this way. The Truman Doctrine of 1947 had as its object the provision of military and economic aid to governments threatened by subversion. Soviet intervention in Hungary in 1956 was justified by reference to the Warsaw Pact and foreign assistance to the insurgents; and American landings in Lebanon in 1958 at the request of the government of President Chamoun were explained as a form of collective defence against indirect aggression.[74]

More recent events demonstrate that this tendency to justify intervention as counter-intervention persists, most notably in Central America.

If the traditional rule has been non-interference when a government faces insurgency with some exceptions to the rule, the exceptions may now

---

[70] Higgins, 'Civil Conflict', 170.
[71] Hyde, i. 203–4.
[72] Friedmann, 'Intervention', 72–3; Wright, 'Lebanon', 121; Hall, 346.
[73] Wright, 'Lebanon', 122.
[74] Brownlie, *Force*, 323.

be more relevant than the rule. Certainly, there is no obligation to assist the government. But when aid is given to the established government it also seems to be a matter of policy justified by an applicable interpretation of international law. Wolfgang Friedmann notes,

[T]he history of recent civil war conflicts [e.g. Cyprus, the Congo, Yemen, and Vietnam] with international implications shows that intervention by a foreign state on behalf of one side has invariably produced counter-intervention by some other state in favour of the other side. In these moves and counter-moves, legal considerations have played a minimal part.[75]

Just as there is no widespread agreement on what characteristics qualify rebels as insurgents, there is no agreement on whether a third State is justified in aiding a government fighting an insurgency. Certainly they may when the insurgency is fomented by yet another State. This, and other exceptions to the general rule of non-intervention which some authors espouse, has become the loophole large enough to swallow the rule itself.

International law seems to have taken two paths in the case of insurgency, one opposed to any intervention and the other opposed only to aiding the insurgents. These paths rejoin in the case of belligerency. Under traditional rules, when belligerency is recognized the recognizing State is entitled to neutral rights. As a neutral, it is obliged to refrain from aiding either side in the conflict.[76] Thus, those who hold that it is lawful to aid the established government in the case of insurgency maintain non-intervention is the rule when belligerency is recognized. Of course, the same exceptions apply. If the belligerents are supported by an outside power, intervention seems to be acceptable under the traditional rules.

Because governments have not recognized belligerency since World War II even in the case of widespread conflict like that in Nigeria in 1967, the traditional rules which prohibit intervention in the case of belligerency are outdated. In fact, it has become common practice for States to ignore the requirement of neutrality, and to continue supplying arms, even in a major civil war.[77]

In addition to customary law, the Habana Convention on the Duties and Rights of States in the Event of Civil Strife of 20 February 1928, one of the few efforts at codification of the law of civil war before Protocol II of 1977, indicates that the principle of non-intervention in case of internal armed conflict is widely accepted in Latin America. According to the Convention, foreign States are prohibited from aiding revolutionaries whether or not

[75] Friedmann, 'Intervention', 73.
[76] Starke, 147; Schwarzenberger, *International Law*, 693; Higgins, 'Civil Conflict', 171; Briggs, 992.
[77] Higgins, 'Civil Conflict', 173.

recognized as insurgents. If the insurgents are recognized as belligerents third States must remain strictly neutral.[78]

The relationship of third States to the parties fighting a civil war is controversial. It suffers from the same problem of artificiality that the recognition of rebellion, insurgency, and belligerency suffers from. Despite the disagreement in specific cases and the tendency to make exceptions to the general rules, one theme remains clear: international law has favoured the established government in an internal war by prohibiting assistance to rebels and allowing assistance to the government except in cases of recognized belligerency when outside States must remain neutral. Traditional international law favoured repression over revolution. This predisposition has been seriously challenged in the last forty years.

The following is an attempt to summarize the relationship of outside States to an internal war.

1. In the case of rebellion, a third State may aid the government but not the rebels. Whether it does so is a matter of policy rather than obligation.

2. In an insurgency, the position of third States is not agreed upon. Either,

  (*a*) third States must remain neutral, or
  (*b*) third States may aid the government but not the rebels. If the insurgents are aided by another State, aid to the government is acceptable.

3. In the case of belligerency third States should remain neutral, although this is no longer common practice.

4. Intervention by a third State on one side or the other in a civil conflict has become so common and has been justified by so many exceptions to the general rule that the exceptions seem to have become the rule.

The traditional law of war is divided into two branches. The first concerns the authority to resort to the use of force addressed in this chapter. The second branch concerns humanitarian protection in armed conflict. It is to this second branch which I now turn.

---

[78] Castren, *Civil War*, 81; Schwarzenberger, *International Law*, ii. 715.

3

Humanitarian Protection in International Law

3.1 Introductory

In a city taken by storm almost any licence was condoned by the law. Only churches and churchmen were technically secure, but even they were not often spared. Women could be raped, and men killed out of hand. All the goods of the inhabitants were regarded as forfeit. If lives were spared, it was only through the clemency of the victorious captain; and spoliation was systematic.[1]

Keen's description of being on the losing side in a war of the Middle Ages shocks the sensibilities of those who accept as commonplace that victors do not have unlimited rights over vanquished. Gradually, over 500 years, a consensus has developed that the methods and means of warfare are not unlimited, that those not taking active part in the hostilities should not be made the target of attacks, and that combatants placed *hors de combat* have certain rights including the right not to be punished for their legitimate acts of warfare.

In large part, this humanitarian law of war applied between States. However, some parts of the traditional law of humanitarian protection applied to non-State entities and combatants in civil wars like national liberation movements. This chapter explores the law of humanitarian protection as it applied to these groups.

It is more difficult to separate the 'old' law of humanitarian protection from the 'new' law than it is to separate the 'old' law on the authority to use force from the 'new' law. In addition to the effects of the right of self-determination, one must consider the development of an international law of human rights which also contributed to the idea that the humanitarian law of war should apply to wars of national liberation. Ultimately, one must acknowledge that the distinction is artificial. The transition was gradual, with a number of cumulative developments rather than an abrupt change. This chapter attempts to describe the state of the law of humanitarian protection before the rapid decolonization of the late 1950s and 1960s with its effects on international politics and international law.

3.2 Humanity and Warfare: An Introduction to Paradox

Military necessity and humanitarian protection for the victims of warfare

---

[1] M. H. Keen, *The Laws of War in the Late Middle Ages* (London: Routledge and Son, 1965), 121–2.

are often antipodal forces in war, each moderating the influence of the other. On the one hand, there is the desire to win and the consequent tendency to use all necessary means to secure victory; on the other, there is the creditable human awareness that life has value, that torture is inhumàne, and that war is an abnormal state of affairs fought not to destroy a civilization, but to achieve a better peace. G. I. A. D. Draper has called this dichotomy between the purposes of the law of war and the nature of war 'probably the most acute point of tension between law and life'.[2] To the sceptical, the conduct of war by its very nature is beyond the control of law. It represents the breakdown of law after which rules cease to apply. All too often those expressing this point of view are combatants most directly responsible for the application of the law of war. On the eve of battle, Prince Andrew Bulkhonsky in Tolstoy's *War and Peace* vented this bitter scepticism. He said,

They talk to us of the rules of war, of chivalry, of flags of truce, of mercy to the unfortunate and so on. It's all rubbish. . . . War is not courtesy but the most horrible thing in life; and we ought to understand that, and not play at war. . . . The aim of war is murder; the methods of war are spying, treachery, and their encouragement, the ruin of a country's inhabitants, robbing them or stealing to provision the army, and fraud and falsehood termed military craft. . . .[3]

It is not only in literature and drama that we find these sentiments. Clausewitz, in his book *On War*, does not consider humanitarian constraints when distinguishing real war from absolute war. In Book I, Chapter 1, he wrote,

Kind-hearted people might of course think there was some ingenious way to disarm or defeat an enemy without too much bloodshed, and might imagine this is the true goal of the art of war. Pleasant as it sounds, it is a fallacy that must be exposed: war is such a dangerous business that the mistakes which come from kindness are the very worst. The maximum use of force is in no way incompatible with the simultaneous use of the intellect. If one side uses force without compunction, undeterred by the bloodshed it involves, while the other side refrains, the first will gain the upper hand. . . . [T]he only limiting factors are the counterpoises inherent in war.[4]

Of course, Clausewitz does contend that the military means must be governed by the political end, but he does not devote even one brief chapter to humanitarian or legal restraints on war. It is with some justification, then, that total warfare unrestrained by mercy is often called 'Clausewitzian'.

[2] G. I. A. D. Draper, 'The Implementation and Enforcement of the Geneva Conventions of 1949 and of the Two Additional Protocols of 1978', *Recueil des cours*, 164 (1979-III), 10.

[3] Leo Tolstoy, *War and Peace*, bk x, ch. 25. Quoted in Geoffrey Best, *Humanity in Warfare* (London: Weidenfeld and Nicolson, 1980), 13.

[4] Carl von Clausewitz, *On War*, ed. and trans. Michael Howard and Peter Paret (Princeton: Princeton Univ. Press, 1976), bk i, ch. 1, sect. 3, 75.

However strongly Tolstoy appeals to our visceral knowledge of how things are, and however strongly Clausewitz appeals to our logic of military necessity, it is a fact of the twentieth century that the rights of the victor over the vanquished are not unlimited. There are restraints in war, however inconsistent this may appear to be.

While humanity and military necessity are often opposing forces in warfare, they are not always so. There is a strong element of practicality and national interest in the observance of humanitarian rules. The threat of retaliation in kind is strong motivation for restraint. Furthermore, if the bitterness caused by inhumanity will linger after the end of hostilities it may be in one's national interest to act with restraint. Clemency is often in\ the interests of the victor as much as to the benefit of the vanquished.

For all their apparent incompatibility, there is a fragile partnership between humanity and warfare, the result of which is the humanitarian law of armed conflict, or *jus in bello*.

3.3 Humanitarian Protection When Belligerency is Recognized

As noted in the previous chapter, the Hague and Geneva Conventions on the law of war restricted the protections and privileges of legitimate combatancy to the representatives of States. More specifically, the privileges of combatancy were restricted to armed forces, militia or volunteer corps, resistance movements belonging to a party to the conflict and complying with Article 4(2) of the Geneva Conventions, persons accompanying the armed forces, and participants in a *levée en masse*. The only extension of protection to representatives of non-States found in the treaties is Article 3 common to the four Geneva Conventions which will be discussed below.

Given the requirements of wearing fixed distinctive signs recognizable at a distance and carrying arms openly as well as belonging to a party to the conflict, generally assumed to be a State, it is little wonder that, under the 1949 Geneva Conventions and customary international law, liberation movements did not often qualify for humanitarian protection. However, it is generally agreed that the law of war does apply to conflicts which begin as civil wars and thus beyond the realm of international law, if belligerency is recognized. Daoud Khairallah notes that

Unrecognized insurgents come under the ambit of domestic penal law in an uprising against the lawful government and when caught they are brought before the courts on criminal charges in the domain of domestic law. The recognition of belligerency puts an end to this situation; it transforms the 'rebels' into 'belligerents' and suspends application of the penal law. The laws of war then become applicable to both parties in the conflict, not only with regard to the conduct of hostilities, but also for all other war activities, such as the care for the sick and wounded, prisoners of war, etc.[5]

Thus, if a civil war acquires the characteristics of an international dispute, the rules relating to the conduct of hostilities and to the use of weapons apply.[6]

Even though it is generally accepted that *jus in bello* applies in cases of recognized belligerency, the reluctance of States to recognize belligerency even in cases of protracted civil war precludes the automatic application of the law to combatants in wars of national liberation. The fact is that belligerency has not been recognized in any war of national liberation, or even the more questionable cases of secession from self-governing States. Discussion of what rights and duties are applicable under traditional international law when the belligerency of a national liberation movement is recognized is highly theoretical and devoid of practice in support of theory.

3.4 Humanitarian Protection Without Recognition of Belligerency

According to long-established principles of international law, civil violence and civil war were matters for the State involved. Until the adoption of Article 3 of the 1949 Geneva Conventions, governments could treat rebels or members of national liberation movements as criminals under their own municipal laws and prosecute them as such.[7] A brief review of State practice before the adoption of the Conventions will demonstrate that governments generally did treat individuals fighting against the government in a civil war as criminals at the outset of hostilities. As the conflict continued, in some cases, governments moderated their positions.

---

[5] Daoud L. Khairallah, *Insurrection Under International Law: With Emphasis on the Rights and Duties of Insurgents* (Beirut: Lebanese Univ., 1973), 28–9.

[6] See I. Sagay, 'The Legal Status of Freedom Fighters in Africa', *Eastern Africa LR*, 6 (1973), 20–1; Erik Castren, *Civil War* (Helsinki: Suomalainen Tiedeakatemia, 1966), 20; Michel Veuthey, 'The Red Cross and Non-international Conflicts', *IRRC*, 10 (Aug. 1970), 411–23; H. Lauterpacht, *Recognition in International Law* (Cambridge: Cambridge Univ. Press, 1947), 246.

[7] Abdelmadjid Belkherroubi, 'Essai sur une théorie juridique des mouvements de libération nationale', *Revue égyptienne de droit international*, 28 (1972), 23; Georg Schwarzenberger, *International Law* (London: Stevens and Sons, 1968), ii. 677; Michel Veuthey, *Guérilla et droit humanitaire* (Geneva: Institut Henry-Dunant, 1976), 216; Jean S. Pictet (ed.), *The Geneva Conventions of 12 August 1949: Commentary* (Geneva; ICRC, 1952), i. 39; James E. Bond, *The Rules of Riot* (Princeton: Princeton Univ. Press, 1974), 112–13; W. E. Hall, *A Treatise on International Law*, 8th edn., ed. A. Pearce Higgins (Oxford: Clarendon Press, 1924), 612.

3.41 Pre–1949 State Practice

Francis Lieber wrote his *Instructions for the Government of Armies of the United States in the Field* during what some historians consider to be the first war of the modern era. It was also a civil war unlike many post-World War II civil wars because the fighting took place between two entities that from the start had many State-like qualities. It was a war of secession between armies who for the most part used conventional tactics, who generally wore uniforms, and who professed allegiance to governments which controlled territory. The American Civil War began with the rupture of the State rather than the growth of an insurgent movement. Lieber's instructions suggested that members of an opposing army in a rebellion should be treated as prisoners of war, but that this does not prevent the government from trying their leaders, nor does it imply recognition of the rebellious people. In Section X on Insurrection, Civil War and Rebellion, Article 153 states:

Treating, in the field, the rebellious enemy according to the law and usages of war, has never prevented the legitimate government from trying the leaders of the rebellion or chief rebels for high treason, and from treating them accordingly, unless they are included in a general amnesty.

The Union was not as lenient with persons in an occupied territory who rose in arms against the occupying power. Article 85 of Lieber's *Instructions* orders that

War-rebels are persons within an occupied territory who rise in arms against the occupying or conquering army, or against the authorities established by the same. If captured, they may suffer death, whether they rise singly, in small or large bands, and whether called upon to do so by their own but expelled government or not. They are not prisoners of war; nor are they, if discovered and secured before their conspiracy has matured to an actual rising, or to armed violence.[8]

With the exception that those indistinguishable from civilians were not treated as prisoners of war, the American Civil War was remarkably similar to an international armed conflict and the combatants on both sides were generally treated as legitimate combatants and as prisoners of war.[9]

Likewise, at the turn of the century, the Boers were treated by the British as prisoners of war, until the annexation of the Boer Republics. After annexation those continuing to resist 'could no longer be regarded as regular combatants but only as rebels'.[10]

[8] Francis Lieber, *Instructions for the Government of Armies of the United States in the Field* (New York: D. van Nostrand, 1863). General Order No. 100, Adjutant-General's Office.

[9] See L. Nurick and R. W. Barrett, 'Legality of Guerrilla Forces Under the Laws of War', *AJIL*, 40 (1946), 572–3.

[10] W. J. Ford, 'Resistance Movements and International Law', *IRRC*, 79, 80, 81 (1967), 579.

Despite this tendency in the nineteenth century to treat combatants opposed to the government in a civil war as prisoners of war when captured, the official position of governments and jurists remained that, although it might be in the interests of the government to extend this analogous treatment, there was no obligation to do so when belligerency was not recognized.

In March 1912 the Acting Secretary of State of the United States, Mr Wilson, wrote to the Mexican ambassador at Washington, 'In this connection I am constrained to call to your attention the obvious fact that since there is now no recognized state of belligerency in Mexico the rules and laws governing warfare and the conduct of neutrals are not involved.'[11] This position was not restricted to governments. Even the Red Cross, whose role has always been a humanitarian one, ran aground on this issue in the 1912 Conference. The Conference was unable to reach a decision on the applicability of the laws of war in internal conflicts. According to one delegate, 'National Red Cross Societies have no duty whatever towards rebel or revolutionary troops who, under the laws of my country, can only be considered as criminals.'[12]

The Spanish Civil War of 1936–9 was a potent example of a civil war with very little humanitarian restraint. Both sides in the conflict refused to treat the other side as lawful belligerents. According to Dr Ford,

Hostages were shot and women and children were not spared. The parties to the conflict treated one another as murderers. The insurgents were not accorded the status of belligerents, because the government feared that by doing so they would weaken the position of the Spanish Republic.[13]

It was during the Spanish Civil War that the conviction began to take shape that some of the rules of war, at least in a general form, should apply to civil conflicts regardless of the recognition of belligerency.[14] The flames of this conviction were fanned by the experiences of occupied territories in World War II. The treatment received by resistance movements operating in occupied territories led to the inclusion of organized resistance movements in the 1949 Geneva Conventions. Arguably, it also laid the

---

[11] Mr Wilson, Acting Secretary of State, to the Mexican ambassador at Washington, 8 Mar. 1912, For. Rel. 1912, 740–1, quoted in C. C. Hyde, *International Law Chiefly as Interpreted and Applied by the United States*, 2nd rev. edn. (Boston: Little, Brown and Co., 1947), i. 203.

[12] Jean Pictet, *Humanitarian Law and the Protection of War Victims* (Leiden: Sijthoff, 1975), 55.

[13] Ford, *IRRC*, 584; see also Jean Siotis, *Le Droit de la guerre et les conflits armés d'un caractère non-international* (Paris: Librairie Générale de Droit et de Jurisprudence, 1958), 150.

[14] Antonio Cassese, 'The Spanish Civil War and the Development of Customary Law Concerning Internal Armed Conflicts', in *Current Problems of International Law* (Milan: Dott. A. Giuffre, 1975), 287–8.

foundation for the application of the laws of war to national liberation movements.

The policy of the Third Reich with regard to captured partisans was extremely harsh. According to Veuthey, pursuant to an order of the Führer signed by Marshal Keitel of 13 May 1941, *francs-tireurs* were to be executed.

Ainsi un ordre du 13 mai 1941, émanant du quartier général du 'Führer', et signé par le maréchal Keitel, énonce que les francs-tireurs sont à liquider sans pitié par la troupe en combat ou s'ils fuient.

Un ordre du Haut-Commandement de l'Armée, du 4 juin 1941, sur les instructions pour le comportement de la troupe en Russie, assimile dans ce traitement sans ménagement et cette politique d'extermination les 'agitateurs bolcheviques, francs-tireurs, saboteurs, juifs'.[15]

There is evidence that these orders were carried out. In 1943, during an offensive of the Yugoslav partisans, General Kuebler, the German Commander of the 118th division, ordered that every partisan taken prisoner was to be shot immediately and all wells were to be poisoned.[16] Similarly, Slovak partisans were not regarded as prisoners of war and were deported to Germany.[17] Their Polish counterparts, in contrast, were regarded as prisoners of war and subject to the 1929 Red Cross Convention, as provided in the Warsaw capitulation agreement.[18] Finally, on 11 June 1944 the Germans announced via Radio-Paris that the French Forces of the Interior (FFI) would be executed despite the declaration made by General Eisenhower on 9 June 1944 that he considered the FFI to be an integral part of the Allied Expeditionary Corps.[19] In this case, the International Committee of the Red Cross intervened and pressed the Germans to grant prisoner-of-war status to members of the FFI complying with Article 1 of the Hague Regulations. Eventually, the German authorities gave their verbal assurance to the Red Cross that members of the FFI would be treated like prisoners of war, but this assurance was never confirmed in writing.[20] Similarly, in Yugoslavia some of the local commanders treated captured Yugoslav partisans like prisoners of war even though orders from higher headquarters refused to recognize them as belligerents. Veuthey noted that,

Ainsi, même le IIIe Reich avait dû, sur la fin de la Deuxième Guerre mondiale, se résoudre à traiter les partisans capturé comme des prisonniers de guerre: tandis que jusqu'alors les instructions—citées plus haut—promettaient la mort aux partisans

[15] Veuthey, *Guérilla,* 221.
[16] Ford, *IRRC,* 584.
[17] Ibid. 582–3.
[18] Ibid.
[19] Veuthey, *Guérilla,* 227; Ford, *IRRC,* 581.
[20] Veuthey, *Guérilla,* 227; Ford, *IRRC,* 581.

capturés, à fin 1942, les autorités militaires allemandes en Yougoslavie proposent au commandement supérieur de la *Wehrmacht* (OKW) de reconnaître Tito comme belligérant; bien que cette proposition ait été repoussée, des commandements locaux traiteront les partisans capturé qui avaient respecté les lois et coutumes de la guerre comme des prisonniers de guerre.[21]

Although one may note conflicts where the established government after a period of repression treats captured rebels as prisoners of war, there are also cases where this did not happen. The civil wars in Spain and Greece are the overture and reprise in this respect. The Greek Civil War (1946–9) was characterized by the absence of any application of the humanitarian law of war. According to Siotis, at the start of the conflict the government passed a number of repressive measures designed to choke the rebellion. Aiding the insurgents was a crime punishable by death; insurgents captured with weapons in their hands were court-martialled and most were sentenced to death; the rebels, adopting equally ruthless practices, killed captured prisoners who refused to join them. As Siotis described:

Dès le début de l'activité des guérillas, sous les ordres du général Marcos, le gouvernement prit une série de mesures législatives en vue de résister aux activités subversives aussi bien que de faire face à la situation militaire qui était alors plus que précaire. L'aide ou le secours apporté aux insurgés étaient considérés comme des crimes punissables de la peine de mort et tous les guérillas pris les armes en mains étaient traduits devant les cours martiales et condamnés le plus souvent à la peine de mort. Les rebelles, de leur côté, adoptaient des mesures analogues à l'égard des prisonniers tombés entre leurs mains qui refusaient de se rallier à leur cause.[22]

The International Committee of the Red Cross was generally unsuccessful in its attempts to ameliorate the suffering on both sides by appealing to the provisions of the draft of what was to become the 1949 Geneva Conventions.

The record of State practice when confronting organized resistance movements or secessionist movements is not entirely Draconian. Governments may eventually treat captured persons in an internal armed conflict as prisoners of war, even if they do not recognize them as such. It was generally agreed that according to accepted principles of international law there was no obligation for them to do so, and no government granting analogous treatment to captured prisoners prior to the 1949 Geneva Conventions in an internal armed conflict where the rebels were not recognized as insurgents claimed to do so out of any legal duty. It was a matter of policy and expediency rather than legal obligation.[23] As Veuthey notes, there has been a slowly evolving trend in this direction for the past 150 years:

[21] Veuthey, *Guérilla*, 226.
[22] Siotis, 171.

Un survol de quelque cent cinquante ans (depuis les guerres napoléoniennes) ·
pourrait montrer *une évolution, qui se manifeste pratiquement dans chaque conflit,
vers un respect des guérrilleros capturés pouvant aller jusqu'à leur reconnaître un
statut de prisonnier de guerre.*[24]

Despite this trend, governments have usually pursued extraordinary
criminal processes at the beginning of a conflict and have only moderated
their positions once it has become clear that the rebellion has not been
crushed in its egg.[25] As we shall see in later chapters, this tendency to pass
'législation d'exception' still exists. There is little doubt that under
traditional international law, prior to any recognition of belligerency, such
legislation was acceptable and any more favourable treatment accorded to
captured rebels was at the discretion of the established government.

3.42 Article 3 Common to the 1949 Geneva Conventions

Since the 1912 Conference when the Red Cross had not been able to agree
on its role in civil war, there had been a gradual trend within the Red Cross
movement toward a more active involvement in civil wars.[26] The 1921 Red
Cross Conference passed a resolution 'affirming the right to relief of all
victims of civil wars or social or revolutionary disturbances in accordance
with the general principles of the Red Cross'.[27]

At the seventeenth International Red Cross Conference, which immediately preceded the 1949 Diplomatic Conference, the International Committee proposed that the following paragraph be added to the Draft
Conventions:

In all cases of armed conflict which are not of an international character, especially
cases of civil war, colonial conflicts, or wars of religion, which may occur in the
territory of one or more of the High Contracting Parties, the implementing of the
principles of the present Conventions shall be obligatory on each of the
adversaries.[28]

The Conference deleted the the clause 'especially cases of civil war,
colonial conflicts, or wars of religion'.

The draft text presented by the International Committee to the
Diplomatic Conference at Geneva in 1949 had no chance of passing.
Governments felt that

[23] See Bond, *Riot*, 114; Michel Veuthey, 'La Guérilla: Le Problème du Traitement des
prisonniers', in *Annales d'études internationales*, 3 (1972), 127.

[24] Veuthey, *Guérilla*, 217.

[25] See Bond, *Riot*, 37 and 113; Veuthey, *Guérilla*, 227.

[26] Michel Veuthey, 'Implementation and Enforcement of Humanitarian Law and Human
Rights Law in Non-international Armed Conflicts: The Role of the ICRC', *Am. Univ. LR*, 33
(1983), 83–97.

[27] Pictet, *Commentary*, i. 40.

[28] Quoted in Bond, *Riot*, 54.

[B]y committing themselves to applying the Geneva Conventions in a civil war, States would be jeopardizing their security and their very existence. The view was held that such a solution would lead to more revolts and anarchy, to the strengthening of insurgent groups by promoting belief in their belligerent status, and to the legal government's inability to undertake legitimate repressive measures.[29]

There were several alternative drafts proposed at the Conference. The one accepted, and now Article 3 common to the four Geneva Conventions of 1949, is an attempt to apply the fundamental principles of the Conventions to non-international armed conflicts while not making the Conventions applicable in their entirety. Article 3 provides,

In the case of armed conflict not of an international character occurring in the territory of one of the High Contracting Parties, each Party to the conflict shall be bound to apply, as a minimum, the following provisions:

(1) Persons taking no active part in the hostilities, including members of armed forces who have laid down their arms and those placed *hors de combat* by sickness, wounds, detention, or any other cause, shall in all circumstances be treated humanely, without any adverse distinction founded on race, colour, religion or faith, sex, birth or wealth, or any other similar criteria.

To this end, the following acts are and shall remain prohibited at any time and in any place whatsoever with respect to the above-mentioned persons:

- (*a*) violence to life and person, in particular murder of all kinds, mutilation, cruel treatment and torture;
- (*b*) taking of hostages;
- (*c*) outrages upon personal dignity, in particular, humiliating and degrading treatment;
- (*d*) the passing of sentences and carrying out of executions without previous judgement pronounced by a regularly constituted court affording all the judicial guarantees which are recognized as indispensable by civilized peoples.

(2) The wounded and sick shall be collected and cared for.

An impartial humanitarian body, such as the International Committee of the Red Cross, may offer its services to the Parties to the conflict.

The Parties to the conflict should further endeavor to bring into force, by means of special agreements, all or part of the other provisions of the present Convention.

The application of the preceding provisions shall not affect the legal status of the Parties to the conflict.

Article 3 of the Geneva Conventions was a milestone in the development of the law of war. Although the Article does not grant any legal status to the rebels, as evidenced by the final paragraph, its adoption affirmed that internal wars are not entirely beyond the scope of international law. Each of the States party to the Conventions has the right to demand that its

---

[29] Pictet, *Humanitarian Law*, 56.

provisions be respected by a government engaged in a civil war. To this degree at least, humanitarian protection in non-international armed conflicts was effectively internationalized.

Article 3, sometimes called the convention in miniature, is only a shadow of the full Geneva Conventions. It resembles the full Conventions in that it is only concerned with individual and physical treatment regardless of the political cause the rebels may be fighting for, but its protections fall far short of those applicable in international armed conflicts.

The Article provides that 'persons taking no active part in the hostilities' be treated humanely and lists four prohibitions in particular: violence to person, the taking of hostages, humiliating treatment, and sentencing without trial. Nothing in the Article prevents governments from suppressing the rebellion, or from prosecuting captured rebels under its domestic laws. Detainees must be treated 'humanely' and given a regular trial, but this does not prevent punishment, up to death, under domestic criminal laws.

Although torture is prohibited by Article 3, 'coercion' is not. The protection accorded to prisoners of war in international armed conflicts is much more specific. Article 17 of the 1949 Geneva Prisoner of War Convention declares that

No physical or mental torture, nor any other form of coercion, may be inflicted on prisoners of war to secure from them information of any kind whatever. Prisoners of war who refuse to answer may not be threatened, insulted, or exposed to unpleasant or disadvantageous treatment of any kind.

One may argue that threats, insults, and other unpleasant treatment which is coercive are forbidden by the prohibitions on humiliating or degrading treatment included in Article 3, but the Article does not specifically prohibit them. Article 3 also does not list the information a prisoner is required to provide when questioned, which the full Conventions do. This is presumably left to the domestic law of the country concerned.

A further shortcoming of the Article is that it does not specifically limit the methods and means of warfare. As James Bond has noted:

One could plausibly equate 'cruel treatment' with the infliction of 'unnecessary suffering', the standard found in Article 23 of the Hague Rules and the basis for outlawing almost all illegal weapons of war. But since Article 3 protects only non-combatants ('persons taking no active part in the hostilities'), it would not prohibit the commander from using chemical or biological weapons—not because they do not constitute cruel treatment, . . . but because combatants fall outside the protective ambit of the article. Article 3 simply does not require that government forces treat resisting rebels humanely.[30]

[30] Bond, *Riot*, 92.

Because Article 3 only protects persons not taking part in the conflict, there are no restrictions on the conduct of combat itself. The standard in international armed conflicts is, again, much clearer. For example, the 1925 Geneva Protocol prohibits 'the use in war of asphyxiating, poisonous or other gases', 'all analogous liquids materials or devices', and the 'use of bacteriological methods of warfare'.[31] Thus, there is the paradoxical situation that the use of poisonous gas is prohibited in international wars, but its use is not prohibited in civil wars.

The humanitarian protection envisioned by the letter of the law in Article 3 is very limited. The Red Cross or other aid societies may offer their services, but the parties need not accept. Even if they do accept, there is no provision in the Article for respect of Red Cross personnel or facilities beyond the brief statement that 'the wounded and sick shall be collected and cared for'.

Article 3 is a set of minimum rules which would have been applicable to wars of national liberation as, until recently, these were considered to be non-international armed conflicts. The representative of Switzerland highlighted the inapplicability of the full Conventions to internal conflicts in a statement in the Final Record of the Diplomatic Conference at Geneva. He said,

The provisions embodied in Article [3] are intended to constitute a complete and exhaustive code of the obligations assumed by the Contracting States in the event of non-international conflicts; apart from this text, no other Article of the four Conventions applies to civil wars.[32]

Despite the shortcomings of Article 3, its inclusion was a great step forward. For the first time, States openly declared that there is an international responsibility for victims in internal armed conflicts. However, the greatest barrier to its application has been that 'armed conflict not of an international character' is not defined. The armed conflict referred to certainly must be less than recognized belligerency because recognition of belligerency would bring the entire body of humanitarian law into force. But below that level one may travel a spectrum from riots to insurgency and the Article itself leaves this an open question.

Pictet, in his *Commentary*, put forth the Red Cross position when he wrote, 'we think, on the contrary, that [Article 3] should be applied as widely as possible.'[33] This statement is of little help in clarifying exactly what it was that States agreed to. G. I. A. D. Draper noted in a 1958 book that

---

[31] 1925 Geneva Protocol for the Prohibition of the Use in War of Asphyxiating, Poisonous or Other Gases, and of Bacteriological Methods of Warfare.

[32] Mr Bolla (Switzerland), Final Record of the Diplomatic Conference at Geneva, 1949, vol. II-B, 336, quoted in M. Greenspan, *The Modern Law of Land Warfare* (Los Angeles: Univ. of California Press, 1959), 621–2.

[33] Pictet, *Commentary*, i. 50.

Varying criteria were suggested during the lengthy debates on [Article 3]. Examples of these criteria were: (*a*) that the Party in revolt against the legitimate government has an organized military force, an authority responsible for its acts, acting within a determinate territory and having the means of respecting and ensuring respect for the Conventions; (*b*) that the legal government is obliged to have recourse to its regular military forces against insurgents operating with a modicum of organization and in possession of a part of the national territory.[34]

The first set of criteria, (*a*), sounds suspiciously similar to those qualities considered necessary for the recognition of belligerency. The second set is wider in scope. Both seem to exclude banditry and riots and it is generally accepted that it was not the intention of States present at the Conference to include low-level violence of this kind within the scope of 'armed conflicts not of an international character'.[35]

The best measure of the Article is the State practice which followed its acceptance. The case of *Public Prosecutor* v. *Oie Hee Koi* (1968) arising out of the 1963 to 1966 armed conflict between Indonesia and Malaysia clarified the law relating to nationals who take arms against their own State even when a state of war is recognized.[36] Twelve Chinese Malays, born in or settled in Malaysia, were captured as members of an Indonesian paratroop force sent to Malaysia to engage in guerrilla warfare. They were tried and convicted of violating the Internal Security Act of 1960 including the unauthorized possession of firearms, and sentenced to death. Upon appeal, the Federal Court of Malaysia upheld all but two of the convictions. The Court assumed that a state of 'armed conflict' existed between Malaysia and Indonesia so that the Geneva Conventions were operative. However, they held that, despite the silence of Article 4 of the Convention on the point, nationals of the Detaining Power are not entitled to protection as prisoners of war, and may be tried under municipal law.[37]

In this case, the defendants were fighting with the opposing army in an international war. Even this did not entitle them to the humanitarian provisions of the full Conventions. Though they were given a trial and presumably treated humanely in accordance with Article 3, this did not prevent their execution under municipal law.

[34] G. I. A. D. Draper, *The Red Cross Conventions* (London: Stevens and Sons, 1958), 15–16.

[35] See Bond, *Riot*, 57–8; Donald W. McNemar, 'The Post-independence War in the Congo', in *The International Law of Civil War*, ed. Richard A. Falk (London: Johns Hopkins Press, 1971), 258; Greenspan, 624–5.

[36] See R. R. Baxter, 'The Privy Council on the Qualifications of Belligerents', *AJIL*, 63 (1969), 290.

[37] Although Baxter criticized the Court, which held that it is the responsibility of the prisoner to prove the applicability of the Geneva Conventions, he ultimately concludes that if 'they had been found to owe allegiance to Malaysia, they could properly have been treated like any other nationals of that country and prosecuted under the Internal Security Act, 1960, of the Federation of Malaya'.

With regard, more specifically, to strictly internal armed conflicts, there have been ample opportunities for the application of the minimal humanitarian provisions of Article 3. Yet, like the archaic system of recognition of belligerency, Article 3 has not proved to be a great success for the same reasons: governments are unwilling to admit that any internal disturbance they face is serious enough to be called an armed conflict. They 'continue to insist that they may in internal conflicts deal with their own citizens as they wish without reference to external—that is, international —standards.'[38]

Examples of this reluctance to apply Article 3 are numerous. In Malaya and Cyprus the United Kingdom was unwilling to admit the applicability of the Article.[39] In Malaysia, both the government and the rebel groups refused inspections by agencies such as the Red Cross.[40] At least in Malaya, unlike the French in Algeria, the British did not torture rebels and attempted to offer incentives for them to surrender.

When the struggle for independence began in Algeria in 1954 the French government claimed they were conducting a police action. When the FLN threatened reprisals for the execution of detained rebels, the French attitude changed, and in June 1956 France accepted the applicability of Article 3.[41]

The Biafran secession led to a bloody civil war. The Nigerian government at no time acknowledged the applicability of Article 3, even though it often acted as though the humanitarian provisions were applicable. It did permit ICRC assistance although it often interfered with that assistance. At the end of the war, a general amnesty was proclaimed.[42]

The Portuguese never acknowledged any obligations under Article 3 in their African colonies of Angola and Mozambique. They were not alone. As James Bond notes,

In the recent past both Pakistan and Ceylon have had to employ regular military units against rebel forces. Neither has publicly recognized any obligations under Article 3; and press reports indicate what would appear to be widespread violations of its basic provisions.[43]

Thus, the record of humanitarian protection in armed conflicts not of an international character is mixed. The International Committee of the Red Cross has offered its assistance in innumerable cases and has often been

[38] Bond, *Riot*, 61.
[39] Tom J. Farer, 'The Laws of War 25 Years After Nuremberg', *International Conciliation*, 583 (May 1971), 52.
[40] Bond, *Riot*, 123.
[41] Allan Rosas, *The Legal Status of Prisoners of War* (Helsinki: Suomalainen Tiedea-katemia, 1976), 148.
[42] Rosas, 196; Farer, 'Laws of War', 191; Bond, *Riot*, 59; John De St Jorre, *The Nigerian Civil War* (London: Hodder and Stoughton, 1972), 282–3.
[43] Bond, *Riot*, 59.

allowed to visit prisoners, to deliver messages, and, in some cases, to provide relief to the civilian population or support to the families of detainees. But, as Professor Draper noted in his 1979 lectures at the Académie de Droit International,

Article 3 has not proved a success although the standards it demands are valuable. Monitoring implementation has rarely proved possible. Sovereignty renders the implementation of international armed conflicts difficult; *a fortiori*, is this the case with internal conflicts.[44]

In conclusion, thanks largely to the persistence of organizations like the International Committee of the Red Cross, there are minimal protections for persons taking no active part in hostilities in armed conflicts not of an international character. These provisions, limited as they are in comparison to those applicable in international armed conflicts, have been sporadically applied. Traditional international law does not protect rebels fighting the established government from trial and conviction under the municipal laws of the country involved. Although in some cases the established government has treated captured rebels as prisoners of war—though they have rarely called them such—there is no obligation for them to do so. As in Algeria, the decision to treat detainees as prisoners of war is made more likely when there is a fear of reprisal.

The extensive provisions for protection of hospitals and medical personnel; the rules for internment of prisoners, their quarter, food, and hygiene; the records required for the dead and detained; and the lengthy and specific rules about treatment of civilians, which exist for international armed conflicts—however fragile they may be—do not exist for internal armed conflicts, including wars of national liberation.

3.5 National Liberation Movements: The Basis of Obligation

One of the most commonly voiced objections to the application of the humanitarian law of war to conflicts other than those between sovereign States is that to do so would introduce an element of discriminatory application. States would be bound by certain rules, but the movement opposing the established government would not be bound by them. Article 3 of the Geneva Conventions provides that 'each Party to the conflict shall be bound to apply' its humanitarian provisions. Yet, the rebel movement which is one of the parties involved is not a signatory of the treaty. It is therefore worth examining briefly the basis of obligation of liberation movements both resulting from recognition of belligerency and under Article 3 of the Geneva Conventions.

[44] Draper, 'Implementation and Enforcement', 27.

There are a number of differing views on how recognized belligerents can be bound by treaties they have not signed. Indeed, Norman Padelford suggests that in the case of belligerency there is no obligation.

Once belligerency has been recognized, it is expected that both sides will conduct themselves accordingly, although there seems to be no obligation according to international law to apply the international rules, in as much as the rules and conventions have been developed to apply to and are only legally binding during war between States.[45]

This view is not generally accepted and it is difficult for this author to distinguish between an expectation that both sides will conduct themselves according to the law of war, and an obligation that they do so.

Some legal scholars claim that non-State parties to conflicts are only bound by customary international law like that contained in the Hague Regulations and not by that in international conventions. Hans Wehberg wrote, 'As the insurgents were not signatories of the international conventions concerning the laws of war, it is only the principles of customary law on the subject that can, as a rule, be applied.'[46] Wehberg is opposed in this contention by Lauterpacht who claimed that, when belligerency was recognized and

the conflict has assumed an international complexion, the rules of the Geneva Conventions apply *in toto* if the legitimate Government is a party to them and if the recognized insurgents formally accept and apply the provisions of these Conventions. Failing this the accepted customary rules of war apply as between the parties in this as in other spheres.[47]

Lauterpacht bases his argument on three premisses to which other scholars also appeal. First, unlike an Article 3 conflict, in the case of recognition of belligerency the rebel faction has many of the characteristics of a State, including conducting its operations in accordance with the laws of war. If this is a condition of recognition of belligerency, it is difficult to see how a rebel faction could have the status of lawful belligerents without acting in compliance with the law of war. As long as international status is conceded, the international rules apply.

The second premiss, and one which is also raised in Article 3 conflicts, is the idea of succession. If the established government was a party to the Conventions, then the opposing guerrilla force, vying for control of the State or secession of part of it, is bound by the Conventions by the theory of succession. Shigeki Miyazaki explained that, according to this law of

[45] Norman Padelford, 'International Law and the Spanish Civil War', *AJIL*, 31 (1937), 229.

[46] Hans Wehberg, 'Civil War and International Law', in *The World Crisis*, 176, quoted in Khairallah, 29.

[47] H. Lauterpacht (ed.), Oppenheim's *International Law*, vol. ii, 7th edn. (London: Longman, 1963), 211–12.

succession, 'the revolutionary authority succeeds the government and occupies the legal position of that government'.[48] Since the established government signed the agreement, the succeeding government assumes its obligations.

Lauterpacht's final premiss, which is echoed by other scholars, is based on Article 2 paragraph 3 common to the four Geneva Conventions. This paragraph provides that,

Although one of the Powers in conflict may not be a party to the present Convention, the Powers who are parties thereto shall remain bound by it in their mutual relations. They shall furthermore be bound by the Convention in relation to the said Power, if the latter accepts and applies the provisions thereof.

In other words, the recognized belligerent need not be a signatory of the Conventions in order for the law of Geneva to apply. Observance of their provisions is enough to establish a mutual obligation.

Those provisions of the Geneva Conventions which are the codification of customary law rather than completely new developments are binding on recognized belligerents. Parties need not be signatories to the Conventions to be subject to this established law because it is independent of contractual obligation.

The case of internal conflicts under Article 3 of the Geneva Conventions is slightly more difficult because the international status of the rebellious party has not been established and is not affected by the application of the Article itself.

One must first note that the rules set out in Article 3 are not subject to reciprocity. They are minimum standards of conduct which the parties 'shall be bound to apply', regardless of the actions of their opponent. Even in the event that a rebel movement fails to observe the provisions of Article 3, the State is presumably still bound to do so, and vice versa.[49]

In general, there seem to be two arguments on the obligation of rebel movements to apply Article 3 when they are not parties to the Conventions.

First, some scholars claim that the Conventions bind people as well as States. Sydney Bailey wrote in 1972,

There is, moreover, a strong body of legal opinion which considers that the humanitarian Conventions do not simply bind States, but that they also bind people. In other words, irregular fighters have the same obligation to apply international humanitarian law as do the official governmental authorities which they seek to undermine or supplant.[50]

---

[48] Shigeki Miyazaki, 'The Application of the New Humanitarian Law', *IRRC*, 217 (July–Aug. 1980), 187.

[49] Ford, *IRRC*, 516–17.

[50] Sydney D. Bailey, *Prohibitions and Restraints in War* (London: Oxford Univ. Press, 1972), 88.

Greenspan and Miyazaki present similar views.[51] If all subjects of a State are bound by the Conventions, then they remain bound even though subsequently some of them may rebel against the established government.

A second and more conventional proposition on the basis of rebel obligation under Article 3 is that of succession. As in the case of obligation by recognized belligerents, the revolutionary government assumes the obligations of its preceding government including those contained in the Geneva Conventions. This is more difficult to accept in the case of an 'armed conflict not of an international character' because the non-State party to such an internal conflict may not yet have a government or even claim to be a legitimate government. In such a situation it would seem artificial indeed for the rebellious faction to assume obligations based on succession.

Finally, the fundamental humanitarian principles enshrined in Article 3 may be of so basic a nature as to be part of customary international law and therefore, the rebels need not be signatories of the Conventions in order for the resultant obligations to apply. This, of course, may be objected to on the grounds that the principles embodied in Article 3 are customary law as far as States are concerned, but their application to internal conflicts was novel, and therefore not customary law for civil war.

In practice, the legal basis of obligation in traditional international law for national liberation movements under Article 3 or as recognized belligerents has been more of an intellectual conundrum than a practical problem. The difficulty has more often been insuring respect for Article 3 by States and the practical ability of liberation movements to carry out its obligations rather than the unwillingness of liberation movements to accept any obligation. The reason for this is obvious. The liberation movement, desirous of international support and recognition, is eager to accept, or at least to appear to accept, its obligations as an international person. Indeed, far from there being difficulty over obligations under Article 3, liberation movements have on occasion declared their intention to comply with the Conventions in their entirety. In Algeria, for example, the FLN in 1956 and again in 1958 declared its intention to apply the Geneva Convention on Prisoners of War to French prisoners.[52] In 1960 the Gouvernement Provisoire de la République Algérienne (GPRA) notified the Swiss government of its accession to the Conventions. The Swiss government circulated this notification to the other signatories, much to the dismay of the French, but the Swiss also made a 'reservation' to this accession based on its non-recognition of the GPRA.[53]

[51] Greenspan, 623; Miyazaki, 188.
[52] Veuthey, *Guérilla*, 202.
[53] Georges Abi-Saab, 'Wars of National Liberation and the Laws of War', *Annales d'études internationales*, 3 (1972), 104–5; Michel Veuthey, 'La Guérilla', 125.

The application of the complete Geneva Conventions to wars of national liberation has been an important theme of the so-called struggle for self-determination. The willingness of national liberation movements to assume obligations, or to appear to assume them, has been less of a problem than their practical ability to do so.

In summary, the following points may be made.

1. In the case where belligerency is recognized, humanitarian law *in toto* applies to the conflict as if both sides were States.

2. When belligerency is not recognized, State practice has been mixed. There is often a period of repression under municipal law sometimes followed by gradual moderation if the conflict is prolonged. Under traditional international law this 'législation d'exception' is permissible and more favourable treatment is discretionary.

3. Article 3 common to the Geneva Conventions provides some basic humanitarian protections in internal conflicts for persons taking no active part in the hostilities. This Article does not prohibit any conduct in combat, nor does it prevent trial of the rebels for offences under the municipal law of the State concerned.

4. In practice, the provisions of Article 3 have been difficult to enforce and sporadically applied.

5. The legal basis of obligation for liberation movements to comply with the humanitarian law of war is not agreed upon by scholars. Its basis may be a matter of succession, of individual responsibility, or of customary law. This is more of a theoretical problem than a practical one.

This concludes the examination of the law of war before the development of the idea that self-determination is a legal right. This idea has challenged the distinction between internal and international armed conflicts; it has extended the humanitarian law of war in its entirety to new realms; and it has eroded the prohibition of the use of force espoused in the Charter of the United Nations. Part II of this book will explore the historical development of self-determination from a principle of political thought to a right in international law.

PART II

Self-Determination

4
Self-Determination in International Law

4.1 Introductory

One of the most controversial issues in international law since the end of World War II has been whether self-determination is a right in international law or simply a principle of political thought which has assumed great prominence in international affairs at various periods since the late eighteenth century. Certainly the principle has a highly charged political content leading one author to contend that it is a 'convenient plaything both for international politics and propaganda'.[1] Whether a 'convenient plaything' or a powerful tool, self-determination has profoundly affected ideas about the relationship between people and their governments. It is not my intention to chronicle the development of the idea of self-determination. The history of the idea may be found elsewhere.[2] Rather, this chapter examines how self-determination developed into a legal right, and secondly, who the 'self' is that can exercise this right.

4.2 Early Development: Wilson and the League

The relationship between a government and its people is a subject as old as political theory itself. In the Western world, the principle of self-determination owes its existence to at least two threads of philosophical thought. First, the principle of equality of men, and second, the idea of a social contract between the government and the governed.[3] Despite these ancient roots, it was not until the birth of democracy in its modern form in the second half of the eighteenth century that the idea of self-determination or national self-determination really began. In the French Revolution

[1] J. H. W. Verzijl, *International Law in Historical Perspective* (Leiden: A. W. Sijthoff, 1968), i. 321.

[2] Ian Brownlie, 'An Essay in the History of the Principle of Self-determination', in *Grotian Society Papers: Studies in the History of the Law of Nations,* 1968, ed. C. H. Alexandrowicz (The Hague: Nijhoff, 1970); Rupert Emerson, *From Empire to Nation: The Rise to Self-assertion of Asian and African Peoples* (Cambridge, Mass.: Harvard Univ. Press, 1960); A. Rigo Sureda, *The Evolution of the Right of Self-determination* (Leiden: A. W. Sijthoff, 1973); Alfred Cobban, *The Nation State and National Self-determination*, rev. edn. (London: Collins, 1969); Hugh Seton-Watson, *Nations and States* (London: Methuen, 1977).

[3] Emerson, *From Empire to Nation*, 3; Brownlie, 'History of the Principle of Self-determination', 93.

the doctrine was a guiding principle in the annexation of enclaves. The first plebiscites were held in Avignon, Savoy, and Nice shortly after the Revolution.[4] On the other side of the Atlantic, the idea that communities may choose their identity and their form of government as argued by men like John Locke, Jean -Jacques Rousseau, and Thomas Paine did not fall on deaf ears. The American Declaration of Independence of 1776 declared,

We hold these truths to be self-evident, that all men are created equal, that they are endowed by their Creator with certain inalienable rights, that among these are life, liberty and the pursuit of happiness. That to secure these rights Governments are instituted among men deriving their just powers from the consent of the governed; that whenever any form of Government becomes destructive of these ends, it is the right of the people to alter or abolish it and institute new Government.

Similarly, the emancipation of Latin America from Spanish control was at least partially due to the idea of self-determination and the example of the French Revolution.[5] It was not until the twentieth century that the principle of self-determination developed beyond this embryonic stage of justifying the resort to self-help or unilateral action.

Although Woodrow Wilson championed the principle of self-determination of peoples, the League of Nations Covenant did not specifically mention self-determination. Article 10 guaranteed territorial integrity and political independence, but it is an unacceptable leap in logic to assume that this sanctioned the principle of self-determination within national borders.[6] Two articles of the Covenant were particularly important.

Article 1(2) of the Covenant concerns membership of the organization. In addition to States, which one would expect to find in a list of prospective members, self-governing territories could join the League. The Article provides: 'Any fully self-governing State, Dominion or Colony not named in the Annex may become a Member of the League if its admission is agreed to by two-thirds of the Assembly.'[7]

The framers of the Covenant agreed that self-governing colonies which did not yet possess complete sovereignty had a status in the international community separate and distinct from the State administering them.[8]

The second and more important idea embodied in the Covenant was that the well-being and development of the people in the colonies formerly held by the defeated powers was a 'sacred trust' accepted by the victors. At this

---

[4] Sarah Wambaugh, *A Monograph on Plebiscites* (London: Oxford Univ. Press, 1920), 33–45.

[5] Brownlie, 'History of the Principle of Self-determination', 92.

[6] S. P. Sinha, 'Has Self-determination become a Principle of International Law Today?', *Indian JIL*, 14 (1974), 332–61.

[7] Article 1(2), League of Nations Covenant, 28 June 1919.

[8] This is an interesting forebear of the 1970 UN Declaration on Principles of International Law which recognized this distinction for non-self-governing territories. *Infra*, sec. 4.44.

point, they did not acknowledge a similar obligation in their own territories. Article 22(1) provides,

To those colonies and territories which as a consequence of the late war have ceased to be under the sovereignty of the States which formerly governed them and which are inhabited by peoples not yet able to stand by themselves under the strenuous conditions of the modern world, there should be applied the principle that the well-being and development of such peoples form a sacred trust of civilization and that securities for the performance of this trust should be embodied in this Covenant.[9]

This Article, while not mentioning any principle, let alone right, of self-determination, does appear to envision these colonies and territories one day able to 'stand by themselves under the strenuous conditions of the modern world'.[10] It does not, however, place any obligation upon administering powers to ensure eventual political independence.

Despite this reference to a 'sacred trust', the Covenant of the League remained firmly rooted in the territorial integrity and political independence of its members, as set out in Article 10. The right to dispose of national territory remained a matter for the individual State concerned and self-determination remained, as it had been before, a right of self-help. There was no legal principle under the League arrangement, nor any substantive political support for developing such a legal principle.[11]

In 1920 the International Committee of Jurists confirmed this interpretation of the Covenant in their advisory opinion to the League of Nations on the *Aaland Islands Question*. Finland had declared its independence in December 1917, following which a separatist movement had arisen on the Aaland Islands, whose inhabitants wanted to be attached to Sweden. The question was taken to the League and the Committee held that,

Although the principle of self-determination of peoples plays an important part in modern political thought, especially since the Great War, it must be pointed out that there is no mention of it in the Covenant of the League of Nations. The recognition of this principle in a certain number of international treaties cannot be considered as sufficient to put it upon the same footing as a positive rule of the Law of Nations.[12]

In the inter-war period there were a number of plebiscites in Europe including Upper Silesia, Schleswig, and the Saar.[13] However, the momen-

---

[9] Article 22(1), League of Nations Covenant, 28 June 1919.

[10] The interpretation of the ultimate objective of the 'sacred trust' was affirmed in the Namibia Advisory Opinion, *ICJ Rep.* (1971), 19.

[11] See Sinha, 'Self-determination', 332–3; Michla Pomerance, *Self-determination in Law and Practice* (London: Martinus Nijhoff, 1982), 7–8; Emerson, *From Empire to Nation*, 3.

[12] The Aaland Islands Question: Report of the Committee of Jurists, *League of Nations Official Journal*, Special Supp. 3 (Oct. 1920), 5; see also Verzijl, 328–32; James Crawford, *The Creation of States in International Law* (Oxford: Clarendon Press, 1979), 85–7.

[13] See Sarah Wambaugh, *Plebiscites Since the World War*, vol. i (Washington: Carnegie Endowment for International Peace, 1933).

tum generated for the principle of self-determination by the Allied war aims and the Russian Revolution never spread beyond Europe to the vast colonial empires. It is generally true to say that there was little development of the principle, used to justify the realignment of borders in Europe after World War I, into a legal right of universal application.

The eight points of the Atlantic Charter of 14 August 1941 as agreed by Roosevelt and Churchill and ascribed to by twenty-six Allied States on 1 January 1942 contained two points relevant to the principle of self-determination.

First, their countries seek no aggrandizement, territorial or other.

Second, they desire to see no territorial changes that do not accord with the freely expressed wishes of the peoples concerned.[14]

These principles were later appealed to when the Charter of the United Nations was drafted. At the time the Atlantic Charter was signed Mr Churchill, at least, did not envision the application of these principles beyond Europe. In September 1941, in the House of Commons, he said,

At the Atlantic meeting we had in mind primarily the extension of the sovereignty, self-government and national life of the states and nations of Europe now under the Nazi yoke and the principles which should govern any alterations in the territorial boundaries of countries which may have to be made. That is quite a separate problem from the progressive evolution of self-governing institutions in regions whose peoples owe allegiance to the British crown. We have made declarations on these matters which are complete in themselves, free from ambiguity and related to the conditions and circumstances of the territories and peoples affected. They will be found to be entirely in harmony with the conception of freedom and justice which inspired the joint declaration.[15]

The vision of the Atlantic Charter as a declaration of war aims destined to drift into obscurity after the redrawing of European boundaries was a vision which would remain unfulfilled.

4.3 The UN Charter

The Dumbarton Oaks proposals which were the basis of the UN Charter made no mention of self-determination either in Chapter I(2), which later became Article 1(2), or Chapter IX(1), which became Article 55.[16] It was not until the San Francisco consultations that the Soviet Union proposed

---

[14] *The Atlantic Charter and Africa from an American Standpoint*, Study by the Committee on Africa, the War, and Peace Aims (New York: no pub. 1942), 32–3; Brownlie, 'History of the Principle of Self-determination', 97.

[15] Quoted in *The Atlantic Charter*, 31.

[16] U. O. Umozurike, 'Self-determination in International Law', (D.Phil. Thesis, Oxford, 1969), 106.

an amendment which included in the text of these two sections the words 'based on respect for the principle of equal rights and self-determination of peoples'. The final text as signed by the participants has several important articles.

Chapter I of the Charter containing Articles 1 and 2, establishes the principles and purposes of the body. Article 1(2) lists as one of the four specified purposes of the UN: 'To develop friendly relations among nations based on respect for the principle of equal rights and self-determination of peoples, and to take other appropriate measures to strengthen universal peace.' In Article 55, part of Chapter IX on International Economic and Social Co-operation, the United Nations assumed the obligation of promoting higher standards of living, full employment, cultural co-operation, and observance of human rights with a view to 'the creation of conditions of stability and well-being which are necessary for peaceful and friendly relations among nations based on respect for the principle of equal rights and self-determination of peoples'. Contrary to what polemics in the following decades might suggest, the Charter of the United Nations nowhere mentions a 'right' of self-determination, nor does it clearly define who the 'self' is that enjoys this principle which should be respected by nations.[17]

Although Articles 1(2) and 55 of the Charter are the only ones which specifically mention self-determination, the Charter contains two chapters, XI and XII, on decolonization. Chapter XI, the Declaration Regarding Non-self-governing Territories, embodies a recognition of the principle that the interests of the inhabitants of these territories are paramount, and an obligation to 'accept as a sacred trust' the promotion of 'the well-being of the inhabitants'. To achieve these goals the members agreed to develop self-government, promote development, and submit regular reports to the Secretary-General.[18]

Chapter XII of the Charter established an International Trusteeship System under the authority of the United Nations to promote 'progressive development towards self-government or independence as may be appropriate to the particular circumstance of each territory'. In practice, many members of the United Nations have sought to deny any distinction between trust territories and non-self-governing territories, and to have all non-self-governing territories treated as trust territories. A Carnegie Foundation inquiry on the UN received a reply from the Indian Council of World Affairs which stated:

The division of dependent areas into non-self-governing and trust territories was

[17] See Pomerance, 12.
[18] David Kay, 'The Politics of Decolonization: The New Nations and the UN Political Process', *International Organization*, 21 (1967), 788.

merely an accident of history; the former were the possessions of the victors of the two world wars and the latter those of the defeated.[19]

The principle of self-determination and the corollaries which were to develop from it in the decades following the signing of the Charter were gradually applied to non-self-governing territories as well as trust territories.[20]

It is in Chapter XII, not Articles 1(2) and 55, that one can most clearly see the fundamental forces that would change the colonial order. Umozurike commented that, with the signing of the Charter, the international community turned away from the protection of empires and toward the 'final liquidation' of colonialism 'in the interest of humanity at large'.[21] Although the Charter was the basis for subsequent developments, I think Umozurike has overstated his case. The League of Nations Covenant had also referred to a 'sacred trust', but this trust did not lead to decolonization in the inter-war period. Moreover, there are other elements in the Charter which counter the subsequent emphasis on self-determination, and suggest that self-determination was not originally perceived as an operative principle of the Charter.

Self-determination of peoples is listed as a 'purpose' in Article 1(2) and the reference to the principle in Article 55 is preambular to a list of social, economic, and political rights that the United Nations 'shall promote'. Sovereign equality, the obligation to refrain from the threat or use of force, and the domestic jurisdiction clauses of the Charter are principles in accordance with which members 'shall act'.[22] The emphasis of the Charter is on the maintenance of peace and security and the basis of the organization is the principle of sovereign equality. It is difficult to reconcile the wording of the Charter with its subsequent interpretation. This is not to say that these subsequent developments are not important indicators of international law in their own right. But 'self-determination, in contrast to sovereignty and all that flows from it,' wrote Yehuda Blum, 'was not originally perceived as an *operative* principle of the Charter. It was regarded as a goal to be attained at some indeterminate date in the future; it was one of the *desiderata* of the Charter rather than a legal right that could be invoked as such.'[23] Since 1945 the Charter has undergone a process of 'progressive interpretation' so that its general exhortations have become prescriptive standards for State conduct.

[19] Indian Council of World Affairs, *India and the World*, (1957), 101, quoted in Umozurike, 164.
[20]e.g. UNGA Res. 1514(XV), the Declaration on Colonialism, includes both trust and non-self-governing territories.
[21] Umozurike, 163.
[22] See Pomerance, 9–13; L. C. Green, 'Self-determination and Settlement of the Arab-Israeli Conflict', *ASIL*, 65 (1971), 43–4.
[23] Yehuda Blum, 'Reflections on the Changing Concept of Self-determination', *Israel LR*, 10 (1975), 511.

4.4 Post-war Acceleration and Metamorphosis

The United Nations was the focal point for the heated debates which surrounded the development of the principle of self-determination. Its rapid expansion reflected the post–1945 process of decolonization and throughout the post–1945 era it remained the primary forum for debate. The General Assembly in particular was a means for newly independent countries to amplify their voices and gain legitimacy for their views.

The political pressure caused by the changing composition of the United Nations was an important factor in the shifting interpretation of the Charter and the development of the right of self-determination in international law. In the first ten years of its existence the United Nations admitted ten new States. In 1960, at the high point of decolonization, seventeen new States, sixteen of which were African, joined the organization. In 1955 13.2 per cent of UN members had achieved independence since 1945. By 1966 this figure had jumped to 45 per cent.[24]

4.41 The Early Years

In its first session, the General Assembly unanimously adopted Resolution 9(I) requesting the Secretary-General to include in his Annual Report a summary of the information on non-self-governing territories extended to him by administering powers under Article 73(e).[25] The Assembly further adopted Resolution 66(I) which provided for an *ad hoc* Committee on Information to study that summary.[26] The voting record on Resolution 66(I) reflected a division which would exist at least until 1960. The Asian and Eastern European States voted in favour; the Western powers, concerned about preventing intrusions on issues that were essentially within the domestic jurisdiction of the country involved, generally voted against the Resolution or abstained. This relatively moderate resolution, with its implication that the issue of self-determination was not essentially within the domestic jurisdiction of individual States, was the beginning of the Third World's efforts to outlaw colonialism and elevate self-determination from a principle to a right.

In its third session the General Assembly passed Resolution 217(III), the International Bill of Human Rights.[27] The Universal Declaration of

---

[24] Kay, 786.

[25] UNGA Res. 9(I), 9 Feb. 1946, unanimous. United Nations resolutions are published in a supplement to the Official Records of each session. Until the thirty-first session the number of the session was in parentheses in roman numerals after the number of the resolution (e.g. 1514(XV)). Starting with the thirty-first session, the number of the session came first in arabic numerals followed by the number of the resolution (e.g. 31/154). Alternatively, the resolutions are published with voting records in *United Nations Resolutions*, ed. Dusan J. Djonovich (Dobbs Ferry, NY: Oceana).

[26] UNGA Res. 66(I), 14 Dec. 1946, 28:15:7.

[27] UNGA Res. 217(III), 14 Dec. 1948, 48:0:8.

Human Rights, contained in Part A of this Resolution, does not specifically mention self-determination. Article 21 does establish that 'everyone has the right to take part in the government of his country', and the will of the people 'shall be expressed in periodic and genuine elections which shall be by universal and equal suffrage'. However, a Russian amendment to the Declaration that 'every people and every nation has the right to national self-determination' was rejected.[28]

In 1950, the fifth session of the Assembly adopted Resolution 421(V), which called on the Commission on Human Rights to 'study ways and means which would ensure the right of peoples and nations to self-determination'.[29] On the basis of those recommendations, the Assembly adopted Resolution 545(VI) of 5 February 1952 in which it decided

. . . to include in the International Covenant or Covenants on Human Rights an article on the right of all peoples and nations to self-determination in reaffirmation of the principle enunciated in the Charter of the United Nations. This article shall be drafted in the following terms: 'All peoples shall have the right of self-determination', and shall stipulate that all States, including those having responsibility for the administration of Non-Self-Governing Territories should promote the realization of that right. . .[30]

This Resolution was voted on in phrases. The phrase 'This article shall be drafted in the following terms: "All peoples shall have the right of self-determination" . . . ' was adopted by roll-call vote by 36 votes to 11, with 12 abstentions. Generally, the Western States voted against or abstained. In this Resolution the Assembly also requested the Commission on Human Rights to draw up recommendations concerning 'international respect for the self-determination of peoples'. When the Assembly addressed these recommendations in the following year, objections were raised on the grounds that how a State ensured respect for self-determination within its own borders and in territories under its authority was a matter essentially within its own jurisdiction and therefore should not be the subject of UN recommendations.[31] Despite these objections the Assembly passed Resolution 637A(VII). Paragraph 2 stated that

The States Members of the United Nations shall recognize and promote the realization of the right of self-determination of the peoples of Non-Self-Governing and Trust Territories who are under their administration and shall facilitate the exercise of this right by peoples of such territories according to the principles and

---

[28] 'Draft Declaration on the Universal Declaration on Fundamental Human Rights', Commission on Human Rights of the Economic and Social Council, UN Document A/784; Umozurike, 112.

[29] UNGA Res. 421D(V), 4 Dec. 1950, 30:9:13.

[30] UNGA Res. 545(VI), 5 Feb. 1952.

[31] Higgins, *The Development of International Law Through the Political Organs of the United Nations* (London: Oxford Univ. Press, 1963), 91.

spirit of the Charter of the United Nations in regard to each territory and to the freely expressed wishes of the peoples concerned, the wishes of the people being ascertained through plebiscites or other recognized democratic means . . . [32]

The argument that the manner in which individual States implemented the principle of self-determination was a domestic matter did not win the day despite the prohibitions of Article 2(7).

4.42 French North Africa

The composition of the international system as reflected in the member States of the United Nations had not changed much by the end of 1952. Only two new flags flew outside UN Headquarters in New York— Indonesia and Israel. The great wave of decolonization had yet to break. It was at about this time that nationalist fervour in French North Africa gave very practical meaning to the principle of self-determination.

French Morocco had been a protectorate of France since the 1912 Treaty of Fez. In October of 1950 Mohammed ben-Youssef, the sultan of Morocco, presented a memorandum to the French government suggesting a number of administrative reforms including the abolition of Press censorship, relaxation of French control over the appointment of chieftains and magistrates, and the modification of the Treaty of Fez. These reforms were rejected.[33] Tensions increased between the Moroccan nationalist Istiqlal or Independence Party and the French administration. In March 1951 the Political Committee of the Arab League decided that its members should ask France to 'take into consideration the national aspirations of the Moroccan people, with a view to the realization of their independence and their admission to the U.N.'. The note, delivered through diplomatic channels in identical language by the governments of Egypt, Syria, Iraq, Jordan, and Saudi Arabia, described French administration in Morocco as 'incompatible with the principle of self-determination of nations and the rights of man'.[34] The French government replied that this was a purely domestic matter.

In 1950 and in 1951 the question of Morocco appeared on the agenda of the General Assembly but no debate took place. In November of 1950 the Egyptian delegate proposed the discussion of French–Moroccan relations. He withdrew agreeing to an indefinite postponement after a vitriolic attack by the French delegate, supported by a number of Western countries, charging interference in French domestic affairs. Following the rejection of the Arab League's notes to the French Foreign Minister in March 1951, the

[32] UNGA Res. 637A(VII), 16 Dec. 1952, 40:14:6.
[33] *Keesing's Contemporary Archives* (Harlow: Longman), 16–23 Feb. 1952, 12023.
[34] Note from the members of the Arab League to the acting French Foreign Minister M. Schneiter, quoted in *Keesing's Contemporary Archives*, 16–23 Feb. 1952, 12024.

Arab League decided to place the Moroccan question on the agenda of the forthcoming UN General Assembly. On 13 November 1951, the Assembly again postponed discussion on the matter.

In 1952 the tensions in Morocco led to violence. In February 1952 the nationalist parties of Tunisia, Morocco, and Algeria met in Paris and decided to form a 'North African Front of Unity and Action' to 'meet the new situation in North Africa and the coalition of the Colonial Powers'.[35] In March the sultan requested the establishment of a provisional government responsible to him to negotiate a new Franco-Moroccan agreement to replace the Treaty of Fez. By December there were anti-European riots and bombings in Casablanca. In 1952, the Arab States again proposed a resolution calling upon France 'to enter into negotiations to reach an early and peaceful settlement in accord with the sovereignty of Morocco, the aspirations of her people, and the U.N. Charter'. An alternative resolution proposed by the Latin American States which was eventually adopted by the Assembly expressed the hope that 'the parties will continue negotiations on an urgent basis towards developing the free political institutions of the people of Morocco, with due regard to legitimate rights and interests under the established norms and practices of the law of nations'.[36] The French delegation was not present for the debate in protest over interference in what it considered to be a domestic issue.

In August 1953 Sultan ben-Youssef was exiled by the French government and there were widespread arrests of supporters and sympathizers of the nationalist party. In its eighth session, the First Committee of the UN adopted a draft resolution which recognized

the right of the people of Morocco to complete self-determination in conformity with the Charter, [and renewed] its appeal for the reduction of tension in Morocco and [urged] that the right of the people of Morocco to free democratic political institutions be ensured.[37]

The Resolution failed in plenary session, 32:22:5, because it did not garner the necessary two-thirds majority. The French delegation was, again, absent in protest.

In August of 1955 agreement was reached between the French and Moroccan parties concerned for the creation of a Moroccan government. On 15 February 1956, that government, with Mohammed ben-Youssef as sultan, signed a joint declaration with France 'recognizing the independence, sovereignty, and integrity of Morocco, and the right of Morocco to appoint her own diplomatic representatives and to control her own armed

[35] *Keesing's*, 16–23 Feb. 1952, 12026.
[36] UNGA Res. 612(VII), 19 Dec. 1952, 45:3:11.
[37] UN Draft Res. A/2526, 22 Oct. 1953, GAOR: 8th session.

forces'.[38] The General Assembly, recognizing that negotiations were imminent, did not take up the matter again.

Similar issues were raised in the Tunisian case.[39] At its seventh session the Assembly considered whether France was violating human rights and the principle of self-determination in the territory. The French, again claiming that the matter was within the domestic jurisdiction of France, boycotted the meetings of the First Committee. The Assembly adopted Resolution 611(VII), a relatively mild statement expressing hope that negotiation would continue 'with a view to bringing about self-government for Tunisians'.[40] In the eighth session of the Assembly the First Committee presented a draft resolution which referred to the right of self-determination for Tunisia. This Resolution failed to receive the necessary two-thirds majority. Both Morocco and Tunisia were admitted to the United Nations in its eleventh session in 1956.[41]

Although in both of these cases the relevant resolutions failed to be adopted in the Assembly where a two-thirds majority was required, they are significant because they received majority support in the First Committee. The rising tide of new States in the organization would make it difficult for the Western powers to defeat such resolutions in later years.

The growing support of the newly independent States for the right of peoples to self-determination was evident at the 1955 Bandung Conference of Afro-Asian Countries which affirmed that, '[T]he subjection of peoples to alien subjugation, domination and exploitation, constitutes a denial of fundamental human rights, is contrary to the Charter of the United Nations and is an impediment to the promotion of world peace and co-operation.'[42]

The case of Algeria is particularly interesting and important as it spanned the years 1954 to 1962, during which time the membership of the United Nations grew dramatically and the organization was deeply involved in the problems of decolonization. For this reason, an examination of the views of States on this one case illuminates well the changing role of self-determination in world politics.

Arnold Fraleigh has argued that, 'By their actions as well as by their votes in the political organs of the United Nations the member states of the United Nations during the period of the Algerian conflict established the

---

[38] *Keesing's*, 31 Mar.–7 Apr. 1956, 14781.

[39] Higgins, *Development*, 94.

[40] UNGA Res. 611(VII), 17 Dec. 1952, 44:3:8.

[41] Higgins, *Development*, 94.

[42] Wil D. Verwey, 'Decolonization and Ius ad bellum', in *Declarations on Principles: A Quest for Universal Peace*, ed. Robert J. Akkerman (Leiden: A.W. Sijthoff, 1968), 134; see also the statement of Mr Quaison-Sackey (Ghana), GAOR: 15th session, 927th mtg. 29 Nov. 1960.

legitimacy of the decolonization war.'[43] Ultimately this may have been true as the Assembly finally recognized the right of the Algerians to self-determination in 1960.[44] However, from 1955, when the question first came before the Assembly, until 1960, resolutions in support of Algeria's right to self-determination were consistently defeated.[45] In its tenth session in 1955 the question of Algeria was included on the agenda, but the Assembly decided to remove it and declared it was no longer 'seized' of the issue.[46] When the matter was brought before the Security Council in June of 1956 on the grounds that it was a threat to peace, a violation of human rights, and a violation of the Charter provisions on self-determination, the Council decided against including it on its agenda.[47] At the eleventh session of the Assembly the supporters of the Algerian national liberation movement, the FLN, were only marginally more successful in gaining recognition for their cause. A resolution in the First Committee which called on France to recognize Algeria's right to self-determination and negotiate a peaceful settlement failed, and two more moderate resolutions were presented to the plenary meeting.[48] Neither received the necessary two-thirds majority. The Assembly did pass Resolution 1012(XI), which expressed hope that a 'peaceful, democratic and just solution would be found'. At the twelfth session, even less was achieved. The Assembly merely noted in Resolution 1184(XII) that good offices had been offered.[49] The Assembly did, however, pass Resolution 1188(XII) which, although it did not relate specifically to Algeria, did relate to self-determination. In it, member States agreed to 'give due respect to the right of self-determination' and 'promote the realization and facilitate the exercise of this right' in non-self-governing territories.[50]

By 1958 the Afro-Asian States were demanding the right of the Algerian people to *independence*, not just self-determination. A resolution to this effect was passed by the First Committee but failed to get a two-thirds majority in plenary session by one vote. But there was an interesting trend taking place. According to Higgins, 'The voting records show that not only was the cause of Algeria gaining support, but that so was the idea that there might be a legal right to self-determination in these circumstances, even in spite of objections based on domestic jurisdiction.'[51]

---

[43] Arnold Fraleigh, 'The Algerian Revolution as a Case Study in International Law', in *The International Law of Civil War*, ed. Richard Falk (London: Johns Hopkins Press, 1971), 184.

[44] UNGA Res. 1573(XV), 19 Dec. 1960, 63:8:27. France was absent.

[45] See Higgins, *Development*, 95–7.

[46] UNGA Res. 909(X), 25 Nov. 1955, without vote.

[47] The vote was 7:2:2.

[48] Draft Resolutions A/C.1/L166 and A/C.1/L167.

[49] UNGA Res. 1012(XI), 15 Feb. 1957, 75:0:1, the United Kingdom abstaining; UNGA Res. 1184(XII), 10 Dec. 1957, 80:0:0.

[50] UNGA Res.1188(XII), 11 Dec. 1957, 65:0:13.

[51] Higgins, *Development*, 96.

By 1959 President de Gaulle had announced proposals for self-determination for Algeria. Many members of the Assembly were understandably reluctant to pressure France, and therefore abstained on resolutions relative to Algeria. The draft Resolution on Algeria presented in the 1959 session called for holding talks to arrive at 'a peaceful solution on the basis of the right to self-determination'.[52] Although the Resolution got a simple majority, it failed.

The fifteenth session of the General Assembly was a milestone in the development of the right to self-determination. The Assembly recognized the right of the Algerian people to self-determination in Resolution 1573(XV) by a vote of 63:8 with 27 abstentions. In opposition were the French community in Africa as well as South Africa and Portugal. Spain, Belgium, the United Kingdom, and the United States abstained.[53] In the sixteenth session of the Assembly a similar resolution, 1724(XVI), was passed with no opposing votes and 38 abstentions.[54] Whereas in the fifteenth session the Algerian situation was described as a threat to peace as well as a breach of the right to self-determination, in the sixteenth session there was no mention of a threat to peace and the Resolution was based solely on the right to self-determination for Algeria. Higgins commented,

[T]he basis of the Assembly resolution, which is addressed to two specific parties, lies squarely on an international legal right to self-determination, and, by implication, the inapplicability of Article 2(7) to any situation concerning this right.[55]

4.43 The Fifteenth Session

It would not have been difficult for an observer at the opening of the fifteenth session of the General Assembly to predict that the admission of seventeen newly independent States would have a decisive effect on the organization. On 23 September 1960, the Soviet Union, conscious of this change, requested the addition of a 'declaration on the granting of independence to colonial countries and peoples' to the agenda.[56] The Soviet draft, whose operative paragraphs were 'demands', proclaimed that all colonial countries 'must be granted forthwith complete independence'. The language of the draft was not likely to persuade wavering States to vote affirmatively. In response, the Afro-Asian States drafted a Declaration on Colonialism which eventually became Resolution 1514(XV).

---

[52] Draft Res. A/L276, GAOR: 14th session, 856th mtg., quoted in Higgins, *Development*, 96.

[53] See Fraleigh, 191; Higgins, *Development*, 97.

[54] UNGA Res. 1724(XVI), 20 Dec. 1961, 62:0:38.

[55] Higgins, *Development*, 97.

[56] UN Doc. A/4501, 23 Sept. 1960; see Kay for a discussion of the Soviet draft.

After a lively debate the Soviet draft was defeated, and the Afro-Asian draft was adopted by 89 votes in favour, none against, and 9 abstentions.[57] The trend toward acceptance of self-determination as a legal right was accelerated sharply by the adoption of 1514(XV) which declared:

1. The subjection of peoples to alien subjugation, domination and exploitation constitutes a denial of fundamental human rights, is contrary to the Charter of the United Nations and is an impediment to the promotion of world peace and co-operation.
2. All peoples have the right to self-determination; by virtue of that right they freely determine their political status and freely pursue their economic, social and cultural development.
3. Inadequacy of political, economic, social or educational preparedness should never serve as a pretext for delaying independence.
4. All armed action or repressive measures of all kinds directed against dependent peoples shall cease in order to enable them to exercise peacefully and freely their right to complete independence, and the integrity of their national territory shall be respected.

The final operative paragraph of the Resolution stated:

7. All States shall observe faithfully and strictly the provisions of the Charter of the United Nations, the Universal Declaration of Human Rights and the present Declaration on the basis of equality, non-interference in the internal affairs of all States and respect for the sovereign rights of all peoples and their territorial integrity.[58]

One of the more moderate members of the Afro-Asian group which presented the draft commented that, 'in order to rally all currents of opinion in the Assembly in favour of a text acceptable to all the Members of the UN, [we] have, in a spirit of conciliation accepted certain phrases of a much more moderate nature.'[59] Nevertheless, one could not accuse its authors of ambivalence. Indeed, some have described Resolution 1514(XV) as a revolutionary attempt to revise the provisions of the Charter without formally amending it.[60] There is merit in this argument. The Charter spoke of a principle of self-determination, not a right, and certainly not a right to independence. Independence was only one of several possible paths which might be 'appropriate to the particular circumstances'.[61] The Charter did not outlaw colonialism, require 'immed-

---

[57] Australia, Belgium, the Dominican Republic, France, Portugal, Spain, South Africa, the United Kingdom, and the United States abstained.

[58] UNGA Res. 1514(XV), 14 Dec. 1960, 89:0:9.

[59] Mehdi Vakil (Iran), GAOR: 15th session, 926th plenary mtg., 28 Nov. 1960, 995–6, quoted in Kay, 790–1.

[60] See Pomerance, 11; C. J. R. Dugard, 'The Organisation of African Unity and Colonialism: An Inquiry into the Plea of Self-defence as a Justification for the Use of Force in the Eradication of Colonialism', *ICLQ*, 16 (1967), 174.

[61] Article 76(*b*), UN Charter.

'immediate steps' to be taken for independence, or proscribe armed action against dependent peoples. But to raise these objections in concert with the argument that resolutions of the General Assembly are not binding *per se* and thereby brand the Declaration as an 'essentially . . . political document'[62] gives too little credit to the Declaration. It must be acknowledged that the Resolution was adopted without any opposing votes and very few abstentions. Furthermore, the generality and political aspect of the principle do not deprive it of legal content.[63] This is not to say that the legal content of the principle is precise, nor has it been fully explicated in the intervening twenty-seven years. Rather, the Resolution represented the wishes and beliefs of a large number of States in the United Nations and is strong evidence of a legal right to self-determination.

Resolution 1514(XV) was directed most obviously at the administering powers of the remaining trust and non-self-governing territories. The Resolution has been interpreted more broadly since 1960 and applied to situations which most observers would not immediately identify as colonial subjugation. Although 1514(XV) does not mention apartheid, in its preambulatory paragraphs it does state that an end must be put to colonialism 'and all practices of segregation and discrimination associated therewith'. There is room for the argument that South Africa's brand of apartheid is a form of colonialism, and at least a denial of self-determination—an argument put forth in the General Assembly and in the Third Report on the UN Commission on the Racial Situation in the Union of South Africa.[64] Likewise, the refusal of the international community to recognize the independence of Southern Rhodesia because it was a State created without regard to the principle of self-determination is evidence that, in addition to the more generally accepted qualifications for recognition of States, there may also be an obligation to respect the freely expressed will of the people.

4.44 The Maturation of the Right to Self-determination

The Declaration on Colonialism was a significant milestone. It was also the beginning of the accelerated development of the right to self-determination within the organs of the United Nations and beyond. In its sixteenth session the Assembly established a Special Committee of Seventeen (expanded to twenty-four in 1962 by Resolution 1810(XVII)) to examine the implementation of the 1960 Declaration.[65] This session also passed

[62] R. Y. Jennings, *The Acquisition of Territory in International Law* (Manchester: Manchester Univ. Press, 1963), 83; see also Pomerance, 12.

[63] Brownlie, *Principles of Public International Law*, 3rd edn. (Oxford: Clarendon Press, 1979), 594.

[64] Dugard, 'The Organisation of African Unity', 159.

[65] UNGA Res. 1654(XVI), 27 Nov. 1961, 97:0:4.

resolutions condemning Portugal's refusal to co-operate with the Committee on Information for Non-self-governing Territories, and made declarations on the inalienable right to independence and self-determination for the peoples of Angola and South West Africa.[66] The reaffirmation of Resolution 1514(XV) and the reaffirmation of the right to independence or self-determination of particular peoples still subject to colonial authority became 'almost an annual ritual for the General Assembly.[67] Without reciting the entire litany, there are some events and resolutions since 1960 which are of particular importance.

It is possible that the real turning-point in the approach to self-determination was not the 1960 Declaration on Colonialism, but the crisis in Goa the following year, when the abstractions of the Resolution were put to the test. In December 1961 Portugal brought a complaint to the Security Council accusing India of aggression because it had occupied the Portuguese enclaves of Goa, Damão, and Diu. The United States, the United Kingdom, France, Turkey, China, Ecuador, and Chile supported a draft resolution calling for a cease-fire and withdrawal of Indian forces from the territory, and urging the parties to work out a permanent solution by peaceful means in accord with the principles of the Charter.[68]

The Resolution was not passed and the use of force by India was not condemned because the Soviet Union, supported by Ceylon, Liberia, and the UAR, vetoed the Resolution. More importantly, a large majority of States immediately acquiesced in the annexation of these former Portuguese territories. Self-determination, although not yet justifying the use of force in the minds of the majority of the representatives to the Security Council, did justify the tacit acceptance of the annexation. James Crawford points out,

The significance of self-determination in [the Goa case] is not so much that it cures illegalities as that it may allow illegality to be more readily accommodated through the processes of recognition and prescription, whereas in other circumstances aggression partakes of the nature of a breach of jus cogens and is not, or not readily, curable by prescription, lapse of time or acquiescence.[69]

Five years after the Goa incident, Resolution 2160(XXI) linked the right

[66] UNGA Res. 1699(XVI), 19 Dec. 1961, 90:3:2; UNGA Res. 1742(XVI), 30 Jan. 1962, 99:2:1; and UNGA Res. 1702(XVI), 19 Dec. 1961, 90:1:4.

[67] See UNGA Resolutions 1810(XVII), 1815(XVII), 1807(XVII), 1819(XVII), 1805(XVII), 1775(XVII), 1760(XVII), 1904(XVIII), 1899(XVIII), 1889(XVIII), 1970(XVIII), 1956(XVIII), 2022(XX), 2105(XX), 2106(XX), 2262(XXII), 2270(XXII), 2288(XXII), 2326(XXII), 2383(XXIII), 2395(XXIII), 2396(XXIII), 2403(XXIII), 2425(XXIII), 2465(XXIII), 2508(XXIV), 2548(XXIV), 2554(XXIV), 2625(XXV), 2652(XXV), 2678(XXV), 2707(XXV), 2708(XXV), 3314(XXIX), 3236(XXIX), 3246(XXIX), 3411(XXX), 3382(XXX), 31/63, 31/20, 31/143, 31/146, 31/154, 32/9D, 32/14, 32/36, 32/42, 32/105J, 32/116, and 35/118.

[68] Quincy Wright, 'The Goa Incident', *AJIL*, 56 (1962), 617.

[69] Crawford, 112–13.

of self-determination to the prohibition of the threat or use of force in international relations. This linkage also had the effect of emphasizing the separate status of self-determination 'units' in international law. The Resolution affirmed that

Any forcible action, direct or indirect, which deprives peoples under foreign domination of their right to self-determination and freedom and independence and of their right to determine freely their political status and pursue their economic, social and cultural development constitutes a violation of the Charter of the United Nations. Accordingly, the use of force to deprive peoples of their natural identity, as prohibited by the Declaration on the Inadmissibility of Intervention in the Domestic Affairs of States and the Protection of Their Independence and Sovereignty contained in General Assembly Resolution 2131(XX), constitutes a violation of their inalienable rights and the principle of non-intervention.[70]

Until 1970, several Western States had consistently abstained on resolutions recognizing a right to self-determination. The adoption of the Declaration on Principles of International Law by consensus in October 1970 marked the first departure from this policy.[71] For the first time, the United Nations unanimously proclaimed,

By virtue of the principle of equal rights and self-determination of peoples enshrined in the Charter of the United Nations, all peoples have the right freely to determine, without external interference, their political status and to pursue their economic, social and cultural development, and every State has the duty to respect this right in accordance with the provisions of the Charter.[72]

The idea that 'peoples' pursuing a right to self-determination have a status distinct in international law from the metropolitan State administering them was clearly stated in the Resolution.

The territory of a colony or other non-self-governing territory has, under the Charter, a status separate and distinct from the territory of the State administering it; and such separate and distinct status under the Charter shall exist until the people of the colony or non-self-governing territory have exercised their right of self-determination in accordance with the Charter . . .

The passage of Resolution 2621(XXV) contributed to the significance of the 1970 session. For the first time, by a vote of 86:5:15, the Assembly proclaimed that the continuation of colonialism in all its forms and manifestations was a 'crime'.[73]

---

[70] UNGA Res. 2160(XXI), 30 Nov. 1966, 98:2:8.

[71] The full title of this Resolution is 'The Declaration on Principles of International Law Concerning Friendly Relations and Co-operation among States in Accordance with the Charter of the United Nations'. This Resolution is often referred to as 'The Declaration on Friendly Relations', 'The Declaration on Principles of International Law', or simply 'The Declaration on Principles'.

[72] UNGA Res. 2625(XXV), 24 Oct. 1970, unanimous.

[73] UNGA Res. 2621(XXV), 12 Oct. 1970, 86:5:15.

By 1970 there were 127 member States in the United Nations and the idea that there was a right to self-determination was firmly established. The demand for the independence of the non-self-governing territories which remained did not abate. It was 1974 before a coup in Portugal led that country to co-operate with the United Nations and arrange for the independence of its African territories of Angola, Mozambique, and Guinea-Bissau.[74] Before 1974, Portugal was continually criticized for its intransigence both in the General Assembly and the Security Council. In November 1972 the Security Council unanimously adopted Resolution 322 which not only recognized the right of the peoples of Guinea-Bissau and Cape Verde, Angola, and Mozambique to self-determination, but affirmed the legitimacy of their struggle to secure it.[75]

Following the decolonization of the Portuguese territories, the spotlight of international concern intensified on those territories where self-determination was still denied. One of the most controversial 'peoples' which captured the attention of the international community in the 1970s and still holds that attention today is the Palestinians.

The Palestine Liberation Organization was created by a National Congress of Palestinians in May 1964, and it immediately became involved in international politics. Sanford Silverburg notes that,

In May 1964, the Palestine National Congress sent formal notification to the U.N. Secretary-General U Thant, regarding the establishment of the PLO and the Palestine Congress, and claimed representation for the PLO in matters dealing with the Palestine people . . . . In March 1965, Shukairy led a PLO delegation to the People's Republic of China where it . . . formally established a representative office. Representative status in China was followed by diplomatic status in Damascus with the creation there of a permanent office, and thereafter by opening offices in other states in the Middle East and elsewhere.[76]

The Palestinian people, as represented by the PLO, were not considered to have a right of self-determination in these early years as much as a right to return to their occupied homeland. In 1965 the General Assembly agreed that the PLO should be involved in considering the Arab refugee question. For the first few years the Palestinians were generally considered to be refugees and the PLO consulted more in the capacity of expert witness than as representative of a people.[77] The Second Conference of

---

[74] *The United Nations and Decolonization: Highlights of United Nations Action in Support of Independence for Colonial Countries and Peoples* (New York: United Nations, 1980) 31; Allan Rosas, *The Legal Status of Prisoners of War* (Helsinki: Soumalainen Tiedeakatemia, 1976), 162–3.

[75] UN Sec. Res. 322 (1972), 22 Nov. 1972, unanimous; see also UN Sec. Res. 312 (1972), 4 Feb. 1972, 9:0:6.

[76] Sanford Silverburg, 'The Palestine Liberation Organization in the United Nations: Implications for International Law and Relations', *Israel LR*, 12 (1977), 382.

[77] See Catherine Burke, 'International Recognition of a Non-State Nation: The Palestine Liberation Organization and the United Nations' (M.Phil. Thesis, Oxford, 1979), 30.

Non-aligned Countries did, however, call for 'full restoration of all the rights of the Arab peoples of Palestine to their homeland, and their inalienable right to self-determination' as early as October 1964.[78]

It was in 1969 that the UN first referred to the Palestinians as a 'people' and not as refugees.[79] In the following year the Assembly recognized that '[R]espect for the rights of the Palestinians is an indispensable element in the establishment of a just and lasting peace in the Middle East.'[80]

In the next year the Assembly took the significant step of including the Palestinian people in a resolution on decolonization. Resolution 2728(XXVI) of 6 December 1971

Confirm[ed] the legality of the peoples' struggle for self-determination and liberation from colonial and foreign domination and alien subjugation, notably in southern Africa and in particular that of the peoples of Zimbabwe, Namibia, Angola, Mozambique and Guinea (Bissau), *as well as of the Palestinian people*, by all available means consistent with the Charter of the United Nations.[81] (Emphasis supplied.)

The Resolution received less support than customary for resolutions of this type, presumably because of the attachment of this controversial clause. The sentiments expressed in this Resolution were reaffirmed by a larger majority in 1973.[82]

The PLO, acting as the representative of the Palestinian people, has been actively involved in diplomacy since its creation. It participated in the International Telecommunication Union Conference, the ICRC Diplomatic Conference, the World Health Assembly, the Third Law of the Sea Conference, and the World Food Conference, as well as many other international and transnational forums.[83] Its biggest political victory was in 1974 when it was invited to participate in the General Assembly deliberations on the question of Palestine in plenary meetings, and then to participate in the sessions and work of the General Assembly as an observer.[84] This move caused tremendous furor despite the fact that the

[78] Silverburg, 373–4.

[79] UNGA Res. 2535B(XXIV), 10 Dec. 1969, 48:22:47. Significantly, Resolutions A and C of this set which dealt with refugee problems passed by 110:0:1 and 108:0:3 respectively.

[80] UNGA Res. 2628(XXV), 4 Nov. 1970, 57;16:39; see also M. Cherif Bassiouni, ' "Self-determination" and the Palestinians', *ASIL*, 65 (1971), 31–40.

[81] UNGA Res. 2787(XXVI), 6 Dec. 1971, 50:24:44.

[82] UNGA Res. 3089D(XXVIII), 7 Dec. 1973, 87:6:33.

[83] Silverburg, 382.

[84] UNGA Res. 3210(XXIX), adopted 14 Oct. 1974, 105:4:20 (Bolivia, Dominican Republic, Israel, and the United States opposed); and UNGA Res. 3237(XXIX), 22 Nov. 1974, 95:17:19. On 29 Nov. 1974 the Assembly passed Res. 3247(XXIX), by 105:3:15, which invited not only the PLO to the United Nations Conference on the Representation of States and their Relations with International Organizations but 'the national liberation movements recognized by the Organization of African Unity, and/or by the League of Arab States in their respective regions to participate in the Conference as observers, *in accordance with the practice of the United Nations*'. (Emphasis supplied.)

PLO had been participating in the UN since 1965. The difference was one of status.

Observer status is an informal relationship which grew out of United Nations practice. It was a way for non-member States to participate in the activities of the Assembly before acceptance as members, or, as in the case of Switzerland, without compromising their neutrality. Apart from the Holy See, observers had been States who asked the Secretary-General to accept them. The General Assembly itself did not approve or disapprove observers, let alone invite them to participate.[85] Before 1974, the Secretary-General accepted observers, 'when such an arrangement is proposed in cases where the country in question is recognized diplomatically'.[86] Thus although members did not vote directly on the acceptance of observers, their recognition policies were their indirect votes. The invitation to the PLO was a significant change. First, the PLO was invited to participate as an observer by the Assembly. Second, the criterion for its participation was that it had been recognized not as a State, but as a representative of a people entitled to certain rights including that of self-determination. In effect, the Palestinians were the first nation without a State to be granted status as a 'non-voting member' based on their as yet unrealized right to self-determination.[87]

Although the Israeli government has always refused to negotiate with the PLO, which it considers to be a terrorist organization, it does recognize the Palestinian people as an entity separate from its neighbouring States. In the 1978 Camp David agreement Mr Begin and President Sadat agreed that 'Egypt, Israel, Jordan and the representatives of the Palestinian people should participate in negotiations on the resolution of the Palestinian problem in all its aspects.' They also agreed that 'The solution from the negotiations must also recognize the legitimate rights of the Palestinian people and their just requirements. In this way, the Palestinians will participate in the determination of their own future.[88]

Israel's acceptance of the existence of the Palestinian people with the right to 'participate in the determination of their own future' is an important acknowledgement of the right of a people to self-determination.

---

[85] In the fifth session of the General Assembly, in response to the Security Council veto preventing the membership of some States, El Salvador proposed that States which received seven or more votes in the Security Council be invited to send observers to the General Assembly and its Committees. This was rejected 21:11:16. See UN Doc. A/1585, 2 Dec. 1950, GAOR: 5th session, Annexes, Agenda Item 19, 3–4; Louis B. Sohn, *United Nations Law* (Brooklyn: The Foundation Press, 1967), 5.

[86] Dag Hammarskjöld, press conference of 21 Apr. 1960, quoted in A. Glenn Mower, 'Observer Countries: Quasi Members of the United Nations', *International Organization*, 20 (1966), 273.

[87] See Burke, 77.

[88] Text of the agreement reached at Camp David between President Sadat and Mr Begin, *The Times*, 19 Sept. 1978.

At the same time, the Camp David accord illustrates that the right of self-determination is moderated by other rights, including the territorial integrity and security of neighbouring States. One passage of the agreement describing arrangements for interim administration on the West Bank concluded, 'These new arrangements should give due consideration to both the principle of self-government by the inhabitants of these territories and to the legitimate security concerns of the parties involved.'

Israel and the Arab countries do not agree which entity is the legitimate representative of the Palestinian people. They do agree that such a people exists, and that they have the right to determine their own future. That right is modified by the security concerns of the bordering States.

A large number of States are of the opinion that the Palestinian people have a right to self-determination. The PLO, as their representative, has a status in international politics and international law which seems to spring not from the possession of territory, but from the recognition that the Palestinians are a people, separate and distinct from other Middle Eastern States. This status, and the privileges which go along with it, is a fruit of their recognized right both to return to their homeland and to freely establish their own political institutions. The acceptance of the PLO as an actor in world politics without an established State is strong evidence of the existence of a right to self-determination in international law.

4.5 Self-determination in Positive Law

The accumulation of General Assembly resolutions after 1960 fails to move some jurists more positivistically inclined. Although the General Assembly has been the most active on the issue of self-determination, its resolutions are not the only indications of a developing right of self-determination.

In accordance with the wishes of the Assembly expressed in 1952, the International Covenants on Human Rights adopted in resolutions of the General Assembly in 1966 included the right to self-determination.[89] Widespread adoption of these Covenants would give the right to self-determination legal force established by treaty. Common Article 1 of these Covenants establishes that

1. All peoples have the right of self-determination. By virtue of that right they freely determine their political status and freely pursue their economic, social and cultural development.[90]

[89] *Supra* sect. 4.41.
[90] The International Covenant on Economic, Social and Cultural Rights and the International Covenant on Civil and Political Rights, and the Optional Protocol to the International Convention on Civil and Political Rights, were adopted by UNGA Res. 2200A(XXI), 16 Dec. 1966. The first Covenant was signed by 51 States, the second by 59

Widespread ratification of the Covenants has not occurred, although this is probably not because of Article 1. Without such ratification the Covenants remain a not insignificant piece of evidence suggesting that self-determination is considered to be a legal right as well as a political principle.

The *South West Africa* and *Western Sahara* advisory opinions given by the International Court of Justice provide further evidence of the status of self-determination in international law. In 1971 the International Court of Justice in the *Namibia* opinion advised that

[T]he subsequent development of international law in regard to non-self-governing territories, as enshrined in the Charter of the United Nations, made the principle of self-determination applicable to all of them. . . . A further important stage in this development was the Declaration on the Granting of Independence to Colonial Countries and Peoples. . . . In the domain to which the present proceedings relate, the last fifty years . . . have brought important developments. These developments leave little doubt that the ultimate objective of the sacred trust was the self-determination and independence of the peoples concerned. In this domain, as elsewhere, the *corpus juris gentium* has been considerably enriched.[91]

Michla Pomerance points out that in this extract the Court does not refer to a right in international law.[92] However, the Court does recognize a principle in international law as enshrined in the Charter and its *further* development in the Declaration on Colonialism (1514(XV)), which refers to a right to self-determination.

Elsewhere in the *Namibia* opinion, later cited approvingly in the *Western Sahara* case, the Court held that

[T]he Court must take into consideration the changes which have occurred in the supervening half-century, and its interpretation cannot remain unaffected by the subsequent development of law, through the Charter of the United Nations and by way of customary law.[93]

In the *Western Sahara* case the International Court was asked to advise the Assembly on two questions: the legal status of the area at the time of colonization by Spain, and the legal ties between the area and Morocco and Mauritania. In the course of its opinion the Court had occasion to comment on self-determination in greater depth than the Court in the *Namibia* case. Judge Petren in a separate opinion commented that:

States. They have received 69 and 71 ratifications respectively. The Optional Protocol has been signed by 23 States and ratified by 27.

[91] Legal Consequences for States of the Continued Presence of South Africa in Namibia (South West Africa) Notwithstanding Security Council Resolution 276 (1970), Advisory Opinion, ICJ Rep. (1971), 31–2.
[92] Pomerance, 69.
[93] Namibia Advisory Opinion, ICJ Rep. (1971), 31; Western Sahara Advisory Opinion, ICJ Rep. (1975), 32.

[A] veritable law of decolonization is in the course of taking shape. It derives essentially from the principle of self-determination of peoples proclaimed in the Charter of the United Nations and confirmed by a large number of resolutions of the General Assembly.[94]

As critics have noted, Judge Petren referred to a law of decolonization, not of self-determination, and a *principle* which has been confirmed by UN resolutions.[95] Judge Petren is not talking about a principle of political thought as was the Committee of Jurists in the *Aaland Islands* case which decided the principle was not sufficient to put self-determination on the same footing as a positive rule of the law of nations. On the contrary, though not unequivocally, he seems to suggest that self-determination *does* have a place in international law. Furthermore, his reference to a law of decolonization rather than self-determination suggests that in law, as opposed to political thought, the repositories of a right to self-determination are limited. This 'law of decolonization' is the right to self-determination for colonies.

Elsewhere the Court held that, 'The above provisions [of 1514(XV)] in particular paragraph 2, thus confirm and emphasize that the application of the right of self-determination requires free and genuine expression of the will of the peoples concerned.' [96] Judge Dillard also noted that

The pronouncements of the Court thus indicate, in my view, that a norm of international law has emerged applicable to the decolonization of those non-self-governing territories which are under the aegis of the United Nations. It should be added that the force of those pronouncements is in no way diminished by virtue of the theoretically non-binding character of an advisory opinion.[97]

Because advisory opinions of the International Court are not necessarily binding on the parties involved, the *Namibia* and *Western Sahara* opinions are not binding interpretations of international law in the same way that decisions of the US Supreme Court are binding interpretations of the domestic law of the United States. That said, the function of the International Court is to decide 'in accordance with international law', and in that sense, its opinions are learned explications of the content of the law.

Finally, one of the most recent pieces of evidence in the form of a multilateral treaty which suggests that self-determination is now widely accepted as a right in international law can be found in the First Protocol Additional to the Geneva Conventions of 1949, completed in June of 1977 and signed by 62 States.[98] Article 1(4) of Protocol I, which was added to

---

[94] Judge Petren, Western Sahara Advisory Opinion, separate opinion, ICJ Rep. (1975), 110.

[95] See Pomerance, 69.

[96] Western Sahara Advisory Opinion, ICJ Rep. (1975), 32.

[97] Ibid. 12.

[98] As of Feb. 1987 the Protocol had been ratified or acceded to by 65 States.

the Protocol at the First Diplomatic Conference in 1974, establishes its scope of application:

4. The situations referred to in the preceding paragraph include armed conflicts in which peoples are fighting against colonial domination and alien occupation and against racist regimes in the exercise of their right of self-determination, as enshrined in the Charter of the United Nations and the Declaration on Principles of International Law concerning Friendly Relations and Co-operation among States in accordance with the Charter of the United Nations.[99]

The 1977 Protocols have profound implications for both the authority to use force and the laws of armed conflict which are explored more fully in later chapters. In addition to these deeper and more complex developments, Article 1(4) expressly recognizes self-determination as a right in international law.

4.6 Self-determination as a Right in Law

The idea that the members of a community should choose for themselves a form of political organization, and that they should be free to conduct their internal affairs and their external relations as they see fit, is a principle as old as the study of politics itself. What I have attempted to demonstrate thus far in this chapter is that the principle of self-determination has undergone a metamorphosis, largely in the last forty years, from a principle of political thought to a right in international law. It is all too tempting to grasp seemingly pivotal events like the passage of Resolution 1514(XV) in 1960 or the signing of the 1977 Protocols as evidence of this change and to ignore the gradual evolution of ideas, as evidenced by the practice of States, which led to these major events. In fact, these seemingly major events are often not revolutionary at all but just the codification of less noticeable changes which have taken place over many years.

In 1920 the Committee of Jurists in the *Aaland Islands* case decided that 'the recognition of [the principle of self-determination] in a certain number of international treaties cannot be considered as sufficient to put it upon the same footing as a positive rule of the Law of Nations'. In 1975 the International Court in the *Western Sahara* case decided that 'the application of the right of self-determination requires free and genuine expression of the will of the peoples concerned'. In the intervening 55 years the vast majority of States have accepted that the age of colonization is

---

[99] *Official Records of the Diplomatic Conference on the Reaffirmation and Development of International Humanitarian Law Applicable in Armed Conflicts, Geneva (1974–1977)* (Berne: Federal Political Department, 1978). Paragraph 3, referred to in the text, states that the Protocol shall apply in the situations referred to in Article 2 of the 1949 Geneva Conventions.

over and that 'peoples' have a right to determine their own affairs. There are still those who maintain that self-determination is not a legal right but a political principle inconsistently applied by States.[100] There is, however, a fairly strong consensus that, even if the content of the legal principle is not entirely clear, there is a right of self-determination in international law.[101]

More important than the thoughts of those who analyse the law are the actions of States which make the law. Here too, it is difficult to ignore the emergence of an entire continent of sovereign States in Africa and the gradual acceptance by States, some more reluctantly than others, of the idea that self-determination is an issue not solely within the domestic jurisdiction of the administering power, that non-self-governing territories have a status separate and distinct from the metropolitan community which governs them, and that the obligation to promote the development of these areas is a legal obligation as well as a moral one.

At the same time, one must acknowledge that self-determination is still a principle of political thought. As it is the ideas of political thought which give rise to the obligations of law in any community, this should come as no surprise. Just as sovereignty is both a principle of political thought and a right in international law, so the principle and the right of peoples to self-determination are complementary, not competitive.

However, the existence of both a principle and a right is the source of a great deal of confusion because the right in law is much more restricted in scope. Not every group has a right in international law to self-determination. The remainder of this chapter will be devoted to the analysis of this problem.

4.7 The Concept of 'Self'

The Charter of the United Nations establishes that 'peoples' are the selves

---

[100] R. Y. Jennings, 78; Verzijl, 321; Pomerance, 71; see statement of G. I. A. D. Draper (UK), Committee I of the Diplomatic Conference on Humanitarian Law, 11 Mar. 1974, CDDH/I/SR.2, OR: viii. 13.

[101] See Dan Ciobanu, 'The Attitude of the Socialist Countries', in vol. i of *The New Humanitarian Law of Armed Conflict*, ed. Antonio Cassese (Naples: Editoriale Scientifica, 1979), 411; Brownlie, *Principles*, 593–5; Ian Brownlie, *Basic Documents on Human Rights*, 2nd edn. (Oxford: Clarendon Press, 1981), 28; Crawford, 87; Verwey, 'Decolonization', 127; Umozurike, 119; Asbiorn Eide, 'Sovereign Equality Versus the Global Military Structure: Two Competing Approaches to World Order', in vol. i of *The New Humanitarian Law of Armed Conflict*, ed. Antonio Cassese (Naples: Editoriale Scientifica, 1979), 22; Georges Abi-Saab, 'Wars of National Liberation and the Laws of War', *Annales d'études internationales*, 3 (1972), 99; I. Sagay, 'The Legal Status of Freedom Fighters in Africa', *Eastern Africa LR*, 6 (1973), 25; J. E. S. Fawcett, *The Law of Nations*, 2nd edn. (Harmondsworth: Penguin, 1971), 46; Rosalyn Higgins, 'Internal War and International Law', in vol. iii of *The Future of the International Legal Order*, ed. C. E. Black and R. A. Falk (Princeton: Princeton Univ. Press, 1971), 103; Green, 46; Sureda.

to whom self-determination applies. This choice of subject was used in the Declaration on Colonialism, the 1977 Protocol as well as the vast majority of other resolutions, declarations, decisions, and agreements regarding self-determination. The subjectivity of defining 'peoples' who enjoy this right is one of the more common criticisms of any legal right of self-determination. 'On the surface', wrote Ivor Jennings, 'it seems reasonable: let the people decide. It [is] in fact ridiculous because the people cannot decide until somebody decides who are the people.'[102] Fortunately, much of the ambiguity in the principal documents is clarified by State practice.

State practice as well as opinion expressed through the political organs of the United Nations suggests that the 'self' is not an ethnic or religious group, but a territorial one. 'Self-determination', according to Rosalyn Higgins, 'refers to the right of the majority within a generally accepted political unit to the exercise of power. In other words, it is necessary to start with stable boundaries and to permit political change within them.'[103] This limitation is a significant one as it rules out self-determination in law, as opposed to political theory, by groups or even individuals whose basis of association lacks this territorial element. The State boundaries of post-colonial Africa are largely those inherited from the colonial age; a situation which has been generally accepted by the newly independent States.[104] In general, the principle applies to those territories which are separate political units. But State practice provides an even clearer indication of the subjects of the legal right.

The right of peoples to self-determination attaches most clearly to trust and mandated territories established under Article 22 of the League of Nations Covenant, and Chapters XII and XIII of the UN Charter. The decisions of the International Court in the *Namibia* and *Western Sahara* cases reaffirmed the responsibility of the administering power to promote the 'progressive development towards self-government or independence' of these territories.[105]

Secondly, the right to determine freely one's economic, cultural, and political destiny applies to non-self-governing territories referred to in Chapter XI of the Charter. The meaning of 'territories whose peoples have not yet attained a full measure of self-government' is not entirely clear. At least, the wording of Chapter XI suggests that the principle applies only to

[102] William Ivor Jennings, *The Approach to Self-government* (Cambridge: Cambridge Univ. Press, 1956), 56.

[103] Higgins, *Development*, 104.

[104] See Ian Brownlie, *African Boundaries* (London: C. Hurst & Co., 1979), 6; Conference of Heads of State or Government of the Non-aligned Countries, 'Programme for Peace and International Co-operation: Declaration as Adopted by the Conference, Cairo—October 1964', *Indian JIL*, 4 (1964), 599. The Assembly of Heads of State and Government at Cairo in 1964 adopted a resolution declaring that 'all Member States pledge themselves to respect the borders existing on their achievement of national independence'.

[105] See Brownlie, *Principles*, 594.

'territories' whose 'peoples' are not fully self-governing and therefore it does not apply to minorities within a State. 'Member States are bound in their behavior towards minorities not by Chapter XI,' contends James Crawford, but 'by the more general human rights provisions of Chapter IX, and in particular by Articles 55 and 56'.[106] Article 74 of Chapter XI suggests that there is a distinction between territories 'to which this Chapter applies' and 'metropolitan areas' of the State, but the difficulty of identifying a non-self-governing territory solely on the basis of the Charter's wording remains. Resolution 1541(XV), passed the day after the more famous Declaration on Colonialism, adopted the view that Chapter XI applies prima facie 'in respect of a territory which is geographically separate and is distinct ethnically and/or culturally from the country administering it'. Principle V of the Resolution further explains that,

> Once it has been established that such a *prima facie* case of geographical and ethnic or cultural distinctness of a territory exists, other elements may be brought into consideration. These additional elements may be *inter alia*, of an administrative, political, juridical, economic or historical nature. If they affect the relationship between the metropolitan State and the territory concerned in a manner which arbitrarily places the latter in a position or status of subordination, they support the presumption that there is an obligation to transmit information under Article 73e of the Charter.[107]

The territories qualifying as non-self-governing were originally determined by replies to a letter from the Secretary-General of 29 June 1946 requesting information on non-self-governing territories. Resolution 1541(XV) stated that Chapter XI was to apply only to 'territories, known as colonies at the time of the passing of the Charter'. Although Article 73 is not that restrictive, with one exception, United Nations' practice has conformed with this interpretation. The exception was the declaration contained in Resolution 1747(XVI) that Southern Rhodesia was a non-self-governing territory.[108] The reason that Rhodesia was considered non-self-governing had less to do with the constitutional relationship between the Smith regime and the United Kingdom than with the denial of human rights in Rhodesia. Resolution 1541(XV) lists one of the factors indicative of independence as 'complete freedom of the people of a territory to choose the form of government which they desire'. The problem in Rhodesia, according to J. E. S. Fawcett, was that the government was 'based upon a systematic denial in its territory of certain civil and political rights, including in particular the right of every citizen to participate in the

---

[106] Crawford, 359.
[107] UNGA Res. 1541(XV), 15 Dec. 1960, 69:2:21.
[108] UNGA Res. 1747(XVI), 28 June 1962, 73:1:27, Portugal and the United Kingdom not participating.

government of his country, directly or through representatives elected by regular, equal and secret suffrage.'[109]

In the period from 1945–78 there were approximately 100 territories that were considered to be non-self-governing in the sense of Chapter XI of the Charter. Of these, sixty have achieved joint or separate independence, including Grenada, Surinam, and Singapore, which had a previous status of self-government. Of the others, 'Seven territories were integrated with the metropolitan State; six with other States. Seven are now Associated States. About seventeen are still dependent territories, whether or not reported on'.[110] The status of East Timor and the Western Sahara is controversial.[111]

Given the history of the last quarter-century, it is difficult to deny that mandate and trust territories and non-self-governing territories have a legal right to self-determination. This right has been established through international agreements and the practice of States. A more controversial category of possible repositories of the right to self-determination is territories 'forming distinct political-geographical areas, whose inhabitants do not share in the government either of the region or of the State to which the region belongs, with the result that the territory becomes in effect, with respect to the remainder of the State, non-self-governing'.[112] In 1968 Dr J. H. W. Verzijl wrote that 'the "right of self-determination" has . . . always been the sport of national and international politics and has never been recognized as a genuine positive right of "peoples" of universal and impartial application, and it never will, nor can be so recognized in the future'.[113] This criticism is clearly levelled at the third collection of possible recipients. State practice in this third category is limited. There are, however, some admittedly contentious examples of peoples in such territories which may have a right to self-determination.

East Pakistan had never been considered a non-self-governing territory under the Charter. However, conditions in what would become Bangla-

---

[109] J. E. S. Fawcett, 'Security Council Resolutions on Rhodesia', *BYIL*, 41 (1965–6), 112; see also M. S. McDougal and M. W. Reisman, 'Rhodesia and the United Nations: The Lawfulness of International Concern', *AJIL*, 62 (1968), 18; Crawford, 104.

[110] Crawford, 364 n. 60.

[111] The General Assembly has consistently supported the right of the peoples of East Timor and the Western Sahara to self-determination. East Timor was annexed by Indonesia in 1976. The territory is part of Indonesia, an occupied independent State, or an occupied non-self-governing territory. The Western Sahara was occupied by Mauritania and Morocco in 1976 following the Spanish withdrawal. Mauritania concluded a peace treaty with the Western Sahara liberation movement, Polisario, in 1979. Morocco claims the territory is part of the State of Morocco. The provisional government established by Polisario in 1976, the SDAR, has been recognized by fifty-six States and is an OAU member. The Western Sahara is either an independent State occupied by Morocco with a government in exile, or part of Morocco.

[112] Crawford, 101.

[113] Verzijl, i. 324.

desh were such as to convince many that East Pakistan should have a right to self-determination. In 1972 V. S. Mani wrote,

Twenty-three years of rule by Pakistan had resulted in the worst type of suffering and tribulations to the Bengali population in the Eastern wing. The administration, except for a couple of fleeting glimpses of democracy and representative government, was consistently authoritarian and under the control of by [*sic*] the West Pakistanis. The East Bengalis were discriminated against in all walks of life. In short, it was a pathetic story of political, economic, social, and cultural domination and exploitation of the East by the West partaking of the worst features of colonialism.[114]

East Pakistan was geographically separate and culturally distinct from West Pakistan. The worsening relationship between the two areas culminating in the independence of Bangladesh was generally accepted as a legitimate act of self-determination and Bangladesh was rapidly and widely recognized as a State, even though a large number of States condemned Indian intervention in East Pakistan. The change of sovereignty and legal status was recognized despite the fact that force was used, which one would not expect without the mitigating factor of a right to self-determination.[115] Several authors have supported the right to self-determination in cases such as Bangladesh, where a region not formally considered a non-self-governing territory under the Charter has many of the characteristics described in UNGA Resolution 1541(XV).[116]

Although East Pakistan was never declared a non-self-governing territory by the United Nations, the cases of Southern Rhodesia and East Pakistan are similar. In both cases, the right to self-determination was not based on the colonial status of the territory, but on the denial of human rights in the territory.

The example of Bangladesh, where a large part of the world community recognized its right to self-determination, is countered by other examples where self-determination has not been supported, the two most notable of which are the Katangan secession from the Congo (1960–3) and the Biafran secession from Nigeria (1967–70).

The Congo Civil War went through a number of phases from the independence of the territory from Belgium on 30 June 1960 to the combined American and Belgian intervention to rescue hostages held by

[114] V. S. Mani, 'The 1971 War on the Indian Sub-continent and International Law', *Indian JIL*, 12 (1972), 84.

[115] See Robert Langer, *Seizure of Territory* (Princeton: Princeton Univ. Press, 1947), 100 *et seq.*

[116] See Ved P. Nanda, 'Self-determination in International Law', *AJIL*, 66 (1972), 321–36; M. K. Nawaz, 'Editorial Comment: Bangla Desh and International Law', *Indian JIL*, 11 (1971), 251–66; Chris N. Okeke, *Controversial Subjects of Contemporary International Law* (Rotterdam: Rotterdam Univ. Press, 1974); O. S. Kamanu, 'Secession and the Right of Self-determination', *Journal of Modern African Studies*, 12 (1974), 361.

the Stanleyville government in late 1964.[117] Within five days of its independence, an independence which Patrice Lumumba's biographer described as 'rotten at the roots', sections of the army mutinied.[118] On 11 July 1960 Prime Minister Lumumba asked the United Nations for assistance, which led to the intervention of United Nations forces in the Congo to restore order and prevent the secession of Katanga. Throughout the entire period of UN operations in the Congo there was no support from any quarter for any Katangan right of self-determination. Anthony Verrier notes that, '[N]ot only for the week of 9 to 15 July . . . , but for the entire period of ONUC's operations, the Third World as a whole and the "African Group" in particular believed in forceful measures to preserve the Congo's unitary constitution.' [119] In fact, pressure by these African leaders in particular led to the adoption of Security Council Resolutions on 21 February and 24 November 1961 which gave the UN forces the approval of the Council to end the Katangan secession by force if necessary.[120]

The African leaders were certainly conscious of their own vulner-abilities, and were eager to point out that self-determination is not a right of secession from a self-governing State. The case of Katanga indicates that it is widely believed that different ethnic or cultural groups within an established State have a right to self-determination in that they have a right to participate in the government of that State. Such a group, even if living together in a particular territory or province, does not have a right to sever its ties with the established government solely because they are ethnically, culturally, or linguistically different. There must also be an element of neglect, denial of equal rights, or *carence de souveraineté*.

This distinction between self-determination of peoples and secession from an established State, which has been the source of a great deal of criticism of any legal right of self-determination, was made quite clear at the 1964 Conference of Heads of State or Government of Non-aligned Countries in Cairo. The Cairo Declaration, while urging support to movements fighting against the Portuguese, also declared that

> The countries participating in the Conference, having for the most part achieved their independence after years of struggle, reaffirm their determination to oppose

---

[117] For discussion of the Congo Civil War see Donald W. McNemar, 'The Post-independence War in the Congo', in *The International Law of Civil War*, ed. Richard Falk (London: Johns Hopkins Press, 1971), 244–302; Michael Riesman, 'Humanitarian Interven-tion to Protect the Ibos', in *Humanitarian Intervention and the United Nations*, ed. Richard Lillich (Charlottesville: Univ. Press of Virginia, 1973), 167–95; Howard Weisberg, 'The Congo Crisis 1964: A Case Study in Humanitarian Intervention', *Virginia JIL*, 12 (1972), 261–76; Rosas, 153–4; James E. Bond, *The Rules of Riot* (Princeton: Princeton Univ. Press, 1974), 114; Anthony Verrier, *International Peacekeeping: United Nations Forces in a Troubled World* (New York: Penguin, 1981).

[118] Thomas R. Kanza, *The Rise and Fall of Patrice Lumumba*, quoted in Verrier, 49.

[119] Verrier, 50.

[120] Verrier, 67.

by every means in their power any attempt to compromise their sovereignty or violate their territorial integrity. They pledge themselves to respect frontiers as they existed when the States gained independence . . . [121]

Somalia and Morocco, both involved in territorial disputes, did not accept the Cairo Resolution. Somalia in particular opposed the Resolution because it took the issue of self-determination off the agenda between independent African States.[122]

The Biafran secession and civil war raised similar issues and is often used as an example of the inconsistent application of self-determination, thus casting doubt on its character as a legal right.

Nigeria had been plagued by internal disturbances for more than a year before the secession of Biafra. In January 1966, following a period of continued unrest over irregular elections, young officers of the Nigerian army overthrew the federal government, killed the Prime Minister, and established a military government under the Commander-in-Chief of the army, General Ayuiyi-Ironsi. On 1 August 1966 General Ironsi was kidnapped in a second coup and Lieutenant-Colonel Gowon took control of Nigeria. According to a news report at the time,

Serious and widespread rioting took place at the end of September and in early October in many areas of Nigeria, with the result that there was a large-scale exodus of Ibos from the Northern Region to the Eastern Region and of Northerners from the Eastern Region to their areas of origin in the North. Ibos from the other Regions and from Lagos also returned to the Eastern Region in large numbers . . . [123]

Following the announcement in May 1967 that the country was to be reorganized into twelve States instead of the existing four regions, Lieutenant Colonel Odumegwu-Ojukwu, the military governor of the Eastern Region, announced the secession of his Region and the formation of the Republic of Biafra.

Given the concentration of Ibos in the region and the history of disturbances in the country, one might have expected some support for the fledgeling State based on the right to self-determination. Biafra, conscious of its need for international recognition, lobbied the OAU summit conference in Kinshasa in September 1967 for support. But the OAU passed a resolution which, reaffirmed respect for the 'sovereignty and territorial integrity of member states', condemned secession, and accepted that the solution of the crisis was 'primarily the responsibility of the Nigerians themselves'.[124]

---

[121] 'Programme for Peace and International Co-operation: Declaration as Adopted by the Conference, Cairo—October 1964', *Indian JIL*, 4 (1964), sect. v, para. 2, 610.

[122] Brownlie, *African Boundaries*, 11.

[123] *Keesing's*, 22–9 Oct. 1966, 21678.

[124] John de St Jorre, *The Nigerian Civil War* (London: Hodder and Stoughton, 1972), 191;

The OAU assumed a diplomatic role, but remained firmly determined to support the territorial integrity of Nigeria. Supporting the secession of Biafra would set a dangerous precedent for the political unity of every African country, and, feared the Heads of State, would 'encourage secession on a tribal basis'.[125]

Similarly, the United Nations remained aloof, encouraging the OAU in its mediatory efforts, providing some humanitarian relief to the area, but consistently supporting the territorial integrity of Nigeria. In response to a question at a press conference in Dakar, Senegal, on 4 January 1970, the Secretary-General, when asked whether there was not a 'deep contradiction between the people's right to self-determination—a right recognized by the United Nations—and the attitude of the Federal Government of Nigeria towards Biafra', responded,

[W]hen a Member State is admitted to the United Nations, there is the implied acceptance by the entire membership of the principle of territorial integrity, independence, and sovereignty of that particular State . . . [T]he United Nations' attitude is unequivocable. As an international organization, the United Nations has never accepted and does not accept and I do not believe it will ever accept the principle of secession of a part of its Member State.[126]

The Nigerian Civil War was never placed on the agenda of the General Assembly or the Security Council.[127]

In the early stages of the civil war which followed Biafra's secession, not only did the UN and OAU support the territorial integrity of the central government, but no individual States recognized Biafra. It was not until April 1968 that Tanzania recognized Biafra. Following the lead of President Nyerere, three other States eventually recognized its independence: Gabon, Zambia, and the Ivory Coast.[128] John De St Jorre noted the paradox of reasoning which caused this handful of States to recognize Biafra:

It is one of the major tragedies of the war that the initiator of the snowballing recognition movement, President Julius Nyerere of Tanzania, did not take such a perilous step isolating himself from the rest of Africa, in order to help the Biafrans to *win*, but primarily to give more power to their elbows and drive the Nigerians to

see also Ellen Frey-Wouters, 'The Relevance of Regional Arrangements to Internal Conflicts in the Developing World', in *Law and Civil War in the Modern World*, ed. John Norton Moore (London: Johns Hopkins Press, 1974), 468; Oscar Schachter, 'The United Nations and Internal Conflict', in Moore, *Law and Civil War*, 419.

[125] President Mobido Keita of Mali in a statement on 23 Apr. 1968, in *Keesing's*, 27 Apr.–4 May 1968, 22672.

[126] Secretary-General U Thant, press conference at Dakar, Senegal, 4 Jan. 1970, *UN Monthly Chronicle*, 7 No. 2 (Feb. 1970), 36.

[127] See Schachter, 419.

[128] Frey-Wouters, 468.

the negotiating table to ensure that they *survived*. Kuanda of Zambia, strongly influenced by Nyerere, recognized Biafra for the same reason.[129]

In addition to these declarations of recognition, the government of France shipped arms to the Biafrans. On 31 July 1968 the French Secretary of Information, M. Joel Le Theule, said that

[T]he French Government considered that the Biafrans had 'demonstrated their will to assert themselves as a people', and that the civil war must be resolved by 'appropriate international procedures on the basis of the right of peoples to dispose of themselves',[130]

The federal government of Nigeria responded directly to the claim that the Ibos had a right to self-determination in the Kampala peace talks of May 1968. Chief Enaharo, the Nigerian representative, said,

If the argument is that 7,000,000 Ibos in the eastern part of Nigeria must enjoy the right of self-determination, surely this same right must be accorded to the 5,000,000 Efiks, Ibibios, Ekois, and Ijaws whom secessionist leaders wish to force into the so-called State of Biafra. They cannot deny the long-standing demands of these articulate minorities for their own State . . . [131]

This argument was generally accepted by governments, particularly governments of newly independent States which feared similar problems in their own countries.

The Biafran resistance finally collapsed in January 1970 after 2½ years of civil war.

The lack of support for any right to self-determination in Katanga and Biafra contrasts sharply with the situation in East Pakistan and calls into question the impartiality of any right to self-determination. Kurdistan, Chad, Sudan, Ethiopia, and Basque Spain are other examples where regions and ethnic minorities desiring a separate identity receive little international support. At a minimum these differences show that the right is not universal; not all groups enjoy it. In the case of East Pakistan the territory in question was not only geographically separate, but was non-self-governing with respect to the remainder of the State. This subordinate status is an important distinguishing factor in this third category of possible repositories of the right to self-determination. The right to self-determination does not mean a right of secession from a self-governing State unless a part of that State has become effectively non-self-governing with respect to the whole.

Furthermore, these apparent inconsistencies demonstrate that self-determination as a legal principle is not isolated from all other principles of

---

[129] De St Jorre, 193–4.
[130] *Keesing's*, 24–31 Aug. 1968, 22880.
[131] *Keesing's*, 24–31 Aug. 1968, 22874.

international law. It is moderated in particular by the principle of territorial integrity. In many of the most contentious cases where the right of self-determination may apply, the problem is not so much that there is not a reasonable claim for self-determination, but that there are other competing principles of international law. In the Falkland Islands the right of the population to maintain its ties with Great Britain, as it clearly wishes to do, competes with the territorial claim of Argentina. In the Western Sahara there is a boundary dispute and a question of historic title to territory as well as the claim of the Sahrawis to the right of self-determination. The annexation of East Timor by Indonesia, though probably less defensible as a matter of law than some other contentious cases, is also a case of competing legal principles. The cases of minority secession from a State, as in Nigeria or Basque Spain, raise the most obvious conflict—the principle of territorial integrity versus the right to self-determination. In many of these contentious cases there are two or more principles of law in conflict, or there are two competing claims for self-determination. These controversial cases—many as yet unresolved—do not deny the existence of the principle of self-determination of peoples as a matter of law. The right of self-determination is part of a set of rules which impact on one another depending upon the circumstances of a particular case. This interrelationship, where self-determination is not always predominant, does not strip the principle of its legal character.

To summarize the position of self-determination in international law the following points may be made.

1. Self-determination is not a matter essentially within the domestic jurisdiction of a State.

2. It is now generally accepted that there is a right to self-determination in international law.

3. This legal right is not enjoyed by any group desiring independence. In general, it applies to separate political units. In particular, trust and mandated territories and non-self-governing territories under Chapter XI of the Charter have a right to self-determination. In addition, geographically distinct territories which are subordinate to the metropolitan State and are non-self-governing with respect to the remainder of the State may have a right to self-determination. Any right of self-determination for a territory in this third category is usually highly controversial.

4. Self-determination may be achieved by the establishment of a sovereign and independent State, the free association or integration with an independent State, or the emergence into any other political status freely determined by the people of the territory.

5. The territory inhabited by peoples enjoying a right of self-determination has a status in international law separate from that of the metropolitan State.

PART III

Right Authority

5

The Authority to Use Force by National Liberation Movements

5.1 Introductory

Thus far I have concentrated on the twentieth century development of the idea that there are entities, most often referred to as 'peoples', who have a right to self-determination in international law. It does not automatically follow that the denial of this right justifies the use of force to secure self-determination; but it is little wonder that persistent denial of demands for self-determination led to calls for remedies, including the use of force.

In practice it has been national liberation movements which have claimed to have the right to exercise this authority on behalf of a people. Or, perhaps in reverse, entities which use force ostensibly on behalf of a 'people' are usually called national liberation movements.

There are exceptions to this general rule. Some liberation movements have been non-violent; some 'peoples' do not have liberation movements; and some neighbouring States have claimed to resort to the use of force on behalf of a people whose right of self-determination has been denied. Although these situations are important, particularly the relationship of other States to a people denied self-determination, they are not the focus of this book. Rather, this chapter examines whether the authority to use force is expanding to include not only States, but national liberation movements representing 'peoples' who aspire to be States.

The suggestion that national liberation movements have the authority to use force to secure the right of their peoples to self-determination challenges the idea that sovereign States are the only agents which may legitimately use force.

Article 2(4) of the Charter of the United Nations prohibits the threat or use of force against the territorial integrity or political independence of any State, or in any other manner inconsistent with the purposes of the United Nations. This Article, the most frequently named candidate for the status of *jus cogens*, reflects the strong presumption of illegality whenever force is used.[1] Given the strength of this general prohibition, it is little wonder that the use of force by national liberation movements to secure the right of

---

[1] See generally Ian Brownlie, *International Law and the Use of Force by States* (Oxford: Clarendon Press, 1963) Michla Pomerance, *Self-determination in Law and Practice* (London: Martinus Nizhoff, 1982), 48.

their peoples to self-determination has met considerable resistance. Nevertheless, there is some support for the use of force by national liberation movements to be included on the short list of situations in which the use of force is legitimate. There is also evidence that many States have not only acquiesced to the use of force by these movements, but actively support their use of force both politically and by more practical means.

There have been occasions in the twentieth century before the era of decolonization when States have accepted the use of force by non-State entities, or entities which no longer had all the characteristics of a State. The most conspicuous examples of this kind were the governments in exile in World War II and the resistance forces in occupied territory. In many of these cases the recognizing governments still considered the affected States to be in existence though occupied by Germany. As James Crawford notes, 'It is well established that belligerent occupation does not affect the continuity of the State: as a result, governments-in-exile have frequently been recognized as governments of an enemy-occupied State *pendante bellico.*'[2]

In some cases, the resistance movements were not related to the governments in exile, but were supported none the less. Tito's partisans, for example, were supported by the British from January 1943 even though Tito was not beholden to the government in exile and Britain remained 'bound by legal and moral ties' to the royalist government in exile.[3] Britain was in an awkward position of supporting a government in exile but not its resistance forces in the field led by Mihailovich.

There have also been cases where States have accepted parties as co-belligerents even when a State did not exist at the outbreak of the war. Poland's emergence after World War I is a relevant example. Having been partitioned for a century and a half, Poland had ceased to exist as a State. The war between Germany and Russia reopened the Polish question in a meaningful way for the first time since 1762. In late 1915 Roman Dmowski came from Petrograd to the West to seek recognition of the Polish National Committee, the KNP, as the exclusive representative of a future Polish government. At this stage, the Western governments still considered the Polish question to be an internal matter for their Russian ally.[4] The February Revolution in Russia, followed by the Declaration of the Principle of National Self-determination on 17 April 1917, and the denunciation of secret treaties, coincided with intensifying American interest in the war. Woodrow Wilson's 21 January 1917 State of the Union

[2] James Crawford, *The Creation of States in International Law* (Oxford: Clarendon Press, 1979), 407.
[3] Stephen Clissold (ed.), *A Short History of Yugoslavia* (Cambridge: Cambridge Univ. Press, 1966), 229.
[4] Norman Davies, *God's Playground: A History of Poland*, vol. ii (Oxford: Clarendon Press, 1981), 386.

Address, in which he supported a united Poland with access to the sea, helped to change the attitude of the Western powers.[5] Hackworth described the sequence of events which followed:

On June 4, 1917 the President of the French Republic issued a decree providing for the creation of an autonomous Polish Army, fighting under its own national colors. Shortly thereafter a Polish National Committee was established in Paris, with the approval of the French Government, which was recognized as the Polish official organization by the Governments of France, Great Britain, Italy, and the United States. Finally, on October 6, 1918, the Polish National Committee was recognized by France as the supreme political authority of the Polish Army, and the Army was recognized as autonomous, allied, and co-belligerent. Similar recognition was extended by Great Britain on October 15, [1918].[6]

The irony of these developments was that the Polish National Committee, accorded a certain status by its recognition as a co-belligerent before the formation of an independent Polish State, was ultimately outdone by Marshal Jozef Pilsudski. Pilsudski returned to Warsaw on 10 November 1918 and began to form the Polish State from the ashes without the support of the Allied governments or the Polish National Committee.[7]

Although Poland was formally recognized by the Treaty of Versailles, the Poles had been accepted as co-belligerents and the Polish National Committee had been accorded a certain status in law through recognition by the Western States before the existence of a Polish State. Poland was considered by some governments, if not all, to have the authority to use force before its re-emergence as a State. Krystyna Marek notes in her work on the identity and continuity of States that

The establishment of the Polish State took place in late autumn 1918 by way of a definite delimitation of its separate legal identity, i.e. of its legal order, valid on a given, though not finally delimited, territory, which had up till then formed part of three partitioning States: Russia, Germany and Austro-Hungary.[8]

The rebirth of Poland was not part of a general principle of universal application despite the fact that Allied war aims included national self-determination in Eastern Europe. In the inter-war years, putting down rebellions in colonial territories was still an internal affair, much as the Polish question remained an internal affair until the Russian Revolution changed the political landscape.

As the decolonization of empires gained momentum after World War II, the idea that liberation movements representing peoples who have a right to self-determination may resort to the use of force as a matter of

---

[5] Davies, 387.

[6] G. H. Hackworth, *Digest of International Law* (Washington: GPO, 1940), i. 319.

[7] Davies, 392.

[8] Krystyna Marek, *Identity and Continuity of States in Public International Law* (Geneva: Librairie E. Droz, 1954), 28; see also Crawford, 312.

international right also attracted support. As evidenced by the practice of States during the two world wars, this idea was not entirely new. It was, however, qualitatively different from its antecedents. If the continuance of colonial domination is contrary to the right of self-determination, so the argument went, then the use of force to secure that right should not be condemned. Furthermore, if a 'people' is separate and distinct from the power administering it, then armed conflict between the administering power and a liberation movement fighting for this people must be international, by definition. The implication of this provocative idea is that wars between States are not the only kind of international wars.

5.2 United Nations Resolutions

Although this author does not completely agree with the positivist conception that a right without a remedy for its breach is no right at all, it is not surprising that persistent denial of self-determination prompted calls for remedies, particularly in that forum where the debate on self-determination raged so intensely: the United Nations General Assembly.

Contrary to the protestations of the most radical of contemporary writers, the Charter of the United Nations does not make an exception permitting the use of force to secure self-determination on the model of Article 51 which permits States to defend themselves in case of an armed attack.[9] In 1960, when the General Assembly passed the Declaration on Colonialism, it did not sanction the use of force in the exercise of that right. This fact was emphatically pointed out by Ambassador Stevenson (USA) in the Security Council debates on Goa in 1961.

Resolution 1514(XV) does not authorize the use of force for its implementation. It does not and it should not and it cannot, under the Charter. . . . Resolution 1514(XV) does not and cannot overrule the Charter injunctions against the use of armed force.[10]

In the four years following the adoption of 1514(XV) the resolutions reaffirming this right of peoples to self-determination continued to refrain from any suggestion that self-determination might be attained through armed struggle. However, by 1964 jurists and statesmen from the Third World countries were contending that this use of force was legitimate. A

---

[9] e.g. E. C. Udechuku argues that this authority is implicit in the Charter: 'That there is no express statement in the Charter about the legality or otherwise of liberation "wars" provides no justification for denying the truth of the statement that the Charter authorizes colonial (and other dependent peoples) to engage in armed struggle, when necessary, to achieve independence.' *Liberation of Dependent Peoples in International Law* (London: African Publications Bureau, 1978), 28.

[10] SCOR, 16th year, 988th meeting, 18 Dec. 1961, para. 93, quoted in Dugard, 176.

resolution adopted by the Conference of Jurists of Afro-Asian Countries held in Conakry in October 1964 claimed that 'all struggles undertaken by the peoples for their national independence or for the restitution of the territories or occupied parts thereof, including armed struggle, are entirely legal'.[11] In 1964 the Conference of Non-aligned Countries held in Cairo declared that the 'process of liberation is irresistible and irreversible. Colonized peoples may legitimately resort to arms to secure the full exercise of their right to self-determination and independence if the colonial powers persist in opposing their natural aspirations.'[12] This sentiment was first reflected in a General Assembly resolution in 1965 when, tiring of Portuguese, Rhodesian, and South African intransigence, the Assembly passed Resolution 2105(XX), which

Recognizes the legitimacy of the struggle by the peoples under colonial rule to exercise their right to self-determination and independence and invites all States to provide material and moral assistance to the national liberation movements in colonial territories.[13]

The use of the ambiguous word 'struggle' unmodified by any reference to the use of force characterized the latter half of the 1960s. In fact, although many States interpreted 'struggle' to mean 'armed struggle' this was by no means a universal view.

In 1966 the Afro-Asian States, led by Algeria, tried to gain acceptance of an interpretation of Article 2(4) of the Charter at meetings of the Special Committee on Principles of International Law which would have excluded wars of national liberation from the general prohibition of the Article. Their interpretation was that, 'The prohibition of the use of force shall not affect . . . the use of force pursuant to . . . the right of peoples to self-defense against colonial domination, in the exercise of their right to self-determination.' The Western States opposed such an interpretation because, according to their view, the right of self-defence applied only to States and any so-called right of peoples to self-defence against colonial domination had no basis in either international law or the Charter of the United Nations.[14] The Special Committee was unable to reach agreement.

The question of national liberation struggles was not restricted to the

---

[11] *Le Monde*, 25 Oct. 1964, quoted in W. D. Verwey, 'Decolonisation and Ius ad bellum', in *Declarations on Principles*, ed. Robert J. Akkerman (Leiden: A. W. Sijthoff, 1977), 121; see also U. O. Umozurike, 'Self-determination in International Law' (D. Phil. Thesis, Oxford, 1969), 171.

[12] Declaration adopted by the Conference, *Indian JIL*, 4 (1964), 603.

[13] UNGA Res. 2105(XX), adopted 20 Dec. 1965, 74:6:27. Similar resolutions referring specifically to Portuguese territories and Southern Rhodesia were also passed in this session. See UNGA Res. 2107(XX) and UNGA Res. 2022(XX).

[14] Arnold Fraleigh, 'The Algerian Revolution as a Case Study in International Law', in *The International Law of Civil War*, ed. Richard A. Falk (London: Johns Hopkins Univ. Press, 1971), 190–1.

General Assembly. In 1966 the Security Council took up the matter of Rhodesia and reaffirmed, in Resolution 232(1966), 'the inalienable right of the people of Southern Rhodesia to freedom and independence in accordance with the Declaration [on Colonialism] . . . and recogniz[ed] the legitimacy of their struggle to secure the enjoyment of their rights.' [15] As in 1965, exactly what kind of 'struggle' was considered to be legitimate was not clear.

In 1967 several Third World States sponsored a resolution in the Special Committee on Principles of International Law which declared that 'alien subjugation, domination and exploitation as well as any other forms of colonialism' were a violation of international law. The draft went on to state that

Consequently peoples who are deprived of their legitimate right of self-determination and complete freedom are entitled to exercise their inherent right of self-defense, by virtue of which they may receive assistance from other States. [16]

Another similar resolution was submitted by Czechoslovakia and Yugoslavia. [17] There was no agreement on the draft. In the debates, the representative of the United States, Mr Reis, commented that

The text submitted by Czechoslovakia also contained a provision designed to sanction wars of liberation under the guise of the Charter principle of equal rights and self-determination of peoples under colonial rule. Such provisions were not compatible with the principle under consideration. The notion of liberation by any means was not compatible with the Charter principles of non-intervention and the threat or use of force. [18]

Other representatives argued that self-defence as conceived in Article 51 was a right of States, not of peoples. To extend the authority to use force beyond these original limits set out in the Charter by definitional sleight of hand would be detrimental to the maintenance of international peace and security. [19] Thus, in spite of resolutions recognizing the legitimacy of various 'struggles', in the late 1960s there was still strong disagreement on

[15] SC Res. 232(1966), 16 Dec. 1966, 11:0:4. Bulgaria, France, Mali, and the USSR abstaining; see also Patrick J. Travers, 'The Legal Effect of UN Action in Support of the Palestine Liberation Organization and the National Liberation Movements of Africa', *Harvard ILJ*, 17 (1976), 571–2.

[16] UN Doc. A/AC.125/L48 of 27 July 1967, sponsored by Algeria, Cameroon, Ghana, India, Kenya, Madagascar, Nigeria, Syria, UAR, and Yugoslavia.

[17] UN Doc. A/AC.119/L6 and A/AC.119/L7: 'the prohibition of the use of force shall not affect . . . the right of nations to self-defense against colonial domination in the exercise of the right of self-determination.'

[18] Mr Reis (USA), 1967 Special Committee on Principles of International Law Concerning Friendly Relations and Cooperation Among States, UN Doc. A/AC.125/SR.68, 4 Dec. 1967.

[19] See the statements of Mr Delpach (Argentina), UN Doc. A/AC.125/SR.70, 7 Aug. 1967, 16–17; and Mr Togo, UN Doc. A/AC.125/SR.69, 4 Aug. 1967, 15.

exactly what kind of 'struggle' was being accepted as legitimate.[20] Most of the Third World States would have accepted the modification of the word 'struggle' by the word 'armed'. However, a significant number of States would not and did not accept that a war of national liberation was within the parameters of the Charter's restrictions on the legitimate use of force.

In 1970, celebrating the tenth anniversary of the Declaration on Colonialism, the Assembly changed its approach slightly when recognizing the legitimacy of liberation struggles. The Assembly reaffirmed 'its recognition of the legitimacy of the struggle of the colonial peoples and peoples under alien domination to exercise their right to self-determination and independence by all means at their disposal'.[21] As on many previous occasions, a significant number of Western States abstained or voted against this Resolution.

Before 1970, all resolutions recognizing the legitimacy of any struggle were opposed by the Western States, usually on the grounds that, although they recognized a right of peoples to self-determination, the use of force for anything other than self-defence against armed attack was contrary to the spirit and principles of the Charter. Furthermore, the authority to use force in self-defence applied only to States confronted with an armed attack, not to peoples. The Declaration on Principles of International Law, passed by acclamation in the General Assembly on 24 October 1970, does address the issue of struggles by national liberation movements, but a number of issues remain unclear.[22]

The Declaration was the result of seven years of work by a Special Committee composed of 'qualified jurists' working on the basis of consensus. The Committee was created not only for the codification of existing law, but for the 'progressive development' of international law.[23] The countries represented spanned the whole spectrum of member States of the United Nations and included all the major powers with the exception of the People's Republic of China, which was not yet represented in the

---

[20] Resolutions reaffirming UNGA Res. 2105(XX) using similar language were adopted in the succeeding four years. See UNGA Res. 2189(XXI), 13 Dec. 1966, 76:7:20; UNGA Res. 2326(XXII), 16 Dec. 1967, 86:6:17; UNGA Res. 2446(XXIII), 19 Dec. 1968, 83:5:28; UNGA Res. 2465(XXIII), 20 Dec. 1968, 87:7:17; UNGA Res. 2548(XXIV), 11 Dec. 1969, 78:5:16; UNGA Res. 2383(XXIII), 7 Nov. 1968, 86:9:19, and UNGA Res. 2508(XXIV), 21 Nov. 1969, 83:7:20 on Southern Rhodesia; UNGA Res. 2395(XXIII), 29 Nov. 1968, 85:3:15 and UNGA Res. 2547(XXIV)A, 11 Dec. 1969, 87:1:23 on South Africa; UNGA Res. 2403(XXIII), 16 Dec. 1968, 96:2:16 on Namibia.

[21] UNGA Res. 2708(XXV), 14 Dec. 1970, 73:5:22. See also Resolutions 2707(XXV), 14 Dec. 1970, 94:6:16 on Portuguese territories and UNGA Res. 2652(XXV), 3 Dec. 1970, 79:10:14 on Southern Rhodesia.

[22] UNGA Res. 2625(XXV), 24 Oct. 1970, unanimous.

[23] For a discussion of the methods and the first two years of work by the Committee see P. H. Houben, 'Principles of International Law Concerning Friendly Relations and Co-operation Among States', *AJIL*, 61 (1967), 703–36.

UN. The fact that the Committee was created to consider questions of law, and the fact that the final Declaration was adopted by acclamation, i.e. unanimously, makes it particularly important when we are trying to discern exactly what States consider the law to be.

As noted in Chapter 4, the Declaration on Principles of International Law was the first UN instrument unanimously to recognize a right to self-determination. States were also agreed by 1970 that a colony or non-self-governing territory had a status separate and distinct from the territory of the State administering it.[24] But the Declaration went further than these general pronouncements which were widely accepted much earlier than 1970. According to the Declaration,

Every State has the duty to refrain from any forcible action which deprives peoples referred to above in the elaboration of the present principle of their right to self-determination and freedom and independence. In their actions against, and resistance to, such forcible action in pursuit of the exercise of their right to self-determination, such peoples are entitled to seek and to receive support in accordance with the purposes and principles of the Charter.[25]

Asbiorn Eide and Georges Abi-Saab place particular emphasis on this paragraph of the Declaration. In their view it confirms that national liberation movements have the authority to use force in international law. Eide notes that the Resolution 'makes it clearer than before that armed struggle for self-determination is legitimate', although he admits that the exact scope of this authority remains unclear.[26] Abi-Saab is more specific. From this paragraph in the Declaration on Principles of International Law, combined with the history of State practice, he concludes that

[A]rmed resistance to forcible denial of self-determination—by imposing or maintaining by force colonial or alien domination—is legitimate according to the Declaration. In other words, liberation movements have a *jus ad bellum* under the Charter.[27]

He goes on to describe this as a significant change for Western governments who, until 1970, had rejected the idea that a right to self-determination justified the use of force in international law. Although Professor Abi-Saab's analysis of other points is exceptionally lucid and precise, this author disagrees with the significance attached to this paragraph of the Declaration on Principles of International Law. In fact,

[24] Professor Abi-Saab puts particular emphasis on this separate status. See Georges Abi-Saab, 'Wars of National Liberation and the Laws of War', *Annales d'études internationales*, 3 (1972), 101–3.

[25] UNGA Res. 2625(XXV), 24 Oct. 1970, acclamation.

[26] Asbiorn Eide, 'Sovereign Equality Versus the Global Military Structure: Two Competing Approaches to World Order', in *New Humanitarian Law of Armed Conflict*, vol. i, ed. Antonio Cassese (Naples: Editoriale Scientifica, 1979), 25.

[27] Abi-Saab, *Annales*, 100.

one of the reasons the Resolution was passed unanimously was that its more controversial provisions could be interpreted in a variety of ways, as is often the case when work is prepared on the basis of consensus. Three major objections may be made to these generous interpretations of the Declaration.

First, the above clause does not say that peoples may use force to secure their right to self-determination. It says that when force is used against them they are entitled to receive support 'in their actions against, and resistance to' this illegitimate use of force. It mentions resistance at all *only* when force is used against peoples and not simply when self-determination is denied. Although the paragraph does not specifically mention self-defence, this would be consistent with the idea that the use of force is limited in law to defence against armed attack as opposed to initiating the use of force to secure some right.

Second, although most countries would have accepted the modification of 'resistance' by the word 'armed' the resolution does not specifically mention 'armed resistance', as Professor Abi-Saab suggests. The absence of the word 'armed' leaves the idea of resistance ambiguous, which was no doubt the intention of the participants. Consensus could not have been reached on the legitimacy of the use of force, even as resistance to 'forcible action'. 'Resistance' could refer to civil disobedience, strikes, or political opposition, which need not involve the use of force. It would be incorrect to assume that there was unanimous support for a right to resist by force of arms.

Third, the final clause of this Article of the Declaration enhances its ambiguity. States were agreed that these peoples are entitled to seek and receive support 'in accordance with the purposes and principles of the Charter'. Since the entire controversy revolves around exactly what the purposes and principles of the Charter do and do not allow, the Declaration really does little more than continue the debate. The Resolution was important because it unanimously established a right of peoples to self-determination in international law, but it did not unequivocally declare that peoples may use force in the exercise of that right. Nevertheless, the 1970 Declaration on Principles of International Law was a tremendous political success for those arguing that wars of national liberation are legitimate. The actual content of the Declaration is often disregarded.

Before 1973, then, the resolutions passed by the General Assembly implying that the use of force for self-determination is legitimate never actually referred to *armed* struggle, although the debates on the resolutions, particularly the 1970 Declaration on Principles of International Law, reveal that this is exactly what most members of the Assembly understood the resolutions to mean. Late in the 1973 session the Third Committee passed a resolution, which would become Resolution 3070(XXVIII), which reaffirmed 'the legitimacy of the peoples' struggle for liberation from colonial and foreign domination and alien subjugation by all available means, including armed struggle'.[28] The Resolution was adopted by the General Assembly by 97 votes to 5 with 28 abstentions. This vote in itself would suggest that the ambiguity of the Declaration on Principles of International Law passed three years earlier by acclamation veiled deep divisions not reflected in the consensus.

The more important development to emerge from United Nations practice in 1973 came from the Sixth Committee, which considers legal issues. The Committee passed a draft sponsored by several Third World and Eastern Bloc States, which eventually became Resolution 3103 (XXVIII), Basic Principles of the Legal Status of Combatants Struggling Against Colonial and Alien Domination and Racist Regimes.[29] The Resolution

. . . solemnly proclaims the following basic principles of the legal status of the combatants struggling against colonial and alien domination and racist regimes without prejudice to their elaboration in the future within the framework of the development of international law applying to the protection of human rights in armed conflicts:

1. The struggle of peoples under colonial and alien domination and racist regimes for the implementation of their right to self-determination and independence is legitimate and in full accordance with the principles of international law.[30]

In the debates in the Sixth Committee, those opposing the Resolution generally avoided criticizing liberation movements or the righteousness of their causes as such, and pointed to the inadequacies of the Resolution as a statement of the law. Mr Aldrich of the United States commented that

Whether his Government approved or disapproved of a particular liberation movement was beside the point; the fact was that a liberation movement as such could not negotiate or conclude international agreements. . . . [I]t should be noted that participation in multilateral conferences concerned with the conclusion of treaties relating to the development of international law had always been limited to Governments and international organizations that might become parties to those treaties.[31]

His colleague, explaining the negative vote of the United States in the

---

[28] UNGA Res. 3070(XXVIII), 30 Nov. 1973, 97:5:28; Verwey, 'Decolonisation', 122. The General Assembly reaffirmed the right to struggle in later sessions. See 3246(XXIX), 3382(XXX), 31/6I, 31/34, 31/143, 31/146, 31/154, 32/90, 32/14, 32/42, 32/105, and 32/116.

[29] Introduced by Madagascar as Draft Resolution A/C.6/L969 in the 1452nd meeting of the 6th Committee, 3 Dec. 1973.

[30] UNGA Res. 3103(XXVIII), 12 Dec. 1973, 83:13:19. Austria, Belgium, Brazil, France, West Germany, Israel, Italy, Luxembourg, Portugal, South Africa, the United Kingdom, the United States, and Uruguay in opposition.

[31] Mr Aldrich (USA), GAOR: 28th session, 6th Committee, 1451st mtg., 1 Dec. 1973.

General Assembly, commented 'We consider it wrong in virtually every paragraph as a statement of law.'[32]

On the other side of the division, opinion was equally strong not only that liberation movements should benefit from the protections of the Geneva Conventions, which was the thrust of the Resolution, but that their use of force to secure their right to self-determination was in accordance with international law.

The representative from Kenya stated, 'In [her government's] opinion, peoples fighting for independence and self-determination were combatants in armed conflicts, and no longer insurgents, since they had a fundamental right to fight for their freedom.'[33] Similarly, the representative from Cuba claimed that 'Since the promulgation of the Charter of the United Nations, the resort to armed force had been unlawful except in cases of self-defence in strict accord with Article 51 or in a just struggle for national liberation.' [34] The Eastern Bloc States also supported this interpretation of the law. The representative from the German Democratic Republic claimed, 'It was thus recognized that the struggle of colonial peoples for self-determination was legitimate and in full accordance with the principles of international law.'[35]

As this evidence indicates, by 1973 the governments of the majority of States were of the opinion that 'peoples' who were not yet members of an independent State had the authority to use force to secure their right to self-determination. It is not clear from United Nations resolutions whether this perceived authority was based on a right to self-defence or simply on the right to self-determination overriding any prohibition on the threat or use of force. It was often justified on both grounds.

At the same time, a significant minority in the General Assembly remained opposed to the extension of the authority to use force beyond sovereign States. It is in the debates on resolutions like 3103(XXVIII), which is much less ambiguous than the unanimously accepted Declaration on Principles of International Law, that one can see the disagreements which remained.

In 1974 the Assembly passed the Definition of Aggression which, like the Declaration on Principles of International Law four years earlier, was developed by a special committee working on the basis of consensus. The final draft produced by the Committee after seven years of work was adopted without vote by the General Assembly. Article 3 of the Definition includes the following acts, regardless of a declaration of war, as acts of aggression:

[32] Mr Evans (USA), GAOR: 28th session, 2197th plenary mtg., 12 Dec. 1973.

[33] Miss Githu (Kenya), GAOR: 28th session, 6th Committee, 1453rd mtg., 4 Dec. 1973.

[34] Mr Alvarez Tabio (Cuba), GAOR: 28th session, 6th Committee, 1449th mtg., 28 Nov. 1973.

[35] Mr Meissner (GDR), GAOR: 28th session, 6th Committee, 1453rd mtg., 4 Dec. 1973.

(*a*) The invasion or attack by the armed forces of a State of the territory of another State, or any military occupation, however temporary, resulting from such invasion or attack, or any annexation by the use of force of the territory of another State or part thereof;

(*b*) Bombardment by the armed forces of a State against the territory of another State or the use of any weapons by a State against the territory of another State;

(*c*) The blockade of the ports or coasts of a State by the armed forces of another State;

(*d*) An attack by the armed forces of a State on the land, sea or air forces, or marine and air fleets of another State;

(*e*) The use of armed forces of one State which are within the territory of another State with the agreement of the receiving State, in contravention of the conditions provided for in the agreement or any extension of their presence in such territory beyond the termination of the agreement;

(*f*) The action of a State in allowing its territory, which it has placed at the disposal of another State, to be used by that other State for perpetrating an act of aggression against a third State;

(*g*) The sending by or on behalf of a State of armed bands, groups, irregulars or mercenaries, which carry out acts of armed force against another State of such gravity as to amount to the acts listed above, or its substantial involvement therein.

This Article taken alone, particularly paragraph (*g*), appears to be a blow to liberation movements, as it defines assistance across State borders as aggression. This would condemn the African neighbours of the former Portuguese colonies and the 'front-line' States who were or are providing sanctuaries for 'freedom fighters'. However, there was a saving clause in Article 7 which stated,

Nothing in this Definition, and in particular article 3, could in any way prejudice the right to self-determination, freedom and independence, as derived from the Charter, of peoples forcibly deprived of that right and referred to in the Declaration on Principles of International Law Concerning Friendly Relations and Co-operation among States in accordance with the Charter of the United Nations, particularly peoples under colonial and racist regimes or other forms of alien domination; nor the right of those peoples to struggle to that end and to seek and receive support in accordance with the principles of the Charter and in conformity with the above-mentioned Declaration.[36]

Recalling that the Declaration on Principles of International Law did little to clarify the law, the Definition of Aggression is only a slightly better elucidation of the applicable legal principles as understood by States in 1974. Article 7 is not only a derogation from Article 3(*g*) which includes sending armed bands across borders under the rubric of aggression, but from all of Article 3. Furthermore, although the Third World States generally considered 'struggle' to mean armed struggle, the mention of the

---

[36] UNGA Res. 3314(XXIX), 14 Dec. 1974, consensus.

use of force was deliberately avoided.[37] Of course, the controversy on exactly what the principles of the Charter and the Declaration on Principles of International Law allowed was perpetuated by the Definition of Aggression. The Resolution was sufficiently ambiguous to receive consent without vote from the Western States who generally opposed the legitimization of the use of force by national liberation movements; yet it was specific enough to be a great victory for the Third World States. The legal issue was still not settled definitively, but the political victory was substantial.

The disagreement over the applicable legal principles continues to be reflected in United Nations votes. A large majority of States regularly vote in favour of resolutions accepting the legitimacy of the use of force by national liberation movements in general, and often with specific reference to particular territories or movements. A powerful minority of States, mostly from the West, consistently oppose any extension of legitimate authority and any move to sanction the use of force. Only when resolutions are ambiguous enough to be interpreted liberally by either camp is there any agreement, and this agreement more often is indicated by consensus or acclamation than by recorded vote. For example, in December 1982 the Assembly passed yet another of its reaffirming declarations which took note of 'the legitimacy of the struggle of peoples for independence, territorial integrity, national unity and liberation from colonial and foreign domination and foreign occupation by all available means, including armed struggle'.[38] This Resolution was passed 120:17:6. The strength of the opposing vote suggests that, although there is generally a willingness to accept self-determination of peoples as a right in international law, not all governments are agreed that the representatives of these peoples have the authority to use force to secure their right of self-determination.

5.3 The Practice of States

United Nations resolutions, particularly those specifically addressing questions of international law, provide a wealth of evidence suggesting that national liberation movements may have the authority to use force in international law. But the practice of States in particular cases can be just as illuminating as these general pronouncements, and arguably more so. While a government may be unwilling to recognize the general principle of the legal authority of non-State actors to use force, it may be willing to make exceptions in particular circumstances, sometimes without publicly acknowledging that it is doing so. Indeed, governments need not be aware,

[37] See Pomerance, 58.
[38] UNGA Res. 37/43, 3 Dec. 1982, 120:17:6.

and probably quite often are not aware, that incremental change is taking place which over a period of time represents a change in our ideas about international law and international society.

At the same time, it is important to distinguish between acquiescence in a matter of fact and acceptance of a principle of law. The existence of some kind of relationship between a State and a national liberation movement, while it may imply that the movement has some kind of international status, does not automatically mean that they have the authority to use force under international law. It is important to examine the character of the relationship. A State may only be protecting its nationals and property in territory controlled by a liberation movement. Such a practical relationship is qualitatively different from general acceptance of the political aims of a national liberation movement or direct aid to help it achieve those aims. There is, of course, a varied assortment of positions between these extremes.

The idea of legitimate authority in international law is closely linked with recognition.[39] Recognition is not a formal legal procedure, although it is often written about as though it is. In practice, it takes a variety of forms and is simply the method by which States define their relationship with a new entity claiming some kind of international status. In the case of civil war, States *recognize*, in theory if not in practice, rebellion, insurgency, and belligerency, with legal consequences flowing from this recognition. In the case of national liberation movements there have been two trends in State practice since the end of World War II in regard to recognition.

First, there has been a tendency to recognize prematurely governments which have been formed by liberation movements who represent a people considered to have a right to self-determination.[40] This recognition has sometimes been extended to governments and provisional governments even when they are located outside the territory which they are fighting to control.

The second tendency which has developed in more recent years is to recognize the liberation movement itself, as distinct from a government formed by it, as *a* representative or *the* representative of its people. The legal consequences of this kind of recognition are not clear. It seems to

[39] Martin Wight, *Systems of States* (Leicester: Leicester Univ. Press, 1977), ch. 6; Ti-Chiang Chen, *The International Law of Recognition* (London: Stevens and Sons, 1951).

[40] The term 'premature recognition' prejudges the nature of the act of recognition and is used here both because it is an accepted term of art and because there appear to be no good alternatives. Obviously, the recognizing State does not consider the recognition to be premature. It is only premature based on traditional standards of international law which may be changing in the case of peoples who have a right of self-determination.

[41] On the politicization of international law see Georges Abi-Saab, 'The Newly Independent States and the Rules of International Law: An Outline', *Howard LJ*, 8 (1962), 95–121; S. Prakesh Sinha, 'Perspective of the Newly Independent States on the Binding Quality of International Law', *ICLQ*, 14 (1965), 121–31.

imply that there is a completely new status in international law. Before these attempts to internationalize wars of national liberation it was generally considered that these were internal wars in which the rebels only received the benefits and rights of international law when they had developed characteristics sufficiently analogous to those of States to be granted belligerent rights or to be recognized as the new government in power. It now seems to be the view of a large number of States that there is a second type of authority which may legitimately resort to the use of armed force under international law: the national liberation movement. It is through the practice of recognition that the changes which have taken place regarding national liberation movements can most clearly be seen.

5.31 Premature Recognition

The subtle interplay between international law and international politics on the matter of recognition cannot be denied.[41] It is a controversial subject when analysing the recognition of States. It is a priori even more controversial with regard to national liberation movements. Hersch Lauterpacht argues that recognition is essentially a part of international law.[42] On the other hand, there can be little doubt that recognition is strongly affected by considerations of national interest leading some to conclude that recognition is a matter of policy.[43] This long-running debate tends to over-emphasize the distinction between law and policy. In fact, recognition is a blend of both, since acts of policy form norms of law and norms of law influence decisions of policy. Recognition is essentially an expression of intention by the recognizing State to treat a liberation movement as a subject of international law.[44]

The practice of States since the end of World War II regarding the secession of territories claiming to have a right of self-determination has not been entirely consistent. This should not be surprising given the evolution of the principle of self-determination itself in these years. Some States, particularly the newly independent States, have demonstrated a tendency to recognize governments or provisional governments even before they have complete control over the territory in issue. Indonesia, Algeria, Guinea-Bissau, and the Western Sahara are the most obvious examples of this tendency.

[42] H. Lauterpacht, *Recognition in International Law* (Cambridge: Cambridge Univ. Press, 1947), 87.

[43] See Thomas Galloway, *Recognizing Foreign Governments* (Washington: American Enterprise Institute, 1978), 5.

[44] Theory on the requirements for and effect of State recognition is particularly far removed from the actual practice of States. The *intention* of the recognizing (or, indeed, non-recognizing) State is the important question, rather than the often obfuscating questions of theory. On this point see Ian Brownlie, 'Recognition in Theory and Practice', *BYIL*, 53 (1982), 197–211.

The collapse of the Japanese administration in the Netherlands East Indies in August 1945 left a vacuum which Indonesian nationalists moved quickly to fill. On 17 August 1945 Sukarno declared Indonesian independence in a short radio broadcast. Japan had capitulated on 15 August, but her forces remained in place to keep order until relieved from responsibility by the South-east Asia Command. It was 29 September 1945, six weeks after the declaration of independence, that a British–Indian battalion began landing on Java 'to secure a speedy, orderly re-establishment of civil government as well as to evacuate Allied prisoners of war and civilian internees'.[45] The British acknowledged Dutch sovereignty openly, although they also supported negotiations between the two sides.

Early attempts to secure recognition of the country, deemed essential both as a bulwark for the Republicans' negotiating position with the Dutch and for the firm establishment of authority within Indonesia, were generally unsuccessful. This was at least partially because the nationalists were tainted by their Japanese association. In January 1946 the Ukraine brought the matter to the Security Council as a threat to the maintenance of international peace and security. The British and Dutch governments argued that Dutch sovereignty was not in question and that the troubles there were a matter of domestic jurisdiction. The proposed resolution for a commission of inquiry failed, as did a more specific resolution proposed by Egypt hoping for a rapid resolution inspired 'principally by the right of self-determination of peoples'.[46] Direct appeals by the nationalists for international support were equally unsuccessful. In the summer of 1946 the Republic made arrangements to exchange rice for textiles with famine-stricken India, but such an exchange was a poor substitute for recognition.[47]

After a series of negotiations conducted with the encouragement of Great Britain, the Indonesians and the Dutch signed the Linggajati agreement of 25 March 1947. The Dutch thereby conceded to recognize the government of the Republic 'as exercising *de facto* authority over Java, Madura and Sumatra'. In return, the Republican government agreed to co-operate 'in the rapid formation of a sovereign democratic state on a federal basis to be called the United States of Indonesia'.[48] Despite serious disagreement about the meaning of the provisions of the Linggajati agreement, particularly the clauses relating to the status of Indonesia in the period of transition, the Netherlands was unable to prevent *de facto* recognition of the Republican government by other States which it had apparently conceded. As a result, and with the objections of the Dutch

---

[45] Michael Leifer, *Indonesia's Foreign Policy* (London: George Allen and Unwin, 1983), 4; see also George M. Kahin, *Nationalism and Revolution in Indonesia* (Ithaca, NY: Cornell Univ. Press, 1952).

[46] *Yearbook of the United Nations*, 1946–7, 341.

[47] Leifer, 10.

[48] Linggajati agreement of 25 Mar. 1947, quoted in Leifer, 12; see also Kahin, 196–9.

who claimed *de jure* authority for the whole area, Indonesia concluded treaties of friendship with Egypt and Syria. At the invitation of Jawaharlal Nehru, Sjahrir participated in the non-governmental Asian Relations Conference as the representative of the Republic of Indonesia. Most importantly, *de facto* recognition was extended by Egypt, Syria, Iran, the United States, Britain, Australia, and China, but not the USSR.[49]

The breakdown of the Linggajati agreement led to the first Dutch military offensive in July 1947, which brought in the UN. The Security Council took up the matter in July and August of 1947 despite Dutch claims of domestic jurisdiction.

In August the Council invited Sjahrir to participate in the Security Council discussions. The Dutch, trying to prevent this enhancement of Republican prestige, tried to secure invitations for representatives of the other projected members of an Indonesian Federation but failed to do so.[50]

On 18–19 December 1948 the Dutch made a second military attack on what was left of the Republic, invading the capital and sending the leaders of the regime into internal exile. What originally appeared to be a successful *coup de force* brought strong condemnation from the Security Council, if not in resolutions passed, certainly in the rhetoric of the chamber.[51] It also resulted in the suspension of Marshall Plan aid from the US, and was unsuccessful in defeating the guerrilla resistance movements fighting for the Republic. International pressure, combined with the failure of the military solution, led to the resumption of negotiations at The Hague in May 1949. On 27 December 1949 Queen Juliana signed the Hague Agreements which established the United States of Indonesia in which the Republic was the largest unit.[52]

The Indonesian nationalists declared their independence in August 1945. Although Indonesia was probably not a fully independent State until December 1949, it did enjoy a certain status in international law before December 1949.[53] It was recognized by several governments, including The Netherlands, as the *de facto* authority. The Security Council assumed jurisdiction in the dispute, basing its involvement at least in part on the status of the Republic. The Republican government was also allowed to participate in these proceedings, although other representatives of the future Federation were not, indicating that the Republican government enjoyed a status which other components of the Federation did not enjoy.

At the same time, there is considerable doubt that this acceptance of the

---

[49] Leifer, 14–15; H. W. Briggs (ed.), *The Law of Nations*, 2nd edn. (London: Stevens and Sons, 1953), 79.
[50] Leifer, 16; Kahin, 215–17.
[51] See *Yearbook of the United Nations*, 1948–9, 212–37; Briggs, 79.
[52] Leifer, 25.
[53] See Crawford, 258.

Republican government was on the basis of any right of self-determination. Certainly Indonesia's demand for independence was based on its claim to have a right to self-determination. However, the response of other States to the formation of the Republic and their recognition of it was influenced more by their *de facto* control and the dictates of Cold War politics. Joe Verhoeven claims in his work on recognition that the course of events in Indonesia was not affected by any nascent right of self-determination. He wrote,

Directement lié aux séquelles de l'occupation japonaise, le conflit qui, au lendemain de la seconde guerre mondiale, conduira à l'indépendance de l'Indonésie, ne paraît guère affecté par le droit des peuples à disposer d'eux-mêmes.[54]

It was not until after The Netherlands government recognized the Republican government's *de facto* authority that other governments afforded some kind of recognition and the matter was taken up in the Security Council.

However, in the Security Council debates, and particularly in the statements of Poland, the Ukraine, and the USSR, there were some whispers of an idea in embryo suggesting that a 'people' had some status in the international community even before recognition.[55] Furthermore, even if there was no implication in the Security Council that the Republicans had the authority to use force to secure their independence, there was general consensus that the use of force against them was unacceptable.[56]

The reaction of the international community to the war in Indonesia was coloured largely by traditional practices in international law highlighted by a few new insights. The response to the Algerian war of independence, and particularly the recognition of the provisional government created by the FLN, was a significant step toward premature recognition of governments fighting wars of national liberation.

The Algerian war spanned the formative years when the 'winds of change' began to transform the map of Africa. Unlike the Republican government of Indonesia, the Algerians were not confronted with the returning troops of a colonial power, which would have given more substance to their pleas of self-defence. On the contrary, it was the FLN that first resorted to the use of force on 1 November 1954, when it launched simultaneous attacks mostly on rural French outposts.[57] The

[54] Joe Verhoeven, *La Reconnaissance internationale dans la pratique contemporaine* (Paris: Éditions A. Pedone, 1975), 146.

[55] In the 1946 debate in the Security Council the Ukrainian delegate maintained *inter alia* that 'the Indonesian population should be granted privileges and rights established in the Charter'. *Yearbook of the United Nations*, 1946–7, 338–41.

[56] See the reports on the Security Council deliberations, *Yearbook of the United Nations*, 1946–7, 338–41; *Yearbook of the United Nations*, 1947–8, 212–33.

[57] Fraleigh, 189; James E. Bond, *The Rules of Riot* (Princeton Univ. Press, 1974), 85–6.

FLN knew that internationalizing the war was its way to gain legitimacy which was impossible under the domestic law of France. In a document circulated on 1 November 1954 explaining its aims and the reasons for its resort to armed action against the French, the FLN called for 'internationalization of the Algerian problem. . . . Within the framework of the United Nations, the affirmation of active sympathy with regard to all nations supporting our liberation action'.[58]

The FLN and its supporters concentrated on three goals. First, they wanted recognition of their right to independence from France. Second, they worked to secure practical financial and logistical support from States sympathetic to their cause (particularly Morocco and Tunisia). And third, they consistently promoted the idea that the conflict between the FLN and the French government was not an internal one. Its representatives in the UN and elsewhere concentrated on these areas rather than trying to secure explicit support for the use of force to secure independence. However, as Fraleigh has noted, 'it is a small jump from declaring that a people are entitled to independence to declaring that they may use force if independence is denied'.[59] The FLN and its supporters in the UN also did not seek explicitly to condemn the use of force by France against the FLN, although the passage of Resolution 1514(XV) within five days of the Resolution on Algerian self-determination had largely the same effect.

Even before the creation of the Provisional Government of the Algerian Republic (GPRA) in September 1958, the FLN had considerable success in gaining acceptance of its stature internationally. In April 1955 the FLN attended the Bandung Conference in which 29 States of the emerging Third World supported the principle of self-determination and favoured independence for North Africa. The Algerians, with no recognized government, could only participate as 'unofficial' delegates. Nevertheless, their presence was a significant step toward their objective of internationalizing the problems in Algeria. By December 1957, a year before the formation of a provisional government, the FLN took part in the Afro-Asian People's Solidarity Conference in Cairo on an equal footing with the governments participating.[60] In April 1958, still before the creation of a provisional government, the FLN participated in the Accra conference of free African States, receiving strong support for its independence.[61]

On 19 September 1958 the FLN announced the formation of the Provisional Government of the Algerian Republic (GPRA) which was eventually to be located in Algeria, but for the time being set up ministries

---

[58] In Joan Gillespie, *Algeria: Rebellion and Revolution* (London: Ernest Benn, 1960), 113.
[59] Fraleigh, 190.
[60] Alistair Horne, *A Savage War of Peace: Algeria 1954–1962* (London: Macmillan, 1977), 247; Gillespie, 160.
[61] Gillespie, 162.

in Tunis. By any of the traditional standards of effective government the GPRA, not even located in the territory it claimed to govern, could not conceivably have been recognized as the government of Algeria. This did not prevent 29 States from recognizing the new government.[62] Other countries, though not openly recognizing the government, did maintain some kind of relations, exchanged visits, or designated the government as the authentic representative of Algeria.[63]

Although the most active support for the GPRA came from the Communist and newly independent States, by 1958 Britain and the United States were playing an increasingly ambivalent role. The NATO countries were not willing to recognize the GPRA, but both the US and Britain were also unwilling to support French policy in Algeria.[64] In July 1957, Senator John F. Kennedy challenged the Republican administration

to place the influence of the United States behind efforts . . . to achieve a solution which will recognize the independent personality of Algeria and establish the basis for a settlement interdependent with France and the neighbouring nations.[65]

In his detailed account of the Algerian war, Alistair Horne commented,

No speech on foreign affairs by Senator Kennedy attracted more attention, both at home and abroad, and under such pressure United States official policy on Algeria now began to shift. Henceforth, instead of backing France at the United Nations, the United States would abstain.[66]

The pressure on France to come to terms with Algerian desires for self-determination would increase after John Kennedy became President.

The reaction of States to the events in Algeria from 1954 to 1962 illustrates a change in emphasis on the part of statesmen. The important question was not whether the war was internal or international, but

[62] See Horne, 316 and 464; Gillespie, 167; Erik Castren, *Civil War* (Helsinki: Suomalainen Tiedeakatemia, 1966), 75; Mohamed Bedjaoui, *Law and the Algerian Revolution* (Brussels: International Association of Democratic Lawyers, 1961), 114–17 and 126–7; Crawford, 260. *De facto* recognition had been extended by Ghana, Liberia, the USSR, Czechoslovakia, Bulgaria, and Yugoslavia. *De jure* recognition was extended by the Democratic Republic of Vietnam, Mali, Indonesia, Lebanon, and Libya. Recognition without specifying its character was extended by Tunisia, Morocco, UAR, Sudan, Saudi Arabia, Iraq, Jordan, Yemen, China, Mongolia, North Korea, Guinea, Togo and Congo, Stanleyville. Ethiopia, Nigeria, Somalia, and Ceylon 'took notice' of the government. It is not clear in this context what *de facto* recognition means. Sometimes governments will use the phrase to acknowledge that authority is exercised in a territory while withholding some measure of approval about the methods used, or the character of, the new regime. In Algeria the provisional government did not control territory. *De jure* recognition implies that the recognizing State both acknowledges that a situation exists and considers the new regime to be legitimate.

[63] These included Afghanistan, Malaya, Burma, India, Pakistan, Laos, Cambodia, Japan, and Hungary.

[64] Horne, 316.

[65] Quoted in Horne, 247.

[66] Horne, 247.

whether it was a decolonization war or a secession. Unlike the Portuguese African territories or the Netherlands East Indies, Algeria is not far from metropolitan France. The litmus test of 'salt-water colonialism' revealed very little salt water between France and Algeria. In every other way—its culture, history, language, and religion—it was certainly a distinct territory. During the course of the war, a large number of States gradually accepted that Algeria was a distinct entity which should be allowed to determine its own political future. As such, the Algerian people, represented first by a liberation movement and then by a provisional government created by that movement, should also have a separate status in international law.

Premature recognition of a government, rather than the acceptance of the authority of a liberation movement to use force when it had no provisional government, is more consistent with the traditional law notions of right authority. The FLN was fighting its war of liberation when the international community was just beginning to recognize a right to self-determination in international law. Although a large number of States eventually supported the right of Algeria to independence, the traditional idea of legitimate authority in international law was still firmly entrenched. The use of force by the FLN, even after the formation of the GPRA, was a matter of self-help neither condoned nor condemned by international law even while the right of the people of Algeria to self-determination was gradually gaining support. At the same time, one must note that even after the creation of the GPRA the use of force by the rebels was never condemned. Whereas, by Resolution 1514(XV), 'all armed action or repressive measures of all kinds directed against dependent peoples' was condemned with only 9 States of 98 members of the General Assembly abstaining.

By 1960 international law on the use of force in wars of national liberation was changing. Whereas traditional international law favoured the established government in internal wars, in a war for self-determination international law began to favour the rebels. If States did not openly agree that liberation movements had the authority to resort to force if self-determination was denied, at least they had begun to condemn the use of force by the colonial power, but not the liberation movement.

The second change illustrated by the Algerian case was that recognition of a government seemed to be taking the place of recognition of belligerency, even when that government did not have effective territorial control. Self-determination served to legitimize recognition which would otherwise have been premature. In other words, the degree of effectiveness required was less when the government established advanced the principle of self-determination of peoples.

The case of Guinea-Bissau is a third example of the trend to recognize prematurely governments formed by liberation movements. Amilcar Cabral formed the Partido Africano da Independencia da Guine e Cabo Verde (PAIGC) in 1956. The armed struggle began in earnest in 1963 and was generally conducted by cross-border raiding parties operating from sanctuaries in Guinea and Senegal.[67]

On 26 September 1973 the PAIGC declared the independence of the State of Guinea-Bissau. The Portuguese government called this declaration an act of propaganda not at all reflective of the actual conditions prevailing in the territory.[68]

There is little doubt that the PAIGC did not have firm control in the territory. Under traditional international law, recognition of the State of Guinea-Bissau would probably have been premature. Nevertheless, by the end of 1973 forty States had recognized the Republic, including China, the USSR, and India.[69] On 2 November 1973 the UN General Assembly passed a resolution by 93:7:30 welcoming 'the recent accession to independence of the people of Guinea-Bissau thereby creating the sovereign State of the Republic of Guinea-Bissau'.[70] Several Western States expressed their belief, in the UN and in their own countries, that the prerequisites for recognition of statehood as required by international law did not exist.[71] A month later the General Assembly, accepting the report of the credentials committee, approved

the credentials of the representatives of Portugal, on the clear understanding that they represent Portugal as it exists within its frontiers in Europe and that they do not represent the Portuguese-dominated Territories of Angola and Mozambique nor could they represent Guinea-Bissau, which is an independent State.[72]

By 31 May 1974, 84 States had recognized Guinea-Bissau. It was not until 26 August 1974 that the new government of Portugal, which had come to

---

[67] For the history of the PAIGC and the conflict in Guinea-Bissau see Gerard Chaliand, *Armed Struggle in Africa* (London: Monthly Review Press, 1969); Gerard Chaliand, *The Struggle for Africa: Conflict of the Great Powers* (London: Macmillan, 1982); Thomas Henriksen, 'People's War in Angola, Mozambique and Guinea-Bissau', *Journal of Modern African Studies*, 14 (Sept. 1976); N. Bruce, 'Portugal's African Wars', *Conflict Studies*, 34 (London: Institute for the Study of Conflict, 1973); Basil Davidson, *The Liberation of Guiné* (Harmondsworth: Penguin, 1969); Basil Davidson, *Growing From Grass Roots: The State of Guinea-Bissau* (London: Committee for Freedom, 1974).

[68] See Charles Rousseau, 'Chronique des faits internationaux: Guinée-Bissau', *Revue générale de droit international public*, 78 (Oct.–Dec. 1974), 1168; *Keesing's*, 12–18 Nov. 1973, 26196.

[69] Rousseau, 1168.

[70] UNGA Res. 3061(XXVIII), 2 Nov. 1973, 93:7:30. Brazil, Greece, Portugal, South Africa, Spain, the United Kingdom, and the United States opposing.

[71] See statement by the Under-Secretary of Foreign Affairs (Italy), *Italian Yearbook of International Law*, 1 (1975) 299; US Department of State, Instructions to the Field, *Digest of United States Practice in International Law* (1974), 17; and statements of France, Switzerland, the Scandinavian States, and Great Britain in Rousseau, 1168–9.

[72] UNGA Res. 3181(XXVII), 17 Dec. 1973, 108:0:9.

power in a military coup on 25 April 1974, signed an agreement with the PAIGC recognizing the Republic of Guinea-Bissau *de jure* effective 10 September 1974.

The final example of what might be called premature recognition concerns the ongoing conflict in the Western Sahara.[73] The Western Sahara was known as the Spanish Sahara until Spain's withdrawal from the colony in 1975. A nationalist anti-colonialist movement began in the 1960s and in 1973 the Frente Popular para la Liberación de Saguia el-Hamra y Rio de Oro, or the Polisario Front, was created. From 1973 to 1975 Polisario fought the Spanish to secure Western Saharan independence, the UN General Assembly having recognized the right of the Sahrawis to self-determination as early as 1965. A UN mission of inquiry sent to the territory in May 1975 reported,

[I]t became evident to the Mission that there was an overwhelming consensus among Saharans within the territory in favour of independence and opposing integration with any neighbouring country. . . . The Mission believes, in the light of what it witnessed in the territory, especially the Frente POLISARIO . . . that its visit served as a catalyst to bring into the open political forces and pressures which had previously been largely submerged.[74]

This popular desire for independence was countered by Moroccan and Mauritanian claims to the territory based on historic title. When, in July 1974, Spain announced its intention to withdraw from the territory, these competing claims led the General Assembly to request an advisory opinion from the International Court of Justice on two questions. First, was Western Sahara at the time of colonization by Spain a territory belonging to no one (*terra nullius*)? And second, if the answer to the first question was in the negative, what were the legal ties between this territory and the Kingdom of Morocco and the Mauritanian entity?[75] The Court decided that the territory was not *terra nullius* and that

The materials and information presented to the Court show the existence, at the time of Spanish colonization, of legal ties of allegiance between the Sultan of Morocco and some of the tribes living in the territory of the Western Sahara. They equally show the existence of rights, including some rights relating to land, which constituted legal ties between the Mauritanian entity, as understood by the Court, and the territory of Western Sahara. On the other hand, the Court's conclusion is

---

[73] On the Western Sahara conflict see John Damis, *Conflict in Northwest Africa* (Stanford, Calif.: Hoover Inst. Press, 1983); J. Naldi, 'The OAU and the Saharan Arab Democratic Republic', *Journal of African Law*, 26 (1982), 152–62; International Commission of Jurists, 'The Western Sahara', *ICJ Review*, 32 (1984), 25–32; Ian Brownlie, *African Boundaries* (London: C. Hurst , 1979), 147–59 and 437–44; Western Sahara Advisory Opinion, ICJ Rep. (1975); Thomas M. Franck, 'The Stealing of the Sahara', *AJIL*, 70 (1976), 694–721.

[74] UN Doc. A/10023/Rev. 1, 59 quoted in International Commission of Jurists, *Review*, 32 (1984), 27.

[75] Western Sahara Advisory Opinion, ICJ Rep. (1975), 14.

that the materials and information presented to it do not establish any tie of territorial sovereignty between the territory of Western Sahara and the Kingdom of Morocco or the Mauritanian entity. Thus the Court has not found legal ties of such a nature as might affect the application of resolution 1514(XV) in the decolonisation of Western Sahara and, in particular, of the principle of self-determination through the free and genuine expression of the will of the peoples of the Territory.[76]

Following the publication of the advisory opinion in October 1975, King Hassan of Morocco announced that 350,000 unarmed volunteers would march across the border, Koran in hand, to assert their historical claim. Spain, desirous of avoiding military confrontation, began negotiations with Morocco and Mauritania which led to the 12 November 1975 Tripartite Agreement which circumvented United Nations and OAU attempts to insure the self-determination of the Sahrawi population by referendum.

In February 1976 Spain withdrew from the Western Sahara and on 14 April 1976 Morocco and Mauritania partitioned the territory. From 1976 until 1979 Polisario fought against Moroccan and Mauritanian occupation. Meanwhile, on 27 February 1976, Polisario proclaimed the formation of the Saharan Arab Democratic Republic (SDAR) with a government in exile based in Algiers but claiming to represent 'Sahiet al-Hamra and Rio de Oro, within their historical boundaries'.[77]

Polisario strategy in these early years was to concentrate on Mauritania, the weaker of the two occupying powers. Its strategy worked and in August 1979 Mauritania concluded a peace treaty with Polisario in which it decided 'to withdraw from the unjust war in Western Sahara' and recognized Polisario as the 'sole legitimate representative of the people of the Western Sahara'.[78]

Since 1979 Polisario has been fighting Morocco which, in March 1980, proclaimed that all of the Western Sahara is now an integral part of Morocco, and its annexation 'an irreversible historical fact'.[79] The OAU as an organization and several of its member States in particular did not agree. By July 1980 the SDAR had been recognized by 35 States. According to the OAU Charter, admission to membership 'shall be decided by a simple majority of the Member States'.[80] Twenty-six of the fifty members of the OAU had recognized the SDAR. At the OAU summit in Freetown, Sierra Leone, after a heated exchange, the members decided to postpone the question of SDAR membership and refer the question to an extraordinary summit. This summit, held in September 1980, failed to resolve the problem.

[76] Ibid. 68.
[77] Damis, 43.
[78] Peace Treaty Between the Polisario Front and the Islamic Republic of Mauritania, signed in Algiers on 5 Aug. 1979, reprinted in Damis, 150–1.
[79] King Hassan on 3 Mar. 1980, quoted in Damis, 91.
[80] Article 28 of the OAU Charter, reprinted in Naldi, 152.

On the military front, by late 1980 Morocco realized that it did not have the resources to 'pacify' the whole of the Western Sahara. In September 1980 the Moroccans began to build a triangular security zone in the north of the territory, which includes the phosphate mines. The triangle is bordered by a perimeter sand wall and anti-vehicular ditch. Since the completion of this strategic triangle, most Polisario operations have taken place outside this protective perimeter.

In February 1982, after Morocco had fended off another attempt to seat the SDAR at the 1981 OAU summit, the SDAR representative was seated at an OAU council of ministers meeting. Morocco led 19 members of the OAU in a walk out of the meeting. In August 1982, 21 African States refused to attend the annual summit if the SDAR was allowed to participate. Since two-thirds of the members must be present to have a quorum, the Tripoli summit never took place. In February 1983 the SDAR took its place at the council of ministers meeting and, again, 18 members of the OAU walked out in protest. The issue of the Western Sahara was paralysing the organization.

Faced with a repeat performance of the 1982 summit where the OAU would again adjourn *sine die*, in 1983 the SDAR voluntarily decided not to take its seat, though it did not relinquish its membership. At this summit the OAU passed a resolution which, for the first time, named Morocco and Polisario as the parties to the conflict and urged direct negotiations so that a referendum could be held by December 1983.[81] Morocco continues to refuse to negotiate directly with Polisario, claiming that Algeria is the other party to the conflict and that the guerrillas are just proxy forces. The negotiations never took place.

The 1984 summit again was threatened with the possible walk out of Morocco and its supporters over SDAR participation. The SDAR took its seat and Morocco left, supported by Zaïre. But the other States who walked out with Morocco in 1982 stayed in 1984, thus ensuring that the OAU had a quorum to continue its work.[82]

The question of the Western Sahara caused a serious fracture in the Organization of African Unity. For the first time, a large number of African States had recognized a provisional government of a country claiming a right of self-determination not against a European colonial power, but against another African State. By July 1984, 56 States, 29 of them African, had recognized the SDAR, and at the 1984 OAU summit Nigeria added its name to the list.[83]

---

[81] International Commission of Jurists, 'The Western Sahara', 31.
[82] *International Herald Tribune*, 12 Nov. 1984, 5, and 13 Nov. 1984, 1.
[83] International Commission of Jurists, 'The Western Sahara', 30; *International Herald Tribune*, 12 Nov. 1984, 5; African States recognizing the SDAR include Algeria, Angola, Benin, Botswana, Burundi, Cape Verde, Chad, Congo, Ethiopia, Ghana, Guinea-Bissau, Lesotho, Libya, Madagascar, Mali, Mauritius, Mauritania, Mozambique, Nigeria, Rwanda,

The future of the Western Sahara remains uncertain. The SDAR is a government in exile whose territory is controlled by Morocco, yet it has been recognized as an independent State by fifty-nine other States and has been seated as a member of the Organization of African Unity as an 'independent sovereign African State'.[84] There is little doubt that the recognition of the SDAR, like the recognition of Guinea-Bissau before it, is premature by the traditional standards of effectiveness. There is also little doubt that this recognition is based on the perceived right of the Sahrawi to self-determination and independence.

In Algeria, Guinea-Bissau, and the Western Sahara recognition of a State took the place of recognition of belligerency.[85] But in a larger sense, the recognition of these governments as States when they did not possess all the requirements of statehood was a way for the recognizing States to confer legitimacy on the objectives and actions of the liberation movements fighting for independence. It was also a way for them to discredit the colonial system which they found repugnant and to pressure the administering power to withdraw. In the Western Sahara the effectiveness of these tactics remain to be seen.

Does this tendency to recognize prematurely States fighting for self-determination imply that the liberation movements involved have the authority to use force in world politics analogous to that of sovereign States? In the view of the Third World and Eastern Bloc States it does. A 'people' which has a right to self-determination is, in this Third World and Eastern Bloc view, a separate entity in international law which may legitimately resort to arms to secure independence when that independence is denied by the administering power. Recognizing a government in exile formed by a liberation movement is a way for States to register their approval and enhance the status of the movement.

This tendency to recognize governments prematurely is not universal. Although the Western States now generally accept self-determination as a right in international law, they adhere to the traditional law notions of recognition based on effectiveness, and the prohibition of the threat or use of force in international relations. Sir Colin Crowe of Great Britain, commenting on UN Security Council Resolution 322(1972), was careful to point this out in his explanation of Britain's positive vote. He said,

São Tomé and Príncipe, Seychelles, Sierra Leone, Swaziland, Tanzania, Togo, Uganda, Upper Volta, Zambia, and Zimbabwe. Other States recognizing the SDAR include Afghanistan, Iran, Kampuchea, Laos, North Korea, South Yemen, Syria, Vietnam, Bolivia, Costa Rica, Cuba, Dominica, Mexico, Nicaragua, Panama, St Lucia, Grenada, Guyana, Jamaica, Surinam, Venezuela, Kiribati, Nauru, Papua New Guinea, Solomon Islands, Tuvalu, and Vanuatu.

[84] Article 28, OAU Charter.
[85] See Crawford, 262–3.

Operative paragraph 1 refers to the legitimacy of the struggle of the people of the territories for the right to self-determination and independence. We would have preferred it to have made explicit that this struggle should be pursued only by peaceful means and in accordance with the provisions of the Charter.[86]

The willingness of Third World States to recognize a State prematurely when the territory involved is or was a colony contrasts sharply with the practice of these States when a territory secedes which is part of a self-governing State as in Biafra or Katanga. In these cases, the principle of territorial integrity and fear for their own vulnerability determines their policies.

5.32 Recognition of National Liberation Movements

In addition to the premature recognition of States, since 1969 there has been a tendency to recognize liberation movements as the legitimate representatives of their people and to include them as observers, associate members, and members of international organizations. To some, this suggests that they are authorities in their own right in international law, capable of legitimately resorting to the use of force.

It was not uncommon for members of liberation movements to appear before particular organs of the United Nations as petitioners to testify and provide information. The leaders of national liberation movements had no right to participate or testify. They were invited to do so as private persons with the same status as other petitioners including missionaries, journalists, and representatives of non-governmental organizations. For the liberation movements and their supporters who were trying to internationalize their struggles, this status was quite unacceptable.[87]

The first opportunity for liberation movements to participate in the work of the UN as representatives of their people came in the Economic Commission for Africa. Portugal had been expelled and South Africa had been suspended from the Commission. This meant that Namibia, Angola, Mozambique, Guinea, and Portuguese Guinea were not represented. In 1967 the Commission passed Resolution 151(VIII), later clarified in 1969 by Resolution 194(IX), on associate membership for those territories and recommended that '[T]he Organization of African Unity should propose the names of representatives of the peoples of the countries in question and

---

[86] Sir Colin Crowe (UK), 22 Nov. 1972, UNSCOR S/PV.1677; see also statement of Mr Bush (USA), 22 Nov. 1972, UNSCOR S/PV.1677, 36–8.

[87] Amilcar Cabral, leader of the PAIGC, and Marcellino Dos Santos, Vice-President of FRELIMO, were particularly adamant on this point. See Claude Lazarus, 'Le Statut des mouvements de libération nationale à l'organisation des Nations Unies', *AFDI*, 20 (1974), 178.

inform the Executive Secretary accordingly to enable him to bring the matter before the General Assembly.'[88]

In 1971, pursuant to this Resolution, the OAU recommended the leaders of four liberation movements to represent the peoples of Angola, Mozambique, and Guinea (Bissau). The UN Council for Namibia recommended the representative for that territory.[89] This list was approved by the General Assembly in December 1971, and these representatives began serving as associate members.[90]

The participation of national liberation movements in the Special Committee on the Implementation of the Declaration on Colonialism began in 1971 when the General Assembly approved the Committee's request to allow representatives of national liberation movements to participate 'whenever necessary and in an appropriate capacity, in its deliberations relating to these territories'.[91] In 1972 the Committee invited several liberation movements to participate as observers.[92]

Similar and simultaneous developments took place in the Fourth Committee of the General Assembly and in the UN Council for Namibia. In the twenty-ninth session of the Assembly the Fourth Committee decided to invite the representatives of national liberation movements to participate as observers on the questions of Southern Rhodesia, the Portuguese territories, and Namibia.[93] SWAPO accepted the invitation to participate in the work of the UN Council for Namibia in 1972 and was granted observer status by the Council in 1973. In its Resolution 3111(XXVIII), which approved of the Council's report, the General Assembly recognized 'that the national liberation movement of Namibia, the South West Africa People's Organization, is the authentic representative of the Namibian people.[94]

In addition, by 1973 the UN Educational, Scientific and Cultural

---

[88] ECA Res. 194(IX), 12 Feb. 1969, Economic and Social Council Reports, 47th session, UN Doc. E/4651, 145–6.

[89] For Angola, Mr Agostino Neto, President of the MPLA and Mr Roberto Holden, President of the FNLA. For Mozambique, Mr Marcellino Dos Santos, Vice-President of FRELIMO. For Guinea (Bissau), Mr Amilcar Cabral, Secretary-General of the PAIGC. For Namibia, Mr Sam Nugoma, President of SWAPO. See UN Doc. E/CN.14/511, 27 Jan. 1977.

[90] UNGA Res. 2795(XXVI), 10 Dec. 1971, 105:8:15. Brazil, Costa Rica, France, Portugal, South Africa, Spain, the UK, and the USA in opposition.

[91] UNGA Res. 2878(XXVI), 20 Dec. 1971, 96:5:18. Approval was reaffirmed by UNGA Res. 2908(XXVII), 2 Nov. 1972, 99:5:23, and UNGA Res. 3118(XXVIII), 12 Dec. 1973, 108:4:17. Portugal, South Africa, the USA, and the UK opposed.

[92] In the 1973 session ZANU, ZAPU, FNLA, MPLA, PAIGC, FRELIMO, SWAPO, and MOLINACO participated as observers in the Committee's deliberations. See legal opinion of the Secretariat, *UN Juridical Yearbook: 1974*, 151.

[93] Representatives of ZANU, ZAPU, FNLA, FRELIMO, SWAPO, and the PAIGC were invited to participate. See legal opinion of the Secretariat, *UN Juridical Yearbook: 1974*, 150; UN Docs. A/8957, A/8889, and A/8933.

[94] UNGA Res. 3111(XXVIII), 12 Dec. 1973, 107:2:17. South Africa and Portugal opposed.

Organization, the International Labor Organization, the International Telecommunication Union, the Food and Agriculture Organization, and the Inter-governmental Maritime Consultative Organization had all granted observer status to national liberation movements.[95]

In a relatively short period of time, from 1969 to 1973, the national liberation movements, particularly those recognized by the OAU, had moved from being petitioners providing information to UN bodies to being observers and representatives of their people in much of the UN's work.

It was 1974 when liberation movements were first extended the privileges of observers in the General Assembly itself. In October of that year the General Assembly invited 'the Palestine Liberation Organization, the representative of the Palestinian people, to participate in the deliberations of the General Assembly on the question of Palestine in plenary meetings'.[96] One month later the Assembly expanded upon their invitation when they invited the PLO to 'participate in the sessions and the work of the General Assembly in the capacity of observer'.[97] A few days later the Assembly decided, in a resolution concerning co-operation between the UN and OAU,

[To] invite as observers, on a regular basis and in accordance with earlier practice, representatives of the national liberation movements recognized by the Organization of African Unity to participate in *the relevant work of the Main Committees* of the General Assembly and its subsidiary organs concerned, as well as in conferences, seminars and other meetings held under the auspices of the United Nations *which relate to their countries.*[98] (Emphasis supplied.)

The difference between these two resolutions is that the PLO may participate not only in the work of the committees and subsidiary organs of the General Assembly, but also in plenary sessions. Other liberation movements did not have this privilege.[99] Furthermore, the PLO may participate on any issue, while the other liberation movements may only participate in work relating to their own countries. In practice, the PLO has limited its participation to issues relating to Palestine.

In December 1976 the General Assembly granted observer status in plenary session to SWAPO in similar terms to those it used in 1974 with the PLO.[100] This Resolution was passed with no opposing votes and only thirteen abstentions.

[95] See UNGA Res. 3118(XXVIII), 12 Dec. 1973, 108:4:17, which takes note of these developments.
[96] UNGA Res. 3210(XXIX), 14 Oct. 1974, 105:4:20. Bolivia, Dominican Republic, Israel, and the UK in opposition.
[97] UNGA Res. 3237(XXIX), 22 Nov. 1974, 95:17:19. The Resolution also provided for its participation in any international conferences convened under UN auspices.
[98] UNGA Res. 3280(XXIX), 10 Dec. 1974, adopted by consensus.
[99] SWAPO was given observer status in plenary session in 1976. See below.
[100] UNGA Res. 31/152, 20 Dec. 1976, 113:0:13.

Thus, there are two liberation movements which may participate in the General Assembly like State observers on all issues, although in practice their participation has been restricted to issues directly affecting them: the PLO and SWAPO. In addition, liberation movements recognized by the OAU may participate, though not in plenary session, as observers in the 'relevant work' of the main committees and subsidiary organs concerned. At present, the OAU recognizes two liberation movements in addition to SWAPO: the Panafricanist Congress of Azania (PAC) and the African National Congress (ANC).[101]

The extension of observer status at the UN to national liberation movements recognized by the OAU was certainly a political victory in the drive to internationalize wars of national liberation. It also undoubtedly has certain consequences in international law. Over and above the specific legal consequences, it is important to note that if national liberation movements did not have any legal personality in international law before the extension of observer status to their representatives in the early 1970s, it is certain that they do have some limited rights and duties under international law as a result of these resolutions. This is not to say that they have the same rights and duties as States, because they do not. At least after their assumption of observer status at the UN, if not before, national liberation movements recognized by the OAU do have legal personality in international law. The legal consequences of the extension of observer status can be divided into three areas: their rights within the UN, the question of diplomatic status, and the question of international representation of the territories themselves.

Practice has determined the extent of observers' rights within the UN as the institution was not envisioned in the Charter.[102] National liberation movements are issued appropriate passes by the Protocol Office, and they have the use of the facilities at the UN. At meetings they have the right to make statements and have the right of reply. They may have their documents circulated by the Secretariat. They do not have the right to vote, to sponsor substantive proposals, amendments, or procedural motions, to raise points of order, or to challenge rulings made by the Chairman.[103] These rights are procedural in nature and only relate to practice within the United Nations itself.

[101] Letter received from Mr Dawit G. Egziabher, Director of Political Department, OAU, 29 Nov. 1984. In the past the OAU has recognized the following liberation movements: for the Portuguese territories, PAIGC, FRELIMO, MPLA, FNLA, UNITA; for Namibia, SWAPO; for Southern Rhodesia, ZAPU and ZANU; for South Africa, ANC and PAC; for the Comoros, MOLINACO; for the Seychelles, Seychelles People's United Party (SPUP); for the French territory of the Afars and Issas, Front de Libération de la Côte des Somalis (FLCS). Thirteen in total.

[102] *Supra*, 74.

[103] See the following legal opinions of the Secretariat issued or prepared by the UN Office of Legal Affairs: 31 Jan. 1975, *UN Juridical Yearbook: 1975*, 164–7; 14 Mar. 1974, *UN*

The question of the diplomatic status of observers, and the PLO in particular, was addressed in a legal opinion from the Secretariat to a private lawyer in 1979. Representatives of national liberation movements do not have diplomatic privileges or immunity in the host State although they do enjoy, under the terms of the headquarters agreement, 'immunity from legal process in respect of words spoken or written' and all acts performed by members of the delegation 'in their official capacity'.[104] In addition, delegations from national liberation movements have the right to travel freely to and from the UN regardless of the relationship between the host State and the movement.[105]

The final and most important of the legal consequences to flow from observer status concerns the question of representation. Most obviously, national liberation movements have the opportunity to participate in the work of the United Nations subject to the parameters of the relevant resolution. Whether this adds up to a 'right' of participation is debatable. The extension of observer status by the General Assembly is entirely discretionary and may presumably be withdrawn by a subsequent resolution of the Assembly.[106]

But beyond this question of participation is a more complex question of exactly whom do these movements represent. What does it mean to represent a people which is not a State?

In the first place, it is clear that this representation of a people does not preclude other movements from representing the same people. Unlike States, where there is one and only one legitimate government recognized by another State (although different governments may be recognized by different States), in the case of liberation movements the authority to represent a people is not necessarily exclusive. For example, the PAC and ANC are both recognized as representing the people of South Africa and a similar situation existed in Angola before independence.

Second, although national liberation movements have been admitted as observers to the UN this does not mean formal representation of the territory rests with the national liberation movement. The Legal Office of the Secretariat commented in June 1974 that

Juridical Yearbook: 1974, 149–56; 1 May 1975, *UN Juridical Yearbook: 1975*, 170; 5 June 1980, *UN Juridical Yearbook: 1980*, 188–9.

[104] In Dec. 1980 the General Assembly passed a resolution calling on States to accord 'the facilities, privileges and immunities necessary for the performance of their functions' to recognized national liberation movements 'in accordance with the Vienna Convention on the Representation of States'. The treaty is not yet in force and the Resolution was strongly criticized by Western and Latin American countries. See UNGA Res. 35/167, 15 Dec. 1980, 97:10:29.

[105] 'Legal Basis for the Observer Status of the PLO', *UN Juridical Yearbook: 1979*, 169–70.

[106] See Lazarus, 199, who concludes, 'En ce sens, on peut dire que dans la pratique des Nations Unies, les peuples en lutte *n'ont pas* la personnalité internationale: *elle leur est octroyée*, sous certaines conditions.'

[Participation in the Economic Commission for Africa] would not necessarily mean that the liberation movements in question would formally represent their respective territories, this question being linked with the existence or otherwise of one or more authorities claiming to be the government entitled to represent a State, or recognized as the government having responsibility for the international relations of a non-self-governing territory.[107]

Formal representation remains the responsibility of the administering power which is 'recognized as having continuing responsibility for their international relations, as well as for the implementation of the Declaration on the Granting of Independence to Colonial Countries and Peoples'.[108]

Thus, the responsibility of national liberation movements recognized by the United Nations is to express the views of the people in their respective territories. It does not include conduct of their international relations beyond expressing these views. This distinction is particularly important as it means that within the UN context, where the acceptance of liberation movements has been quite progressive, the international personality of a national liberation movement is strictly limited to the expression of views and not the conduct of international relations. This was made particularly clear in the case of Namibia. On the one hand, the General Assembly has given the UN Council for Namibia the responsibility of representing Namibia 'in international organizations, at conferences and on any other occasion as may be required'. On the other hand, the Assembly recognizes that 'the national liberation movement of Namibia, the South West Africa People's Organization, is the authentic representative of the Namibian people'.[109] The distinction is that SWAPO and the Council for Namibia do not act in the same capacity and in practice both often attend the same conferences and meetings. The Council is supposedly the legitimate administrative and governmental authority for the territory until independence, while SWAPO expresses the views of the people but does not represent Namibia, as a territory, internationally. South Africa is a third authority in Namibia whose international legitimacy is not accepted, but whose practical power must be. The Legal Office of the Secretariat, while acknowledging there may need to be some clarification as to these different types of representation, concluded that the desire of the General Assembly that

Namibia be represented by the Namibian national liberation movement relates more particularly to the representation of the Namibian people, and in no way prejudices or conflicts with the right and the obligation of the United Nations

---

[107] 'The Representation of National Liberation Movements in the Work of the Economic Commission for Africa', 18 June 1974, *UN Juridical Yearbook: 1974*, 168.

[108] Ibid. 169.

[109] UNGA Res. 3031(XXVII) and UNGA Res. 3111(XXVIII).

Council for Namibia to represent Namibia on behalf of the international authority which is legally responsible for the territory until it achieves independence.[110]

The conclusions to be drawn from this distinction between representing the views of a people and administrative and governmental responsibility are twofold. First, it sets a limit on the international personality enjoyed by these movements. Recognition as the representative of a people does not imply that the administering power has lost any of its authority to govern and conduct the international relations of the territory. A second and related conclusion is that the consequences of recognition by the OAU or UN are restricted to the authority to represent the views of the people. UN practice does not suggest that recognition in this way constitutes recognition of the authority to resort to the use of force by these movements in the same way that recognition of a State or government would so do. The administering power retains the authority to govern in the territory and to conduct international relations for the territory.

That said, one must add that this is by no means a unanimous conclusion and is a strictly legal one. The fact remains that the extension of observer status to recognized national liberation movements was a considerable political victory for the movements involved and for their supporters. The tactics of these limited international legal persons, including the use of force, have never been condemned by the UN or any other international organization and they have often been commended for their struggle. The majority of governments do contend that these movements have the authority to use force.[111] The extension of observer status and the recognition of movements as representatives of their people reinforce this idea and enhance the international stature of national liberation movements. However, a powerful minority of States still vehemently oppose the extension of the authority to use force to entities other than States.

5.33 The States in Opposition

One of the most persistent criticisms of any right of self-determination, let alone the authority to use force to secure that right, is that it is a right which many States recognize as operating against other States, but no State acknowledges as operating against itself. This question of how States respond to liberation movements fighting against them is particularly important when examining which entities may legitimately resort to the use of force.

In the case of inter-State wars often one or both sides will accuse the other of aggression, but in this century States have not often questioned

---

[110] 'Representation of National Liberation Movements in United Nations Organs', 14 Mar. 1974, *UN Juridical Yearbook: 1974*, 156.
[111] See e.g. the Statement of Mr Hamad (UAE), UNGAOR 1980 A/C.6/35/SR.74, 12–14.

the *authority* of another State to wage war and therefore claimed that it is not a war at all but some other form of violence.[112] This is characteristic of the twentieth-century acceptance of a system dominated by sovereign States where war is, by definition, a conflict between two or more of these dominant entities. If the States fighting against liberation movements were to accept that these movements are legitimate authorities and concentrate instead, as is the case with inter-State wars, on aggression or respect for the humanitarian law of armed conflict, this would certainly be strong evidence that liberation movements possess the requisite legal personality to use force legitimately in international law. On the other hand, treatment of wars of national liberation as problems of internal public order, prosecuting members of these movements in domestic courts under domestic criminal law, and refusing to apply the Geneva Conventions or allow visits by the International Red Cross are indications that governments do not accept the international character of the armed conflict.

Some States have been willing to acknowledge the application of Article 3 of the Geneva Conventions in wars of national liberation. Some States have given 'analogous treatment' to rebels. No State confronted by a national liberation movement has ever acknowledged that it was fighting an international conflict, nor has any State since the end of World War II accepted the authority of a liberation movement to use force against it.

It is not particularly surprising that an established government denies the legitimacy of an opposition movement using violence to undermine it. Governments, after all, have no interest in enhancing the prestige of their opponents. Nevertheless, it is illustrative of the fact that the authority of liberation movements under international law has not been accepted by the most important group of States involved: those against whom they are fighting.

At the outbreak of violence in Algeria in 1954 the French government regarded the uprising as a problem of restoring law and order not even covered by Article 3 of the Geneva Conventions. In June of 1956 France accepted the applicability of Article 3, but denied to the end the international character of the conflict.[113]

---

[112] In Aug. 1965 the Democratic Republic of Vietnam declared that it considered 'the actions of the US Government and its agents in Saigon as acts of piracy and regard the pilots who have carried out pirate-raids, destroying the property and massacring the population of the Democratic Republic of Vietnam, as major criminals caught *in flagrante delicto* and liable for judgement in accordance with the laws of the Democratic Republic of Vietnam, although captured pilots are well treated.' Letter to the ICRC, Aug. 1965, quoted in Allan Rosas, *The Legal Status of Prisoners of War* (Helsinki: Soumalainen Tiedeakatemia, 1976), 176–7. Although in some ways this statement questions the authority of the United States to use force it is more a condemnation of aggression than a challenge to its legal capacity. It is unique in that it attempts to justify treating the combatants of an aggressor *State* like pirates and criminals under domestic law.

[113] See Tom Farer, 'Humanitarian Law and Armed Conflicts: Toward the Definition of

The government of Malaysia did not accept the authority of its subjects to use force against it, as evidenced by the Court's decision in *Public Prosecutor* v. *Oie He Koi*. The Court acknowledged that the 1963–6 conflict between Indonesia and Malaysia was international and that the Geneva Conventions were in force. Nevertheless, the protections of those Conventions were denied to those who 'owed a duty of allegiance to Malaysia' and therefore the defendants could be and were tried under the 1960 Internal Security Act preventing unauthorized possession of firearms.[114]

In the Vietnam War the situation was slightly different. In 1964 the South Vietnamese government passed Vietnam Law No. 18/64 which provided that terrorists and saboteurs would be sentenced to death in the 'shortest time possible' by military courts without previous hearings and without any right to appeal. One year later the government acknowledged the applicability of the Third Convention (i.e. on *international* armed conflicts) and stopped prosecuting captured members of the National Liberation Front solely for their participation in hostilities.[115] The Americans, consistent with their contention that the insurgents in the south were supported by North Vietnam and that the conflict was international in character, granted prisoner-of-war status to Vietcong as well as North Vietnamese regulars and 'guerrillas, self-defense forces and secret self-defense forces . . . captured while actually engaging in combat or in a belligerent act under arms, other than an act of terrorism, sabotage, or spying'.[116] According to the Red Cross, by 1967 'all combatants captured under arms' in South Vietnam were granted prisoner-of-war status.[117] However, the willingness of the United States to grant prisoner-of-war status to all under arms did not reflect a belief that the liberation forces were an authority in their own right, but that the war was an inter-State war using subversion and guerrilla tactics. The argument that indigenous forces in South Vietnam were supported by the North was one of the bases of US intervention in the conflict. It would therefore be incorrect to characterize US policy as implicitly acknowledging the international authority of the indigenous guerrilla forces themselves.

The attitude of Portugal to its African colonies before the April 1974

"International Armed Conflict" ', *Columbia LR*, 71 (1971), 53; Rosas, 148; Maurice Flory, 'Algérie et droit international', *AFDI*, 5 (1959), 829; Castren, *Civil War*, 74; Jean Charpentier, 'La France et le G. P. R. A.', *AFDI*, 7 (1961), 857.

[114] Richard R. Baxter, 'The Privy Council on the Qualifications of Belligerents', *AJIL*, 63 (1969), 290.

[115] Rosas, 168; Joseph Kelley and George Pelletier, 'Theories of Emergency Government', *South Dakota LR*, 2 (1966), 64.

[116] MACV Directive No. 381–46 of 27 Dec. 1967, Annex A, reprinted in *AJIL*, 62 (1968), 767.

[117] *IRRC*, 4 (1967), 188, quoted in Rosas, 169.

coup was much the same as that of France to Algeria nearly twenty years earlier. The Portuguese government consistently held that the conflicts in Africa were internal disturbances which were not even conflicts not of an international character under the terms of Article 3 of the Geneva Conventions.[118]

The government of South Africa which also controls Namibia certainly does not recognize the ANC, the PAC, or SWAPO as organizations which may legitimately resort to the use of force against it. The ANC and PAC are proscribed organizations and have been since 1960. SWAPO is not a proscribed organization although its activities are limited.[119] Prosecution under successive security laws, including the Suppression of Communism Act of 1950, the Sabotage Act of 1962, the Terrorism Act of 1967, and the Internal Security Act of 1982, has been common.[120]

The Israeli position is slightly different from that faced by South Africa in that it is surrounded by hostile States with whom it has had a succession of wars in addition to its difficulties with militant nationalist Palestinian groups. Nevertheless, as a matter of policy, the Israeli government considers these organizations to be criminal terrorist groups without any legitimate status in international law and not covered by the Geneva Conventions because they do not belong to a party to the conflict.[121]

Thus, despite the ringing cries from a large number of States arguing that national liberation movements are legitimate authorities in world politics and may resort to the use of force to secure their right to self-determination, no State actually confronting one of these movements has acknowledged their legitimacy. This is not surprising, but I think it is none the less important. It could be that these governments are just violating the law. But if the States most intimately involved with a situation which other States claim is subject to new rules of international law deny the existence of these new rules, their denial must cast grave doubt upon the legal character of these rules in a system which depends on practice and consent for its development.

The practice of States since the end of World War II suggests a number

---

[118] Rosas, 162–3.

[119] Personal interview with Mr Jacob Hannai, SWAPO Chief Representative in Western Europe, 15 Mar. 1985.

[120] e.g. *State* v. *Tuhadeleni et al.* (1967), more commonly known as the 'Terrorist Trial' or the 'Trial of the 37'; the 'Trial of the Pretoria Twelve' in May 1977; see I. Sagay, 'The Legal Status of Freedom Fighters in Africa', *Eastern Africa LR*, 6 (1973), 16; John Dugard, 'South West Africa and the "Terrorist Trial" ', *AJIL*, 64 (1970), 19–41; John Dugard, *Human Rights and the South African Legal Order* (Princeton, NJ: Princeton Univ. Press, 1978), 220–1; International Commission of Jurists, 'South Africa', *Review* (June 1978), 15–18; International Commission of Jurists, 'South Africa', *Review* (Dec. 1984), 24–7.

[121] In *Military Prosecutor* v. *Kassem et al.* (Ramallah 1969) the Israeli Court held that the PFLP was an illegal organization and its members were not entitled to prisoner-of-war status. See Georg Schwarzenberger, 'Human Rights and Guerrilla Warfare', *Israel Yearbook on Human Rights*, 1 (1971), 248–9; Rosas, 209.

of conclusions about the authority to use force by national liberation movements.

1. The right of self-determination may legitimize the recognition of a government or a provisional government which otherwise would be premature.

2. National liberation movements can have international legal personality.

3. Some States which recognize the authority of national liberation movements in general do not do so when the movements are arrayed against them or their allies.

4. A large number of States now maintain that national liberation movements may legitimately use force to secure the right of their people to self-determination. The trend in international law over the last four decades and since 1960 in particular has been toward the acceptance of their legitimacy. However, a powerful minority of States, including those that confront national liberation movements, do not accept their authority as a matter of international law. Thus, it cannot be maintained that a customary rule exists.

5.4 The 1977 Protocols

The two 1977 Protocols Additional to the 1949 Geneva Conventions are documents on the humanitarian law of armed conflict. Article 1(4) of Protocol I includes 'armed conflicts in which peoples are fighting against colonial domination and alien occupation and against racist regimes in the exercise of their right of self-determination' in the list of international armed conflicts. Despite the caveat of Article 4 that the Protocol 'shall not affect the legal status of the Parties to the conflict', Article 1(4) does affect the legal rights and obligations of national liberation movements and the States opposing them just as Article 3 of the 1949 Geneva Conventions affected the rights and duties of States and rebel movements in non-international armed conflict.

Following a protracted debate, liberation movements recognized by regional intergovernmental organizations were invited to participate in the Diplomatic Conference convened by the Swiss government in 1974 to consider the Draft Protocols submitted by the ICRC.[122] As a result of this

---

[122] By Resolution 2(I) the Conference decided to invite liberation movements recognized by regional intergovernmental organizations. See CDDH/55, OR: vol. i, Pt II, 5. The 'Official Records' of the Conference were published in 1978 in 17 volumes. Not all the documents issued during the Conference were reproduced and there is no comprehensive index. There are two published commentaries which are useful. The most comprehensive is Michael Bothe *et al.*, *New Rules for Victims of Armed Conflicts: Commentary on the Two 1977 Protocols Additional to the Geneva Conventions of 1949* (London: Martinus Nijhoff, 1982). Addition-

decision, eleven national liberation movements recognized by the League of Arab States and the Organization of African Unity were invited to the Conference.[123]

More important than their participation in the Conference was the inclusion of Article 1(4) in Protocol I on international armed conflicts.[124] The governments who opposed or abstained did so because the criteria were arbitrary and subjective and because they feared that such a provision would lead to the unequal and partial application of *jus in bello*. No delegation suggested that the use of force for self-determination was itself illegitimate. Indeed, the Italian representative stated that 'his delegation had consistently supported the practical application of the principle of self-determination of peoples'.[125] The Canadian delegate added that '[T]he Conference was not seeking through the article to give peoples the right to self-determination. The discussions in the United Nations and elsewhere on colonial domination, alien occupation and racist regimes had already been given [*sic*] an international character.'[126]

On the other hand, those who supported Article 1(4) did not hesitate to note the importance of Article 1(4) for the recognition of the authority of liberation movements to use force. Mr Abi-Saab of Egypt, who ably served as spokesman for the Third World throughout the Conference, explained Egypt's vote:

International practice on the universal, regional and bilateral levels had established beyond doubt the international character of wars of national liberation. The purpose of the amendment which had been adopted as paragraph 4 of Article 1 had not been to introduce a new and revolutionary provision, but to bring written humanitarian law into step with what was already established in general international law, of which humanitarian law was an integral part.[127]

Other delegates were more direct than Mr Abi-Saab, noting that the world has given 'national liberation movements their rightful status and assur[ed]

---

ally, a 4-volume article-by-article summary of the First Protocol only was published in 1979: Howard Levie, *Protection of War Victims: Protocol I to the 1949 Geneva Conventions* (Dobbs Ferry, NY: Oceana, 1979). Citations for particular documents referred to will list the number of the document followed by its location in the 17-volume official records.

[123] CDDH/51/Rev.1, OR: vol. i. 671. These were the African National Congress (ANC), Angola National Liberation Front (FNLA), Mozambique Liberation Front (FRELIMO), People's Movement for the Liberation of Angola (MPLA), Palestine Liberation Organization (PLO), Panafricanist Congress (PAC), Seychelles People's United Party (SPUP), South West Africa People's Organization (SWAPO), Zimbabwe African National Union (ZANU), Zimbabwe African People's Union (ZAPU), African National Council of Zimbabwe (ANCZ).

[124] In the roll-call vote on Article 1(4) of Protocol I the result was 87:1:11. Israel opposed. CDDH/SR.36 para. 58, OR: vol. vi. 41. For the negotiating history of this Article see *infra* sect. 7.41.

[125] Mr Di Bernardo (Italy), CDDH/SR.36, para. 78, OR: vol. vi. 45.

[126] Mr Miller (Canada), CDDH/SR.36, para. 92, OR: vol. vi. 48.

[127] Mr Abi-Saab (Egypt), CDDH/SR.36, para. 7, OR: vol. vi. 44.

them adequate protection',[128] and that the Article 'embodied the fundamental right to self-determination and the right to struggle against alien
domination'.[129]

The aim of the 1977 Protocols is to 'reaffirm and develop the provisions
protecting the victims of armed conflicts' and not to legitimize or authorize
'any act of aggression or any other use of force inconsistent with the
Charter of the United Nations'.[130] It is a treaty of *jus in bello*.
Nevertheless, the participation of national liberation movements in the
Conference with a status distinct from that of other observers and
privileges not given to non-governmental bodies prior to 1974, their
signature of the final act, and, most importantly, the inclusion of Article
1(4) in Protocol I illustrates that many States considered their conduct to
be legitimate. If the use of force by peoples fighting for self-determination
was not considered to be legitimate in international law, or if it was still
considered to be solely an act of self-help beyond the realm of international
law, it is likely that States would have continued to treat national liberation
movements as subject solely to municipal law. The inclusion of wars of
national liberation in Protocol I on international armed conflicts is a
statement of the acceptability of the use of force by national liberation
movements in some circumstances.

On the other hand, those States from the Western Bloc who generally
oppose legitimizing the use of force for any purpose other than the self-
defence of States could defer to the humanitarian purpose of the treaty. Its
provisions apply 'without any adverse distinction based on the nature or
origin of the armed conflict or on the causes espoused by or attributed to
the Parties to the conflict'.[131] It therefore cannot legitimize any use of
force. The humanitarian content of the Protocol, combined with the
injunction of Article 4, allowed the Western States to accept the
international character of wars of national liberation without accepting the
proposition that the Protocols legitimize the use of force by national
liberation movements.

The Western countries who opposed assimilation of wars of national
liberation into the category of conflicts covered by Protocol I, and
especially the legal purists among them who lamented the inclusion of such
ill-defined and subjective concepts as colonial domination, alien occupation, and racist regimes, were more conciliatory after the close of the
first session in 1974.[132] With one exception, no country made a reservation

---

[128] Mr Mbaya (United Republic of Cameroon), CDDH/SR.36, para. 95, OR: vol. vi. 49.

[129] Mr Naoroz (Afghanistan), CDDH/SR.36, para. 118, OR: vol. vi. 54.

[130] Preamble, 1977 Protocol I.

[131] Preamble, 1977 Protocol I.

[132] See Charles Lysaght, 'The Attitude of Western Countries', in vol. i of *The New
Humanitarian Law of Armed Conflict*, ed. Antonio Cassese (Naples: Editoriale Scientifica,
1979), 354.

regarding Article 1(4) on signature, although countries may do so upon ratification. That one exception was the United Kingdom, which understood,

[I]n relation to Article 1, that the term 'armed conflict' of itself and in its context implies a certain level of intensity of military operations which must be present before the Conventions or the Protocol are to apply to any given situation, and that this level of intensity cannot be less than that required for the application of Protocol II, by virtue of Article 1 of that Protocol, to internal conflicts . . .[133]

This reservation is interesting as it attempts to retain the traditional law notion that the status of the parties to a conflict is determined by their political and military success and not by the justness of the cause for which they are fighting. Thus far, Britain has not ratified the treaty.

5.5 The Legal Arguments

In the numerous statements by governments asserting that national liberation movements may legitimately use force there has never been a comprehensive explanation presenting the legal basis of this asserted legitimacy. On the other hand, there have been a number of articles, primarily by Western jurists, refuting any claim to legitimacy under international law.[134] However, the assertion that the authority to use force by national liberation movements is therefore a means of political pressure devoid of legal content gives too little credit to the sincerity of Third World governments who no doubt see it as both a matter of international legal right *and* a means of pressure on those governments still clinging to the vestiges of colonialism. Despite the lack of a comprehensive explanation of the principle, there are several distinguishable arguments put forth in justification of the authority to use force by national liberation movements as a principle of law.

One of the most common justifications of the use of force by national liberation movements is the plea of self-defence. It is not surprising that anti-colonial States have argued that the use of force by liberation

---

[133] Reprinted in Bothe *et al*, 721. In their explanation of vote following the adoption of Article 1 in plenary, the Australian delegate noted, 'In supporting Article 1 as a whole, Australia understands that Protocol I will apply in relation to armed conflicts which have a high level of intensity.' Australia did not make a reservation upon signature but reserved the right to do so upon ratification.

[134] See e.g. C. J. R. Dugard, 'The Organisation of African Unity and Colonialism: An Inquiry into the Plea of Self-defence as a Justification for the Use of Force in the Eradication of Colonialism', *ICLQ*, 16 (1967), 157–90; C. J. R. Dugard, 'SWAPO: The *Jus ad bellum* and the *Jus in bello*', *South African LJ*, 93 (1976), 144–58; Robert E. Gorelick, 'Wars of National Liberation: *Jus ad bellum*', *Case Western Reserve JIL*, 11 (1979), 71–93; George Ginsburgs, ' "Wars of National Liberation" and the Modern Law of Nations: The Soviet Thesis', *Law and Contemporary Problems*, 29 (1964), 910–42.

movements is consistent with the norms of the Charter. The plea of self-defence has been argued in three ways.

First, in some cases liberation movements and States supporting them have justified their use of force based on a right of self-defence against the original colonial invasion. In 1954 the FLN claimed that they were fighting a delayed war of self-defence against the French invasion of 1830.[135] Similarly, in justifying India's annexation of Goa before the Security Council in 1961 the Indian delegate argued that the Portuguese military occupation in 1510 could not confer good title.[136] This argument is not particularly persuasive because of the principle of intertemporal law, by which the acquisition of a territory by force at a time when the use of force to acquire territory was not illegal confers good title. Furthermore, the acquiescence of the people of a territory over a period of time would indicate that the right of self-defence has lapsed.[137] Although the Security Council failed to condemn the Indian action in Goa because of the Soviet veto, a majority of the Council took the view that its annexation was illegal.

The more common argument made to support the plea of self-defence is that colonialism, by its very nature, is permanent aggression and any other conception of colonialism misrepresents its true nature. Therefore colonial peoples have a right, consistent with the Charter's norms, to defend themselves. In 1963 at the Addis Ababa OAU summit conference President Sekou Toure declared, '[I]t is essential that this Conference lays down a dead-line for the end of foreign domination in Africa, after which date our armed forces should intervene in the *legitimate defense* of the African continent against aggressors.'[138] Similar sentiments were expressed by a large number of Third World States in the UN, particularly in the deliberations on the 1970 Declaration on Principles of International Law and the 1974 Definition of Aggression. In these debates the Third World States were generally arguing for a broad interpretation of Article 51 of the Charter. The Syrian delegate speaking in the Sixth Committee deliberations on the Definition of Aggression argued that 'His delegation believed that the right of self-defense should be interpreted in the widest possible sense and should cover the use of force by peoples who were oppressed, colonized or expelled from the land of their birth.'[139]

Such a liberal interpretation of self-defence was not in accord with the views of the Western Bloc nor with many of the Latin American States. In

---

[135] Fraleigh, 190.

[136] Pomerance, 49; Quincy Wright, 'The Goa Incident', *AJIL,* 56 (1962), 617–32; Dugard, 'OAU', 168–9.

[137] Dugard, 'OAU', 168–9; Gorelick, 73.

[138] *Ethiopia Observer,* 7 (1963), 30, quoted in Dugard, 'OAU', 165.

[139] Mr Al-Atrache (Syria), UNGAOR: 25th session, 6th Committee, 1204th mtg., para. 5, 21 Oct. 1970.

the first place, a number of countries were still of the opinion that Article 51 applied to the right of self-defence for States. In 1967 the Argentine representative pointed out that

[His] delegation could not support the idea expressed . . . by the non-aligned countries relating to the exercise of the right of self-defense by a people denied of its legitimate right of self-determination. . . .[His delegation] considers the inherent right of self-defense stated in Article 51 of the Charter [to be] a right which belong[s] to sovereign States.[140]

Secondly, both the Western and Eastern Bloc States were sceptical about such a broad interpretation of Article 51 which, in their view, would undermine the prohibition of the use of force and return the idea of 'self-help' to international law. They supported the view that the important clause of Article 51 was that an *armed attack* must take place for there to be a right of self-defence.[141] Nevertheless, a large number of primarily Third World States do consider colonialism to be a form of aggression which justifies the use of force in self-defence to be rid of it.[142]

Although the Eastern Bloc States were sceptical of a broad interpretation of Article 51 in general and tended to justify the use of force by national liberation movements on other grounds, they did occasionally include nations struggling for self-determination within their limited interpretation of self-defence. In 1965 the Ukrainian delegate, debating the Declaration on Principles of International Law, stated,

The lawful use of force should be strictly limited in accordance with Article 51 of the Charter to measures of individual or collective self-defense by nations against colonial domination in the exercise of their right to self-determination, and the application of a Security Council decision taken in accordance with the Charter.[143]

The Western States, sometimes supported by Latin American States, did not and still do not agree with this interpretation of Article 51, nor do they consider colonialism to be a form of permanent aggression.

There is a third argument posed for the legitimization of the use of force

---

[140] Mr Delpach (Argentina), in 1967 Special Committee on Principles of International Law, 7 Aug. 1967, UN Doc. A/AC.125/SR.70, 16–17.

[141] Brownlie, *Force*, 255; Quincy Wright, 'US Intervention in the Lebanon', *AJIL*, 53 (1959), 116; Gorelick, 75.

[142] See statements of Madagascar, UNGAOR: 29th session, Report of the Special Committee on the Definition of Aggression, Supp. 19, 15; Tunisia, UNGAOR: 29th session, 6th Committee, 1482nd mtg., 22 Oct. 1974, para. 26; Libya, UNGAOR: 29th session, 6th Committee, 1182nd mtg., 25 Sept. 1970, para. 47; Afghanistan, UNGAOR: 29th session, 6th Committee, 1206th mtg., 26 Oct. 1970, para. 50; UAR, UNGAOR: 24th session, 6th Committee, 1168th mtg., 3 Dec. 1969, para. 14; Kenya, UNGAOR: 29th session, 6th Committee, 1474th mtg., 11 Oct. 1974, para. 24.

[143] Mr Sapozhnikov (Ukraine), UNGAOR: 20th session, 6th Committee, 875th mtg., 15 Nov. 1965, para. 19; see also statement of Mr Graefrath (GDR), 11 Mar. 1974, quoted in Levie, 6.

based on a right of self-defence which is less vulnerable to the criticisms of the Western powers although it still has failed to convince that group. By the 1970 Declaration on Principles of International Law, member States of the United Nations agreed by consensus that a people who have a right to self-determination have a status in law separate and distinct from that of the State administering them, and that every State has the duty to refrain from the use of force to deprive such peoples of their right of self-determination.[144] If the colonial power initiates the use of force, some argue that the people, represented by their liberation movement, have the authority to use force in self-defence. In other words, national liberation movements have the same authority as subjects of international law as sovereign States. They are still prohibited from resorting to the threat or use of force in their relations with the colonial power, but they may defend themselves against armed attack in accordance with Article 51 of the Charter.

The Third World States have not been eager to embrace this limited justification because it does not legitimize the eradication of colonialism by force of arms if necessary. However, the argument is occasionally used, although often in conjunction with more strident arguments claiming a right to overthrow colonialism. For example, Professor Abi-Saab has argued that '[A]rmed resistance to forcible denial of self-determination—by imposing or maintaining by force colonial or alien domination—is legitimate according to the Declaration [on Principles of International Law]'.[145]

This strict application of the right to self-defence is much less vulnerable to Western criticism which stems primarily from the reluctance to breach the *jus cogens* norm prohibiting the threat or use of force. Nevertheless, the Western States have not generally accepted this limited interpretation. The Declaration on Principles of International Law refers to resistance, not 'armed' resistance, and the Definition of Aggression refers to struggle not 'armed' struggle. The Western States do not accept the adjectives as implicit.

The plea of self-defence was only one of the legal arguments proposed by the anti-colonial States. In a way, it was a justification within the bounds of the Charter of a more fundamental idea: that the denial of self-determination by colonial domination, alien occupation, or racism is so abhorrent that the use of force to eradicate these evils is justified irrespective of any prohibition of the use of force. In other words, wars of national liberation are an exception to the general prohibition of the use of force and anti-colonialism is part of a higher law.[146]The idea that this basic

---

[144] UNGA Res. 2625(XXV).

[145] Abi-Saab, 'Wars of National Liberation in the Geneva Conventions and Protocols', *Recueil des cours*, 165 (1979–IV), 371–2.

[146] See Sanford Silverburg, 'The PLO in the UN', *Israel Law Review*, 12 (1977), 389; S. N. MacFarlane, 'The Idea of National Liberation' (D.Phil Thesis, Oxford, 1982), 466; Rupert Emerson, 'Self-determination', *AJIL*, 65 (1971), 467.

principle justifies the use of force was argued by the government of Mali in the deliberations on the Definition of Aggression. Mali

was surprised at the continued failure of members of the Special Committee to agree on the legitimacy of the liberation struggle. Failure to recognize that right in so important a text as the one currently being elaborated would be a rejection of one of the basic principles of the Charter.[147]

Several Third World and Eastern Bloc States have argued that wars of national liberation are not prohibited by the Charter because Article 2(4) was referring to territorial aggrandizement. Wars of national liberation, in contrast, are fought to eradicate an agreed evil, and are therefore exempt from this prohibition.

Although the idea that wars of national liberation are exceptions to the general rule prohibiting the threat or use of force is widely accepted by Third World and Eastern Bloc States, it is not accepted by the Western States where sympathy for the ends of securing self-determination does not justify the use of force as a means. Many critics, quite rightly, have seen in this argument overtones of the medieval concept of a just war.

Finally, there is a third legal argument, less challenging of the traditional norms of international law than either the right of self-defence for peoples or the idea of a higher law. Quite simply, it is the explicit acceptance of a right of revolution by national liberation movements. The former representative of the United States to the Special Committee of Twenty-Four, Seymour Finger, explained,

It was not the US view that peoples should be denied the right to resort to any means at their disposal, including violence, if armed suppression by a colonial power required it. . . . The difficulty lay in giving a general endorsement to the UN—an organization dedicated to peace—to such violence. . . . Such action could hardly be reconciled with the requirements of the Charter of the United Nations.[148]

Mr Finger seems to be saying that the United States did not object to the idea of liberation as such, only to granting it legitimacy. This is nearly identical to the traditional conception of international law which neither condones nor condemns internal wars.

This *laissez-faire* approach is not accepted by the Third World and Eastern Bloc States for a number of reasons. First, it does not recognize the international character of wars of national liberation which is essential both to the liberation movements and to their supporters. Second, acceptance of liberation in this manner implies the continuance of traditional ideas of non-intervention on the side of the liberation

---

[147] Mr Maiga (Mali), UNGAOR: 28th session, 6th Committee, 1444th mtg., 21 Nov. 1973, para. 14.
[148] Seymour Finger, 'A New Approach to Colonial Problems at the United Nations', *International Organization*, 26 (1972), 145.

movement, which is clearly unacceptable to the members of the Organization of African Unity which have accepted an obligation to eradicate colonialism from the African continent. Finally, this more limited institutionalized right of revolution would continue to favour the established government whereas, according to a large number of States, in a war of national liberation international law would and should be in favour not of repression, but of revolution.[149]

Thus, the legal arguments proposed are not without substance even if they are not agreed upon by all States as accurate statements of the applicable legal principles.

5.6 Conclusions

International law is still a matter of consent, not consensus. As a matter of law, not all States are agreed that national liberation movements have the authority to use force. Nevertheless, it would be a mistake to overlook the change in ideas which has taken place largely in the last forty years. Wars of national liberation are no longer matters where international law definitely favours the established government to promote international order and protect the status quo. On the contrary, largely due to the influence of newly independent States with the support of the Communist countries, all States have at least recognized the separate international personality of 'peoples' who have a right of self-determination and condemned the use of force against these peoples even if States have not condoned the use of force to effect change.

To contend unequivocally that the various resolutions of the General Assembly, the practice of States, and the 1977 Protocols reflect a change in international law which gives national liberation movements the authority to use force legitimately would be an overstatement. The law as it stands is still not agreed upon. However, some conclusions can be made about the current state of affairs.

1. National liberation movements have an international legal personality unlike that of other non-governmental organizations. This status is based on the right of the peoples which they represent to self-determination.
2. There is general agreement that wars of national liberation are not strictly internal armed conflicts.
3. The use of force to deny the free exercise of a people's right to self-determination is contrary to the principles of international law.
4. The right of a people to self-determination may legitimize the recognition of a government which would otherwise be premature.

[149] Natalino Ronzitti, 'Wars of National Liberation: A Legal Definition', *Italian Yearbook of International Law*, 1 (1975), 192.

5. The authority of national liberation movements to use force is not agreed upon as a matter of international law. Such authority is actively supported by the newly independent States and the Eastern Bloc States, but has never been accepted by an established government confronting a liberation movement, or by the Western States. Practice in the UN, particularly the Declaration on Principles of International Law and the Declaration on Aggression, both adopted without vote, does not resolve the fundamental differences of opinion over the status of national liberation movements and the extent of their authority as a matter of law. However, the trend over the last four decades and since 1960 in particular has been toward the extension of the authority to use force to national liberation movements.

6

National Liberation Movements as Representative Authorities

6.1 Introductory

Chapter 5 addressed the authority of liberation movements to use force as a matter of international law. There is a second question, reminiscent of that explored by Augustine, Aquinas, and their contemporaries, which is separate from that discussed in the previous chapter but related to it: if it is the case that there is a right of 'peoples' to self-determination and some claim that the use of force to secure this right is justified, then how does a particular liberation movement become a legitimate representative of a people? This is a broad and complicated question which could be the subject of a book on its own. The purpose of this chapter is to explore the question in a general way as it relates to the larger issue of the authority to use force in international law.

It is easier to identify the legitimate authority for a State than it is for a 'people'. It is generally accepted that a State must have a permanent population, a defined territory, a government, and the capacity to enter into relations with other States.[1] Since the existence of an effective government is a condition of statehood, the government of a State is obviously the organ which decides to use force and executes that decision once made. But in the case of a people, desirous of statehood but not necessarily having a separate, established government, the answer is not self-evident. In practice it has been liberation movements and the provisional governments sometimes established by these movements which have often been considered to be the authorities representing a people.

The need for governments to choose which entity legitimately represents a people or a territory is not a new problem. During World War II, for example, the Yugoslav Chetniks led by Mihailovich were recognized by the Yugoslav government in exile yet were fighting against Tito's Communist partisans. After sending British liaison officers to Yugoslavia to judge the situation in the field, the British government decided in 1943 to support only Tito. Mr Churchill defended this position in the House of Commons when he declared,

---

[1] See Article 1, 1933 Convention on Rights and Duties of States, 165 *LNTS*, 19; Ian Brownlie, *Principles of Public International Law*, 3rd edn. (Oxford: Clarendon Press, 1979), 74.

The reason why we have ceased to supply Mihajlovic with arms and support is a simple one. He has not been fighting the enemy, and, moreover, some of his subordinates have made accommodations with the enemy, from which have arisen armed conflicts with the forces of Marshal Tito. . . . We have proclaimed ourselves the strong supporters of Marshal Tito because of his heroic and massive struggle against the German armies.[2]

Similar decisions were made concerning resistance movements in Greece. In Greece, the British government even tried to reconcile differences between various movements by negotiating a 'National Bands' agreement. According to E. C. W. Myers, the signatories of the agreement

bound themselves to allow all bands, to whatever organization they belonged, to exist unmolested by them, and to be free to carry out operations against the enemy, in accordance with instructions from the Middle East Command, through me or any of my officers. In return they would be supplied with arms, ammunition and other essentials by the Allies, so far as was within their means.[3]

Choices made between resistance movements fighting in a major war or between different factions in a civil war are not at all uncommon.

6.2 International Recognition

While it is quite common for governments to make choices amongst liberation movements, it is not clear that there are any accepted legal principles by which governments make their decisions. Certainly the act of recognition has legal consequences, whether such recognition is extended by an international organization or by an individual State. But the qualities of liberation movements which apparently lead to this recognition have never been clearly set out by any State or organization. It would be more accurate to say that there are some consistencies in international practice concerning recognition of liberation movements, but this practice is not necessarily a matter of international law. Recognition of an entity representing a people is still a very primitive and tenuous development for which definitive rules do not appear to exist.

It is also important to note that the existence of some kind of relationship between a liberation movement and an outside government is a very practical matter that can occur for a variety of reasons at a variety of levels. A government may negotiate with a liberation movement simply to secure the release of nationals held hostage. At the other extreme, a

---

[2] Quoted in Stephen Clissold (ed.), *A Short History of Yugoslavia: From Early Times to 1966* (Cambridge: Cambridge Univ. Press, 1966), 229.

[3] E. C. W. Myers, *Greek Entanglement*, 130–1, quoted in C. M. Woodhouse, 'Summer 1943: The Critical Month', in *British Policy Towards Wartime Resistance in Yugoslavia and Greece*, ed. Phyllis Auty and Richard Clogg (London: Macmillan, 1975), 123.

government may recognize one movement in particular as 'legitimate' and provide arms, training, and sanctuary to the members of that movement. There is a spectrum of types of contact, some elements of which might be described as recognition.

6.21 United Nations Practice

The tendency of the United Nations to recognize liberation movements as the legitimate representatives of their peoples was discussed in Chapter 5.[4] The question here is, on what basis did the UN choose some liberation movements and not others, from some territories and not others?

The Economic Commission for Africa was one of the first international bodies to consider the problem of choosing representatives of Angola, Mozambique, Guinea-Bissau, and South West Africa to attend sessions of the Commission as associate members. Three years before actually deciding how to choose these representatives, the Commission requested suggestions from African governments on the problem.[5] The responses received by the Commission have several common themes.

First, almost all the governments immediately turned to the existing nationalist organizations in the territories under consideration. The possibility of the peoples of these territories being represented by some other means, independent of the liberation movements, does not seem to have been considered at all.

Only the United Kingdom suggested the possibility of soliciting recommendations from the administering powers. It is not surprising that the views of administering States were not solicited, given that Portugal had been expelled and South Africa suspended from the Economic Commission for Africa; it is none the less important that representation of a people was to be determined completely outside the established governmental structure of a territory. The United Kingdom noted that

[A]lthough a request to appoint representatives may be directed to a territorial government by a United Nations organ, authorization for such a direct approach is required (expressly or by implication) from the competent authorities of the states responsible for the international relations of the territory.[6]

Third, there was no agreement concerning the number of represent-atives which should be invited to participate. Some governments seemed to assume that only one nationalist organization would represent the people

---

[4] *Supra*, sect. 5.32.

[5] On 28 Feb. 1964 the Commission passed Resolution 94(VI) requesting the Executive Secretary to make inquiries into the matter with the Economic and Social Council. On 2 Oct. 1964 a letter requesting suggestions on the way in which non-self-governing territories should be represented was sent to member governments. *Report on Measures Taken in Regard to Resolution 94(VI)*, UN Doc. E/CN.14/340, 9 Feb. 1965.

[6] Statement of the United Kingdom, UN Doc. E/CN.14/340/Add.1, 9 Feb. 1965.

of the territory, while others did not restrict representation to one group.[7]

A final common thread running through many of the responses was the importance of recognition by the OAU. Some governments recommended that the OAU should decide which persons or organizations should represent these territories. Others just suggested they should be consulted.

In 1967 the Economic Commission decided that the OAU should propose representatives. This practice of deferring to the judgment of the OAU as the regional organization concerned has become standard practice in the United Nations since 1967.

The UN Council for Namibia faced similar problems when deciding who would represent the Namibian people. The UN Council was supposed to administer the territory, 'with the maximum possible participation of the people of the Territory'.[8] In 1970 the Council noted that the problem which had so far prevented such participation resulted 'from the existence of several political groupings of Namibians, each claiming that they were more representative than the others on grounds convincing to themselves but difficult for the Council to evaluate'.[9] The Council consulted the OAU, which recognized SWAPO as the only organized representative in South West Africa. They also consulted SWAPO itself and two other nationalist groups, SWANU and SWANUF. The OAU representatives, while accepting that the decision was one for the Council to make, intimated that OAU recognition of SWAPO should be the prime consideration of the Council.[10] Of course, the other nationalist organizations did not agree and argued for their inclusion as representatives. In 1972 the Council reported to the General Assembly that

[It was] not able to resolve the question of participation of Namibians in its work. Nevertheless, it was gratified to note that the opportunity given to representatives of Namibian people to regularly attend the meetings of the Council as observers, was accepted by the representative of SWAPO.[11]

The following year the Council for Namibia granted observer status to SWAPO, 'the Namibian liberation movement recognized by the OAU'.[12] In the same session the General Assembly recognized SWAPO as 'the authentic representative of the Namibian people'.[13] Although one wonders

---

[7] UN Doc. E/CN.14/340, 9 Feb. 1965 and UN Doc. E/CN.14/380, 27 Dec. 1966.

[8] UNGA Res. 2248(S-V), 19 May 1967, 85:2:30.

[9] UN Council for Namibia, Report on its Mission to Africa, 31 Aug. 1970, UN Doc. A/AC.131/20, 21.

[10] UN Doc. A/AC.131/20, 25.

[11] 27th session, Supp. 24 (A/8724), vol. i, para 187, quoted in *UN Juridical Yearbook*, 1974, 152.

[12] UNGAOR: 28th session, Supp. 24(A/9024), para. 280, quoted in *UN Juridical Yearbook*, 1974, 152.

[13] UNGA Res. 3111(XXVIII), 12 Dec. 1973, 107:2:17.

what would have happened if a representative of SWANU or SWANUF had accepted the invitation of the Council to attend the 1972 session, it appears that the Council for Namibia and the General Assembly also deferred to the recognition policies of the OAU. The General Assembly continued this practice in 1974 when they invited representatives of national liberation movements recognized by the OAU to participate as observers.[14]

This general tendency within the United Nations to defer to the OAU on questions of representation for non-self-governing territories is evident when one looks at the territories which have been represented by liberation movements and those which have not.

It appears that the recognition of entities as legitimate representatives of their peoples has only been a topic of discussion for African territories and Palestine. Obviously, a large number of non-self-governing territories were in Africa. However, one cannot discount the importance of pressure brought to bear by members of the Organization of African Unity. In other parts of the world the question of legitimate representation appears to have been avoided in the UN.

The influence of OAU member States in the UN is also evident when one considers that Polisario, the only liberation movement in the Western Sahara, is not recognized in the UN as the 'legitimate' representative of the Sahrawis. The UN has repeatedly recognized the right of the people of the Western Sahara to self-determination, but Polisario does not enjoy observer status. Furthermore, although a majority of the members of the OAU have recognized the provisional government established by Polisario, the OAU never recognized Polisario as it did other liberation movements. Clearly, it is difficult for the UN to recognize a liberation movement which is fighting against a sovereign African State even if the UN has accepted the right of the people of that territory to self-determination.

The only non-African territory which has been recognized by the United Nations as a 'legitimate representative' is the PLO, the liberation movement recognized by the League of Arab States.[15]

This tendency to defer to the regional organization concerned is not restricted to the United Nations. In 1974, when the Diplomatic Conference convened in Geneva to consider the Draft Protocols to the Geneva Conventions, the Conference decided to invite the national liberation movements 'recognized by the regional intergovernmental organizations concerned.'[16] In practice, this meant those recognized by the OAU and the League of Arab States.

[14] UNGA Res. 3280(XXIX), 10 Dec. 1974, adopted by consensus.
[15] See Catherine Burke, 'International Recognition of a Non-state Nation: The Palestine Liberation Organization and the United Nations' (M.Phil. Thesis, Oxford, 1979).
[16] Res. 2(I), CDDH/55, OR: vol. i, Part II, 5.

The absence of formally stated criteria in the UN for recognition of a liberation movement as the legitimate representative of its people was politically expedient. It does not mean, however, that there were no implicit criteria or ideas in the minds of those who decided to defer to the wisdom of the regional organization concerned.

6.22 OAU Recognition

When the OAU was formed in 1963 one of the aims of the Organization, as stated in its Charter, was the eradication of 'all forms of colonialism' from Africa and 'absolute dedication to the total emancipation of the African territories which are still dependent'.[17] To help fulfil this aim, the OAU has a Liberation Committee accountable to the Assembly which provides assistance to liberation movements and administers a special fund to finance these movements.[18] It is this committee which recommends recognition of particular movements.

In 1970 the OAU explained to a UN mission to Africa that its recognition of SWAPO was based on three criteria: the movement must be representative of the people, it must be engaged in a liberation struggle, and it must be effective.[19] No attempt was made to explain what was meant by effectiveness or how the OAU determines the representative character of a movement. These criteria, possessing a certain degree of juridical formalism, were repeated in slightly different form by the Head of the Decolonization and Sanctions Division in 1985:

[I]n order for a liberation movement to be recognized by the OAU, the OAU has to be satisfied on [sic] the activities and objectives of the liberation movement seeking recognition; furthermore it has to be established that the said movement has the support of the majority of its people.[20]

Exactly what these activities and objectives must be was not expanded upon.

In principle, the political orientation of the movement is irrelevant.[21] In practice, since the OAU Liberation Committee relies primarily on neighbouring States to get its information, impartial assessments are difficult.

[17] OAU Charter, Articles 2(1)*d* and 3(6).

[18] C. J. R. Dugard, 'The Organisation of African Unity and Colonialism: An Inquiry into the Plea of Self-defence as a Justification for the Use of Force in the Eradication of Colonialism', *ICLQ*, 16 (1967), 162; Leonard T. Kapungu, 'The OAU's Support for the Liberation of Southern Africa', in *The Organization of African Unity After Ten Years: Comparative Perspectives*, ed. Yassin El-Ayouty (London: Praeger, 1975), 142; G. Chaliand, *Armed Struggle in Africa* (London: Monthly Review Press, 1969), 108.

[19] UN Doc. A/AC.131/20, para. 47, 31 Aug. 1970.

[20] Letter received from Mr Dawit G. Egziabher, Head of Decolonization and Sanctions Division, OAU, 11 Mar. 1985.

[21] Claude Lazarus, 'Le Statut des mouvements de libération nationale à l'organisation des Nations Unies', *AFDI*, 20 (1974), 180.

The procedure used by the OAU Liberation Committee to determine whether or not a liberation movement should be recognized begins with a petition sent to the OAU by the liberation movement seeking recognition. The Liberation Committee then sends a mission to the region to seek information. Based on their report, the Committee makes its recommendation to the Heads of State summit which decides whether or not to recognize the movement.[22] Often these investigations to determine popular support and combat effectiveness are conducted neither in the country concerned, nor on the field of battle, but in the capital of a neighbouring State. In 1964 this practice led to the recognition of the Angolan Revolutionary Government in Exile (GRAE) headquartered in Congo (Libreville), while the MPLA was not recognized at that time. Several African States, in disagreement with the OAU on this decision to recognize the GRAE, continued to support the MPLA.[23]

The criteria used by the OAU to determine which liberation movements are recognized as representatives of their people are highly subjective. However, based on the liberation movements which have and have not been recognized by the OAU, some conclusions can be drawn.

At present, the OAU recognizes three liberation movements as representatives of their peoples: SWAPO, the PAC, and the ANC.[24] This list is more notable for those excluded than those included. The OAU has never recognized Polisario as the representative of the Sahrawi people although it has been actively involved in negotiations to have a referendum in the territory and has been a mediator between Morocco and Polisario. It was not until 1983 that the OAU abandoned its pleas to 'parties to the conflict' and urged direct talks between Morocco and Polisario thereby acknowledging openly that the OAU considered the guerrillas to be the other party involved. As far as Morocco is concerned, Algeria is the other party to the conflict and Polisario is a proxy force.[25] This concession is minor compared with the political and material support given to liberation movements fighting against non-African powers.

In cases where a movement is fighting an African government, there has been no question about the OAU's position: territorial integrity of the self-governing African State is paramount except when the black majority in that State is disenfranchised. Thus, the OAU does not recognize any liberation movements on the horn of Africa. Likewise the OAU supported the territorial integrity of Nigeria and did not recognize Biafra, nor did the

[22] Letter received from Mr Dawit Egziabher, 11 Mar. 1985.
[23] Lazarus, 180–1.
[24] In the past the OAU has recognized the PAIGC, FRELIMO, MPLA, FNLA, and UNITA from the Portuguese territories; ZAPU, ZANU, and ANCZ from Zimbabwe; MOLINACO from the Comoros; SPUP from the Seychelles; and FLCS from the Afars and Issas.
[25] *International Herald Tribune*, 3 Nov. 1984, 1.

African States support Katangan secession from the Congo. The situation in the Western Sahara caused a rift in the OAU because the Sahrawis never became an independent State following the withdrawal of the European colonial power. It seems that in OAU practice a liberation movement can only be the legitimate representative of the people of a territory if the established government is a colonial power or is a minority regime which denies equal rights to the majority.

A second conclusion to be drawn from the practice of the OAU is that being recognized as a legitimate representative of the people does not preclude other movements from representing the same people. The OAU has made efforts to unify disparate groups into a single movement or front. When efforts at reconciliation have failed, the OAU has recognized and assisted more than one liberation movement in the same territory. For the purpose of representing the views of the people of a territory in international forums, recognition of more than one movement seems unusual, but need not cause practical problems. For other purposes, like military training and assistance funnelled through the OAU Liberation Committee, recognition of more than one liberation movement is shortsighted. This assistance may initially be directed against the administering power. In the long term, recognizing and supporting more than one movement foments internecine violence between irreconcilable groups once the administering power is gone. Despite the inadvisability of recognizing more than one movement in a given territory, the OAU has recognized two liberation movements in South Africa and historically has recognized more than one in other territories.[26]

A third observation which can be made about OAU recognition is that the intensity of the armed conflict conducted by liberation movements recognized by the OAU has varied greatly from case to case. At one extreme the OAU recognized the Seychelles People's United Party and at the other extreme it recognized the Portuguese liberation movements, and the PAIGC in particular. Because there is such a broad spectrum of activity which appears to be included in the OAU's definition of 'military effectiveness' and 'the existence of a liberation struggle' it is difficult to say that, in practice, a standard of effectiveness exists. The interpretation of effectiveness appears to be highly subjective and inconsistently applied.

Furthermore, unlike recognition of a State, recognition of a liberation movement by the OAU has not depended upon the control of territory. This represents a notable shift away from the traditional law ideas of recognition of belligerency which required, *inter alia*, control over territory. OAU recognition in furtherance of self-determination seems to emphasize the control of the loyalty of the population rather than control

---

[26] In Angola the OAU eventually recognized the MPLA, the FNLA, and UNITA. In Zimbabwe, both ZANU and ZAPU were recognized.

of land. This is one of the factors that makes OAU decisions so subjective. It may also be more realistic since control of territory is often not an objective of a liberation movement until very late in its struggle.

Because liberation movements have rarely been able to prove their legitimacy through control of territory, one cannot overlook the importance of salesmanship by liberation movements seeking recognition. Their ability to convince neighbouring States as well as the Liberation Committee that they do represent the population of the territory—perhaps better than any other party involved—is an important factor in securing support.

Finally, and most obviously, the liberation movements which have been recognized by the OAU have all claimed to represent a 'people' entitled to self-determination and desirous of independent statehood in an established territory. None have claimed to be representatives of particular tribes, religious or ethnic minorities, or even particular provinces within a colonial territory. In some cases the leaders of a movement have come primarily from one particular tribe or area, as some allege is the case with SWAPO, but in no case have these movements claimed to represent only a certain tribal people or region.[27] In other words, they must claim to represent the whole 'self' and not just a part of it.

From the practice of the UN and OAU some general conclusions may be made concerning the authority of a particular movement to use force on behalf of a people.

1. In general, the United Nations has deferred judgment on the representative character of particular liberation movements and has relied upon recognition by the regional intergovernmental organization concerned. In practice, this has meant the League of Arab States for Palestine and the OAU.

2. The criteria for recognition used by the OAU have a certain judicial formalism, but are open to wide interpretation. The two major requirements are that the movement be representative of the people of a territory and that it be engaged in an armed struggle of unspecified intensity. The movement need not control territory.

3. To be recognized, a national liberation movement must claim to represent the whole of a people identified as having a right to self-determination.

4. The OAU has been very reluctant to recognize a movement as the legitimate representative of a people when this claim conflicts with the territorial integrity of a member State.

---

[27] In 1970, for example, SWANU claimed that SWAPO was 'a regionally oriented organization enjoying support and influence only in the northern part of the Territory, and carrying no support whatsoever in the central and southern part of Namibia, where Hereros, Namas and Damaras are located'. UN Doc. A/AC.131/20, 21.

5. Although attempts are usually made to reconcile disparate liberation movements fighting in the same territory, recognition of more than one liberation movement as representatives of the same people has occurred.

6. In practice, the recognition of particular liberation movements as representatives of their people is a highly subjective procedure affected by the perception of popular support, ideological affinity with neighbouring States, and the territorial integrity of self-governing States.

PART IV

Protection of Victims

7

The Law of Armed Conflict in Wars of National Liberation

7.1 Introductory

The application of the humanitarian law of armed conflict to wars of national liberation has met less resistance than the attempt to legitimize the resort to force by national liberation movements. Whereas the extension of the authority to use force runs directly counter to the general trend of the twentieth century towards a *jus contra bellum*, the idea that the combatants in these wars should have the benefit of certain humanitarian protections is entirely consistent both with the expanding international law of human rights and with increasing concern about the prevalence and brutality of wars of national liberation.[1]

The application of the laws of war to wars of national liberation has also been a more popular subject for study than the question of right authority, particularly since the opening of negotiations which led to the 1977 Protocols Additional to the 1949 Geneva Conventions.[2] The substantive

---

[1] *For a discussion on the relationship between the humanitarian law of war and the law of human rights see G. I. A. D. Draper, 'The Ethical and Juridical Status of Constraints in War', Military Law Review, 55 (1972), 169–85; Dietrich Schindler, 'Human Rights and Humanitarian Law: Interrelationship of the Laws', Am. Univ. LR, 31 (1982), 935–43.*

[2] See Michel Veuthey, *Guérilla et droit humanitaire* (Geneva: Institut Henry-Dunant, 1976); Michel Veuthey, 'La Guérilla: Le Problème du traitement des prisonniers', *Annales d'études internationales*, 3 (1972), 119–36; Michel Veuthey, 'Guerrilla Warfare and Humanitarian Law', *IRRC*, 234 (May–June 1983), 115–37; Georges Abi-Saab, 'Wars of National Liberation and the Laws of War', *Annales d'études internationales*, 3 (1972), 93–117; Georges Abi-Saab, 'Wars of National Liberation in the Geneva Conventions and Protocols', *Recueil des cours*, 165 (1979-IV), 353–445; G. I. A. D. Draper, 'The Implementation and Enforcement of the Geneva Conventions of 1949 and of the Two Additional Protocols of 1978', *Recueil des cours*, 164 (1979-III), 1–54; G. I. A. D. Draper, 'Wars of National Liberation and War Criminality', in *Restraints on War*, ed. Michael Howard (Oxford: Oxford Univ. Press, 1979), 135–62; Antonio Cassese (ed.), *The New Humanitarian Law of Armed Conflict*, vol. i (Naples: Editoriale Scientifica, 1979); Frits Kalshoven, 'Reaffirmation and Development of International Humanitarian Law Applicable in Armed Conflicts', *NYIL*, 8 (1977), 107–35; Howard Levie, *Protection of War Victims: Protocol I to the 1949 Geneva Conventions* (Dobbs Ferry, NY: Oceana, 1979); Jean Salmon, 'La Conférence diplomatique sur la réaffirmation et le développement du droit international humanitaire et les guerres de libération nationale', *Revue belge de droit international*, Part I, 12 (1976), 27–52, and Part II, 13 (1977), 353–78; Dietrich Schindler, 'International Humanitarian Law and Internationalized Internal Armed Conflicts', *IRRC* (Sept.–Oct. 1982), 255–64; Dietrich Schindler, 'The Different Types of Armed Conflicts According to the Geneva Conventions and Protocols', *Recueil des cours*, 163 (1979-II), 116–63; Jean Siotis, *Le Droit de la guerre et les conflits armés d'un caractère non-international*, (Paris: Librairie Générale, 1958); Bothe, Partsch, and Solf,

provisions and protections of the law of war as applied to wars of national liberation is a vast and complex subject far beyond the scope of this book. Rather, the purpose of this chapter is to examine, through recent State practice and the 1977 Protocols, the application of this *body* of law in wars of national liberation. There are, of course, certain salient issues which are emphasized in the text which follows. The treatment of captured belligerents, the protection of civilians, and immunity from prosecution under domestic law for legitimate acts of warfare are central and often controversial problems when considering the application of the law of war in wars of national liberation.

The 1977 Protocols are not as revolutionary as some authors writing in the immediate aftermath of the Diplomatic Conference have suggested.[3] There has been a gradual trend, with some notable exceptions, toward the extension of humanitarian protection to conflicts not of an international character and to wars of national liberation in particular. The purpose of this chapter is to examine this trend.

7.2 United Nations Resolutions

In the realm of humanitarian law United Nations practice has been less important than the practice of States involved in wars of national liberation, the efforts of the International Red Cross, and multilateral treaties. Nevertheless, the application of the law of war to wars of national liberation has been the subject of General Assembly resolutions since 1968.[4] Until 1973 these resolutions called on particular parties, including South Africa, Portugal, and the United Kingdom in Rhodesia, to apply the 1949 Geneva Conventions to the conflicts in their territories. In 1973 the Assembly approached the matter in a general way with Resolution 3103(XXVIII). This Resolution addressed the legal status of combatants in wars of national liberation and declared that

New Rules for Victims of Armed Conflicts (London: Martinus Nijhoff, 1982); B. A. Wortley, 'Observations on the Revision of the 1949 Geneva "Red Cross" Conventions', *BYIL*, 54 (1983), 143–66; James E. Bond, 'Amended Article 1 of Draft Protocol I to the 1949 Geneva Conventions: The Coming of Age of the Guerrilla', *Washington and Lee LR*, 32 (1975), 65–78.

[3] See e.g. David E. Graham, 'The 1974 Diplomatic Conference on the Law of War: A Victory for Political Causes and a Return to the "Just War" Concept of the Eleventh Century', *Washington and Lee LR*, 32 (1975), 25–63.

[4] See UNGA Res. 2383(XXIII), 7 Nov. 1968, 86:9:19; 2508(XXIV), 21 Nov. 1969, 83:7:20; 2547A(XXIV), 11 Dec. 69, 87:1:23; 2678(XXV), 9 Dec. 1970, 95:5:14; 2652(XXV), 3 Dec. 1970, 79:10:4; 2871(XXVI), 20 Dec. 1971, 111:2:10; 2796(XXVI), 10 Dec. 1971, 91:9:12; 2795(XXVI), 10 Dec. 1971, 105:8:5.

[A]rmed conflicts involving the struggle of peoples against colonial and alien domination and racist regimes are to be regarded as international armed conflicts in the sense of the 1949 Geneva Conventions, and the legal status envisaged to apply to the combatants in the 1949 Geneva Conventions and other international instruments is to apply to the persons engaged in armed struggle against colonial and alien domination and racist regimes.[5]

This was the same Resolution which the American representative, Mr Evans, considered to be 'wrong in virtually every paragraph as a statement of law'.[6] He went on to say that the US government believed that

[T]o classify one kind of conflict as international because of motivation or to accord special treatment to a select class of victims of war because of their motivation is frankly the antithesis of international humanitarian law and totally unacceptable.[7]

The Western States generally opposed or abstained on this Resolution and similar resolutions relating to specific territories.

As part of United Nations practice, the extension of the humanitarian law of war to movements fighting for self-determination was a predictable consequence and corollary of the idea that a 'people' fighting for self-determination had a status in international law separate and distinct from that of the administering power. If a war of national liberation is an international war, then the humanitarian law of war should apply. State practice suggests that, for a variety of reasons, the international rules are often used.

7.3 Recent Trends in State Practice

Although States remain reluctant to confer the *status* of legitimate combatancy on their opponents, in some wars of national liberation they have observed the principles of international humanitarian law. In this respect, then, State practice is ahead of the codification of the law and probably will remain so. While States are reluctant to admit that their opponents have certain rights under international law which protect them from the full extent of domestic law, or, in some cases, reluctant even to admit that an armed conflict exists, they are often equally reluctant to appear to be inhumane or to encourage brutality against their own soldiers who may be held by a national liberation movement. Thus, in many cases the established government has allowed the ICRC to visit detainees, to aid the civilian population, and to deliver family messages. In some wars of

---

[5] UNGA Res. 3103(XXVIII), 12 Dec. 1973, 82:13:19.
[6] *Supra*, 101.
[7] Mr Evans (USA), UNGAOR: 28th session, 2197th plenary mtg., 12 Dec. 1973.

national liberation, generally after a period of repression, the State has treated detainees like prisoners of war, refrained from prosecuting them under domestic law, and even exchanged them for their own prisoners of war. Usually the State involved will deny that these 'security detainees' are or have any right to be prisoners of war.

There are also some notable exceptions to this tendency. Some governments have continued to apply domestic criminal law even when the conflict is widespread. This section examines some of these cases, with particular emphasis on recent wars of national liberation.

Practice in this area has been more evolutionary than revolutionary and has a long history.[8] In the post-World War II era the International Red Cross has intervened in numerous internal conflicts with varying degrees of success. In fact, today the Red Cross performs most of its activities in situations that are not recognized as international armed conflicts. By toning down the legal arguments for its involvement in the protection of detainees and emphasizing confidentiality and quiet pragmatic negotiation, the ICRC has had some success in applying the law of war to internal armed conflicts and, in particular, to wars of national liberation.[9] In some cases the established government has applied the law of war, or parts of it, on its own initiative without ICRC encouragement. In other cases the established government has refused to apply anything but domestic criminal law, which may or may not be in harmony with the provisions of international law.

As noted in Chapter 5, at the outbreak of the Algerian war in 1954 the French government regarded the uprising as a matter of restoring law and order not even covered by Article 3 of the Geneva Conventions. After a meeting in January 1955 between the ICRC and the government of Mr Mendes-France, the French government agreed to allow the ICRC to visit detainees of their choice in Algeria. By allowing these visits, the French government implicitly accepted the applicability of Article 3 of the Geneva Conventions.[10] Until June 1956, however, captured members of the FLN were routinely prosecuted under a special powers act which provided for detention without trial and special court jurisdiction for crimes against the security of the State. Members of the FLN prosecuted under this law were

---

[8] See Michel Veuthey, *Guérilla*; Allan Rosas, *The Legal Status of Prisoners of War: A Study in International Humanitarian Law Applicable in Armed Conflicts* (Helsinki: Suomalainen Tiedeakatemia, 1976); Siotis.

[9] See, in general, Michel Veuthey, 'Implementation and Enforcement of Humanitarian Law and Human Rights Law in Non-international Armed Conflicts: The Role of the International Committee of the Red Cross', *Am. Univ. LR*, 33 (1983), 83–97; Jacques Moreillon, 'The International Committee of the Red Cross and the Protection of Political Detainees', *IRRC*, 169 (Apr. 1975), 171–83; Comments by the ICRC, 'Protection and Assistance in Situations not Covered by International Humanitarian Law', *IRRC*, 205 (July–Aug. 1978), 210–14.

[10] ICRC, *The ICRC and the Algerian Conflict* (Geneva: ICRC, 1962), 5.

often executed.[11] In June 1956 France formally accepted the applicability of Article 3. This was at least partially because the FLN threatened reprisals if executions of captured FLN members continued.[12]

On 19 March 1958 the Commander-in-Chief in Algeria ordered that special detention camps should be created to intern members of the FLN captured while under arms. From this point on the French government treated the detainees very much like prisoners of war. Prosecutions ceased, but the French government maintained that, legally, detainees were not prisoners of war.[13] In the autumn of 1961, following repeated requests by the ICRC, the French government adopted a form of 'special penal treatment' for political detainees. This treatment

exempts political detainees from working, separates them from the other detainees, recognizes their right to have spokesmen, enables them to practice their religion, authorizes them to read certain papers and have radio sets and, finally, gives them the possibility of receiving sums of money through the ICRC. Article 18 of the Minister of Justice's circular of November 17, 1961, expressly stipulated that detainees of this category could correspond under closed cover with the International Committee of the Red Cross.[14]

Despite this analogous treatment, the French government maintained to the end that the conflict was an internal one subject only to the provisions of Article 3. Of course, Article 3 does require the parties to the conflict to 'endeavor to bring into force . . . all or part of the other provisions' of the Geneva Conventions.

On the Algerian side, there was a gradual trend toward the full application of the law of war encouraged by the FLN's strategy of internationalizing the conflict. In the first year of the conflict there were cases of executions and maimings of 'traitors' to the nationalist cause, a practice which declined after 1956.[15] In 1958, after two years of requests by the ICRC, the Red Cross was allowed to visit four captured French soldiers. In October of 1958 these soldiers were released and repatriated by the Red Cross. In addition, in February 1956 and again in June 1958 the FLN announced through its offices in Tunis that it intended to apply the Third Geneva Convention in its entirety to captured French soldiers.

[11] See Michel Veuthey, *Guérilla*, 202; Joseph Kelley and George Pelletier, 'Theories of Emergency Government', *South Dakota LR* 2 (1966), 67; Erik Castren, *Civil War* (Helsinki: Suomalainen Tiedeakatemia, 1966), 74. See also the response of the French Foreign Minister to the GPRA's notification of accession to the Geneva Conventions on 25 July 1960 in Arnold Fraleigh, 'The Algerian Revolution as a Case Study in International Law', in *The International Law of Civil War*, ed. Richard Falk (London: Johns Hopkins Univ. Press, 1971), 195.

[12] Rosas, 148.

[13] *The ICRC and the Algerian Conflict*, 7.

[14] *The ICRC and the Algerian Conflict*, 6–7.

[15] Joan Gillespie claims that in the first five months 500 'traitors' were killed and 100 mutilated. *Algeria: Rebellion and Revolution* (London: Ernest Benn, 1960), 122.

The FLN also ordered its soldiers to comply with international law. The commandments which were to govern the conduct of the FLN combatants ordered them to conform to the principles of Islam and the international law of war. According to the tenth commandment, guerrillas were instructed, 'Se conformer aux principes de l'Islam et aux lois internationales dans la destruction des forces ennemies'.[16]

In 1960 the provisional government of Algeria, set up by the FLN in September 1958, sent an instrument of accession to all four Geneva Conventions to the Swiss government, as depository of the Geneva Conventions. The Swiss government circulated the accession although it made a reservation because it did not recognize the GPRA.[17] The French government, in a note to the Swiss Federal Political Department on 25 July 1960, objected to this accession, noting that

[T]he self-styled 'provisional government of the Algerian Republic' . . . cannot, on any grounds, claim the capacity of 'state' or that of 'power'. Consequently, it does not possess the requisite competence to 'adhere' to the said conventions, according to the text itself of these conventions.[18]

Despite these reservations on the legal character of any such accession, its practical meaning was clear. It promoted the idea that the conflict was an international one and it was an unequivocal statement of the intention of the FLN to apply the law of war.

There was less international support for the Biafran secession than for the Algerian war because Biafra was part of a self-governing State. Even so, many of the rules of international humanitarian law were observed.[19] At no time during the civil war did the federal government openly acknowledge the applicability of the Geneva Conventions or even Article 3. Yet some of the government's actions suggested that it considered the Conventions to be applicable in their entirety .

In 1966, before the secession of Biafra in May 1967, the federal government issued decrees stating that

[P]ersons charged with isolated acts of terrorism would be tried by civil courts, whereas acts occurring in widespread form would lead to the proclamation of military areas, where offenders would be tried by military tribunals, the penalty upon conviction being death or imprisonment for up to 21 years.[20]

However, after the outbreak of the war between Biafra and Nigeria, the

[16] Quoted in Veuthey, *Guérilla*, 202.

[17] See Abi-Saab, *Annales*, 104–5.

[18] Note of 25 July 1960 from the French Ministry of Foreign Affairs to the Swiss Federal Political Department, quoted in Fraleigh, 195.

[19] See Michael Bothe, 'Article 3 and Protocol II: Case Studies of Nigeria and El Salvador', *Am. Univ. LR*, 31 (1982), 899–909.

[20] *Keesing's*, 23–30 July 1966, 21517.

Nigerian federal government issued a code of conduct to its soldiers emphasizing the political nature of the war and the need to re-establish confidence in the government. The code required that Biafran prisoners should be 'treated as prisoners of war'.[21] Instructions were given on the protection of civilians, mosques, churches, foreigners, and private property. Foreign mercenaries, however, were 'not to be spared'.

In fact, the Red Cross made fairly regular visits to detainees held by the federal government. In August 1968, in response to allegations of genocide, the Nigerian government invited a group of international observers to the country to inspect operations in the field and the treatment of prisoners. The observers made some recommendations concerning constructive work and exercise for detainees and other relatively minor matters, but Press reports at the time noted that 'prisoners of war and internees appeared to be in good health'.[22]

The problem in Biafra was not the treatment of captured combatants as prisoners of war, but the provision of relief supplies to prevent starvation. The federal government only allowed relief to go to Biafra via night flights to one airport. Ground transport was not permitted and all air shipments had to be inspected by the federal government. In June 1969 an ICRC relief plane, flying at night, was shot down. Shortly thereafter, the federal government decided to 'terminate the role of the ICRC in Nigeria'.[23] Problems like this are common, especially when relief agencies must act on the basis of humanitarian initiative and not on the firmer ground of the full Geneva Conventions.

As far as Biafran actions are concerned, the Biafran government had declared itself an independent and sovereign State. Therefore it considered the conflict to be an international one. Because of the naval blockade of Biafra and the lack of assistance from neighbouring countries, aid from the ICRC to Biafra was controlled by the Nigerian government.

In the Portuguese territories in Africa—Mozambique, Angola, and Guinea-Bissau—Portugal consistently denied that there was even a conflict within the terms of Article 3. In their view, the domestic law of Portugal was applicable to the rebels, not any international law of armed conflict.[24] As a result, thousands of 'suspects' were arrested, imprisoned, and

---

[21] See Rosas, 198; John de St Jorre, *The Nigerian Civil War* (London: Hodder and Stoughton, 1972), 282–3; Alvin Edgell, 'Nigeria/Biafra', in *Civil Wars and the Politics of International Relief*, ed. Morris Davis (London: Praeger, 1975), 50–73.

[22] *Keesing's*, 25 Jan.–1 Feb. 1969, 23159.

[23] Edgell, 51; see also James E. Bond, *The Rules of Riot* (Princeton: Princeton Univ. Press, 1974), 129.

[24] See J. S. Bains, 'Angola, the UN and International Law', *Indian JIL*, 3 (1963), 67; Neil Bruce, 'Portugal's African Wars', *Conflict Studies*, 34 (London: Institute for the Study of Conflict, 1973), 2.

interrogated in an attempt to restore order.[25] The Portuguese High Command ordered that,

According to military practice, a fighting man who is captured out of uniform should be shot. It is important to take prisoners, for they can give useful information; it is for that reason that they should not be shot immediately. . . . The prisoner must be given the opportunity to speak voluntarily but should he refuse to do so, more efficient methods must be adopted that will rapidly persuade him to co-operate. After that, he will be shot in accordance with military practice, given the fact that he is a fighting man out of uniform.[26]

After the April 1974 coup Portugal seemed to recognize the international character of the conflicts in its African territories. The government invited the ICRC to visit captured 'prisoners of war' held by Portugal.[27]

With the exception of Guinea-Bissau after February 1974, no liberation movement in the Portuguese territories openly committed itself to respecting the Geneva Conventions as such. However, the FNLA and MPLA did allow the ICRC to visit their prisoners and unilaterally released some prisoners during the conflict. The liberation movements claim to have treated prisoners humanely, and Rosas and Henriksen find no reason to doubt this claim.[28]

These historical examples illustrate that established governments have sometimes been willing to treat members of liberation movements like prisoners of war and to apply at least the principles of international humanitarian law after an initial period of repression. These governments have usually been careful to point out that they do so as a matter of humanity and self-interest and not because of any legal obligation. The legal basis for the involvement of humanitarian organizations like the ICRC has been a 'right of humanitarian initiative' or, at most, Article 3 of the Geneva Conventions. Their continued presence has depended on the beneficence of the established government. While some governments have applied international law, there have been wars of national liberation in which international humanitarian law was not applied.

The most important question is to what extent these trends in the practice of States are apparent in recent wars of national liberation, particularly since the conclusion of the 1977 Protocols Additional to the Geneva Conventions.

The provisional government established by Polisario in the Western Sahara, the SDAR, has not transmitted a formal instrument of accession to

---

[25] Eduardo Mondlane, *The Struggle for Mozambique* (Harmondsworth: Penguin, 1969), 158.

[26] UN Working Group on the Situation in Portuguese Territories, UN Doc. E/CN.4/1020/ Add. 1, 56–7, quoted in Rosas, 164.

[27] Rosas, 162–3.

[28] Rosas, 162; Thomas Henriksen, 'People's War in Angola, Mozambique and Guinea-Bissau', *Journal of Modern African Studies*, 14 (Sept. 1976), 382–3.

the Geneva Conventions to the Swiss government. However, there can be little doubt that the SDAR considers the conflict to be an international one since it claims status as an independent State with a government in exile in Algiers. Should the SDAR accede to the Conventions, one would assume, based on the precedent of Algeria, that the Swiss government would circulate this accession. Despite the lack of any instrument of accession, Polisario has made it known through a declaration to the International Committee of the Red Cross that it intends to abide by the Conventions. The ICRC has been able to visit Moroccan prisoners held by the Polisario Front. According to the *Bulletin* of the ICRC, in June 1984,

Delegates recently visited 210 Moroccan prisoners of war held in five places of internment by the Polisario Front.

Ten of the Moroccan POWs were released to the ICRC and repatriated on May 9, [1984].[29]

Despite the widespread nature of the conflict in the Sahara, the position of Morocco seems to be that the Western Sahara is an 'integral part' of Morocco.[30] The Moroccan authorities allow the ICRC to visit detained Algerian prisoners of war, but negotiations to allow the ICRC to visit detained Polisario combatants have been unsuccessful.[31] The Red Cross conference in Manila in 1981 took the unusual step of passing a resolution which declared that the conflict in the Western Sahara is at least subject to Article 3 of the Geneva Conventions. Morocco, while it did not react strongly to this Resolution, still does not consider the Conventions to be applicable and does not allow ICRC visits to its Polisario detainees.

Israel is a classic example of a government which vehemently denies any obligation to treat members of Palestinian groups as prisoners of war, even when captured under arms in a conventional engagement, while in practice applying many of the principles of international law to these security detainees. The government acts similarly toward the Fourth Geneva Convention and the occupied territories. Since 1967 the Israeli government has consistently denied that the Fourth Geneva Convention is formally applicable, but it claims to observe the 'humanitarian provisions' of the Convention.[32] In practice, it allows the International Red Cross to operate and observes most of the provisions of the Fourth Convention.[33]

[29] ICRC, *Bulletin*, 101 (June 1984), 3.

[30] John Damis, *Conflict in Northwest Africa* (Stanford, Calif.: Hoover Inst. Press, 1983), 90–1.

[31] ICRC, *Survey of Current Activities* (Geneva: ICRC, Oct. 1984), 27.

[32] See Meir Shamgar, 'Legal Concepts and Problems of the Israeli Military Government: The Initial Stage', in vol. i of *Military Government in the Territories Administered by Israel: 1967–1980*, ed. Meir Shamgar (Jerusalem: Hebrew Univ., 1982), 13–60.

[33] The expulsions of certain Palestinian residents of the occupied territories and the destruction of houses in reprisal for co-operation with the Palestinian resistance are notable exceptions to this generalization. These are clear violations of the Fourth Convention. See particularly Articles 27, 33, 49, and 53, 1949 Geneva Convention IV.

The position of the Israeli government has always been that armed Palestinian groups are 'terrorists'. Since they neither belong to a party to the conflict, nor conduct their operations in accordance with the law of war, they are not entitled to privileged treatment in accordance with the Third Geneva Convention. A statement released by the Israeli Ministry of Foreign Affairs in July 1982 explaining the legal aspects of the Israeli operation in Lebanon specifically stated that

[T]he PLO and its associated terror groups do not fall within any of the categories formulated in the [Third] Convention regarding persons entitled to the status of prisoner of war. They are not 'regular armed forces' and do not constitute an 'organized resistance movement belonging to a party to the conflict'.[34]

In 1969 this position was upheld by an Israeli court when members of the Popular Front for the Liberation of Palestine (PFLP) were tried for armed infiltration, belonging to an unlawful association, and carrying arms and ammunition. They were captured in October 1968 while coming into Israel from the East Bank armed and in uniform. The court held, 'No Government with which we are in a state of war accepts responsibility for the acts of the Popular Front for the Liberation of Palestine.'[35] The court also held that the PFLP did not conduct its operations in accordance with the laws of war, and therefore the defendants were not entitled to prisoner-of-war status. This meant that they were not immune from prosecution for their acts of violence.

The same policy still governs Israeli attitudes toward captured Palestinians. In a High Court case resulting from the 1982 invasion of Lebanon, the Supreme Court of Israel agreed with the government that

[Palestinians detained at the Ansar prison] are hostile foreigners detained because they belong to the forces of the terrorist organizations or, because of their connections or closeness to terrorist organizations, they endanger the security and well-being of Israeli troops still deployed on Lebanese soil.[36]

The High Court did decide that Israel was an occupying power. Therefore, the treatment of the detainees at the Ansar prison was governed by the Fourth Geneva Convention on civilians, not the Third Convention on prisoners of war.

In actual practice, the Israeli government sometimes treats captured Palestinians like prisoners of war, especially when they are captured while

---

[34] Israel Ministry of Foreign Affairs, Information Division, Briefing No. 342, 4, quoted in W. T. Mallison and S. V. Mallison, *Armed Conflict in Lebanon, 1982: Humanitarian Law in a Real World Setting* (Washington: American Educational Trust, 1983), 48.

[35] *The Military Prosecutor* v. *Omar Mahmud Kassem* et al., 1 S M J C 402, 13 Apr. 1969, *Israeli Yearbook on Human Rights*, 1 (1971), 456–60.

[36] *Leah Zemel* v. *Minister of Defense* et al., Israeli High Court of Justice, May 1983. Known as the 'Ansar Prison Case'.

fighting openly alongside the regular armies of other Arab States. Israel often repatriates them with the prisoners of other States.[37] In recent years they have even openly admitted that this is the case. A spokesman for the Israeli Foreign Ministry defending Israel's transfer of prisoners from the Ansar camp in Southern Lebanon said 'The guerrillas had been accorded all the privileges due prisoners of war under the Geneva Conventions, although he said they did not qualify for that status under the convention.'[38]

In March 1968 the Israelis captured 147 members of a Palestinian resistance organization and 12 members of the regular Jordan army at Karameh, east of the Jordan River. The ICRC undertook negotiations to have the former treated like prisoners of war. Eighty-one of these prisoners were repatriated to Jordan within a few months. Fifty-five more were returned to Jordan in May 1970, and one of the last was returned in October 1971.[39] The Israeli government also exchanges Palestinian detainees for Israeli soldiers held by Palestinian groups. In 1971 Palestinian commandos released an Israeli civil guard and the Israelis released a Palestinian detainee.[40] In March 1978 the PFLP-General Command released an Israeli soldier in exchange for 14 detainees held by Israel.[41] The ICRC negotiated a very large prisoner exchange in November 1983 of 4,400 Palestinians held at the Ansar camp for six Israelis held by the PLO in Tripoli.[42] In May 1985, Israel exchanged 1,046 Palestinian and 104 Lebanese prisoners, plus a Japanese terrorist, for three Israeli soldiers. Three hundred and eighty six of the detainees were serving life sentences in Israel. Six hundred of those released returned to their homes in Israeli occupied territory.[43]

In addition to these prisoner exchanges, the ICRC has generally been allowed to visit detained Palestinians, and to distribute relief supplies to them. It has made reports to the Israeli authorities concerning the treatment of detainees and these reports have generally been acted upon.

In January 1978 the ICRC and the Israeli government reached a new agreement which allows the ICRC to visit detainees under interrogation—access was previously denied to them in this period. This agreement was extended to cover Southern Lebanon after the 1982 Israeli invasion.[44] Released detainees have reported that conditions in these camps improved

---

[37] Rosas, 210; Veuthey, *Guérilla*, 228–9.
[38] *International Herald Tribune*, 5 Apr. 1985, 1.
[39] ICRC, *ICRC Activities in the Middle-east, 1967–1979: Extracts from ICRC Annual Reports*, (Geneva: ICRC, 1980), pp. 1968/1, 1970/5, 1971/6. No mention is made in the reports concerning the fate of the remaining ten Palestinians.
[40] *ICRC Activities in the Middle-east*, p. 1971/7.
[41] Ibid. p. 1979/4.
[42] ICRC, *Summary of the Activities of the ICRC: 1983*, (Geneva: ICRC, 1983), 7.
[43] *The Economist*, 25–31 May 1985, 44.
[44] *ICRC Activities in the Middle-east*, p. 1977/1.

considerably after the ICRC obtained access in mid-July 1982.[45] Thus, although the Israeli government has denied that the Palestinians are prisoners of war, they have generally treated them as such.

Like other national liberation movements, the PLO has an interest in adhering to the Geneva Conventions. Adherence enhances its respectability and legitimacy in the eyes of others. Moreover, the practical consequence of mutual respect for the Conventions means more favourable treatment for members of their organization interned by Israel. The PLO has declared its intention to abide by the Geneva Conventions of 1949 and the two 1977 Protocols a number of times since 1969.[46] In practice the ICRC has been allowed to visit Israelis detained by Palestinian organizations, though not always in their place of detention as required by the Geneva Conventions. In particular cases, the PLO and its component groups have openly agreed to grant prisoner-of-war status and treatment to Israelis in their custody.[47] The PLO has far more to gain by according prisoner-of-war status to detained combatants and declaring its adherence to the Geneva Conventions than does the established government.

The situation in South Africa is markedly different from that in Israel. Although African States have committed themselves to the eradication of apartheid and there has been overt and covert support for liberation movements confronting the established governments in South Africa and Namibia, the African States do not question the right of South Africa to exist as an independent State. The succession of inter-State wars in the middle East where Palestinians have also been combatants has forced Israel to address the issue of the law of war when fighting these groups in a situation that is clearly armed conflict and of great international interest. In South Africa the actual existence of an armed conflict is in question.[48]

The South African government does not recognize the applicability of the Geneva Conventions in South Africa or Namibia, including Article 3. Furthermore, unlike Israel—the other 'target' State for Article 1(4) of 1977 Protocol I—the South African government does not apply the provisions or principles of these Conventions in practice. The problem in South Africa and Namibia is even more fundamental than analogous treatment of captured combatants. Basic human rights for those who dissent politically are not even protected.

In South Africa itself the ANC and PAC are proscribed organizations

---

[45] International Commission of Jurists, 'Lebanon', *ICJ Rev* 31 (Dec. 1983), 13.

[46] In 1969 the PLO informed the Swiss federal government of its decision to accede. This was not circulated by Switzerland, presumably because the PLO was not a provisional government. However, such correspondence is transmitted to the ICRC. See Rosas, 308.

[47] For example, in 1978 the PFLP/GC gave POW status and treatment to a captured Israeli soldier who was subsequently visited several times by an ICRC representative and eventually repatriated. *ICRC Activities in the Middle-east*, p. 1978/4.

[48] This is not the case, however, where South African troops have been used in Angola.

and have been since 1960. Detention and prosecution of members of these organizations has occurred under a succession of security and detention laws, the most recent of which is the 1982 Internal Security Act. In 1984, 39 South Africans appeared in court charged with high treason. Of these, 10 were convicted. Another 24 were charged with terrorism of whom 11 were convicted and six cases were still outstanding by the end of the year. Four more people were charged with assisting terrorists and all were convicted.[49] In addition to those charged and convicted, Article 29 and Article 50 of the 1982 Internal Security Act permit detention without charge. In February 1985, 51 people were in detention under these provisions and three others under other security laws.[50]

The trial and imprisonment of those who participate in the activities of the ANC or PAC are well documented.[51] Although the South African government does allow the International Committee of the Red Cross to visit convicted security prisoners and administrative detainees held under Section 28 of the Internal Security Act, the South African government neither recognizes the applicability of the law of war to these individuals nor applies the principles of this law in practice.[52] Those who violate the security laws of South Africa are detained, tried, and treated as criminals under particularly harsh domestic law.

The situation in Namibia where the South West Africa People's Organization is engaged in armed struggle against South Africa is similar. In fact, the 1967 Terrorism Act was introduced and applied retroactively in order to prosecute 37 Namibian members of SWAPO for illegal activities after SWAPO decided to resort to armed struggle in 1966.[53] Unlike the PAC and ANC, SWAPO itself is not a proscribed organization in Namibia.[54]

[49] *Star* (South Africa), 3 Jan. 1985.

[50] Report of the Detainees' Parents Support Committee, 28 Feb. 1985, 1.

[51] See UNESCO Report, 'Violations of Human Rights in Southern Africa', UN Doc. E/CN.4/1985/8, 23 Jan. 1985; Reports of the Detainees' Parents Support Committee, 25 Feb. 1985, 30 Nov. 1984, and 31 Oct. 1984; International Commission of Jurists, *Review*, (June 1978), 15–18; John Dugard, *Human Rights and the South African Legal Order* (Princeton, N.J: Princeton Univ. Press, 1978); Amnesty International Press Release, 'Deportation from Swaziland of Bhabalazi Bulunga', 30 Nov. 1984. See also news reports of the most recent trials, *South Africa Times*, 3 Feb. 1985; *Rand Daily Mail*, 29 Jan. 1985 and 28 Feb. 1985; *Citizen*, 15 Nov. 1984; *Sowetan*, 25 Jan. 1985; *Star*, 12 Dec. 1984.

[52] Section 28 provides for detention to prevent the commission of 'certain offences or endangering of security of State or of maintenance of law and order'. Section 29 is for detention of 'certain persons for interrogation'. Apparently the ICRC does not have access to these detainees, nor those detained without trial under Section 50, 'Action to combat state of unrest'. Recall that in Feb. 1985 the Detainees' Parents Support Group reported 57 persons detained under Articles 29 and 50, and none under Article 28. The ICRC also has not been allowed to visit security detainees in the 'homelands'.

[53] I. Sagay, 'The Legal Status of Freedom Fighters in Africa', *Eastern Africa LR*, 6 (1973), 16; John Dugard, 'South West Africa and the "Terrorist Trial" ', *AJIL*, 64 (1970), 21; Dugard, *Human Rights*, 220–1.

[54] Personal interview with Mr Jacob Hannai, SWAPO representative in Western Europe, 15 Mar. 1985.

In addition to the various South African Security Acts which apply to Namibia as well, Namibians may also be detained under Proclamation AG.9 of 1977, as well as several other proclamations enacted by the Administrator-General.[55] The ICRC has been able to visit security prisoners, people in preventive detention, and those in the Mariental Camp detained under Proclamation AG.9 and there is some evidence that these visits, as well as those to Robben Island, have resulted in some improvement in prison conditions.[56] However, in Namibia as in South Africa, there is no 'analogous treatment' for captured members of SWAPO.

7.4 The 1977 Protocols Additional to the Geneva Conventions

In September 1968 the International Committee of the Red Cross launched a new effort to reaffirm and develop the humanitarian law of armed conflict.[57] The Geneva Conventions were twenty years old. There was widespread agreement that the Conventions had some shortcomings and, at least, needed updating to take into account changes in the character of warfare and weapons since 1949. In 1971 and 1972 the ICRC convened two sessions of a Conference of Government Experts. As a result of this work, it wrote two Draft Protocols Additional to the Geneva Conventions. These two drafts, submitted to governments in 1973, formed the basis of a Diplomatic Conference convened by the Swiss government in 1974 to reaffirm and develop the international humanitarian law of armed conflicts. There were four sessions of the Conference lasting for several months of each succeeding year until 1977.[58] The result of this Conference was two Protocols Additional to the 1949 Geneva Conventions. Protocol I concerns international armed conflicts and Protocol II applies to non-international armed conflicts. The two Protocols supplement the 1949 Geneva Conventions; they do not replace them. Protocol I supplements all four Geneva Conventions and Protocol II supplements only common Article 3.

[55] See UNESCO Report E/CN.4/1985/8, 23 Jan. 1985, 99.

[56] See statement of Mr Herman Toivo Ja Toivo, founder member of SWAPO released on 1 Mar. 1984 after 20 years in prison, before the UN Working Group on Human Rights in South Africa, UN Doc. E/CN.4/1985/8, 23 Jan. 1985, 102; ICRC, *Survey of Current Activities*, 5.

[57] In 1969 the 21st Conference of the Red Cross at Istanbul requested the ICRC to 'pursue actively' its efforts to supplement the existing law.

[58] The Draft Protocols presented by the ICRC are reprinted with an introductory letter in the Official Records of the Diplomatic Conference, OR: vol. i, Part III. See also Bothe, 1–10. The ICRC also published, for the benefit of participating governments, an article-by-article copy of the Draft Protocols with extensive commentary on its origins and development. See *Draft Additional Protocols to the Geneva Conventions of August 12, 1949: Commentary* (Geneva: ICRC, Oct. 1973).

Very early in the first session of the Conference it became clear that antagonism between North and South would overshadow that between East and West. Indeed, these fissures threatened the continuation of the Conference itself. As noted in Chapter 5, after four weeks of discussion the Diplomatic Conference invited national liberation movements recognized by the regional intergovernmental organization concerned to participate in the Conference.[59] The participation of national liberation movements in the Conference was quickly overshadowed by the debates which followed.

7.41 Scope of Application: Article 1(4)

Of the two Draft Protocols submitted by the ICRC, the first dealt with international armed conflicts and the second with conflicts not of an international character. The distinction in the Draft Protocols between national and international conflict was made on 'the factual and objective basis of whether a conflict takes place in the territories of different States or inside one particular State'.[60] Consequently, the scope of Protocol I in the 1973 draft was restricted to 'situations referred to in Article 2' common to the 1949 Geneva Conventions.[61] Draft Protocol II applied 'to all armed conflicts not covered by Article 2.'[62] The ICRC envisioned that Protocol II would apply to wars of national liberation with the possible exception of treatment of prisoners of war. A footnote in the 1973 draft of what would become Article 44 of Protocol I on combatants and prisoners of war recommended that if the Diplomatic Conference should decide to mention armed struggles for self-determination in Protocol I, a third paragraph to the draft could be added providing that '. . . [M]embers of organized liberation movements who comply with the aforementioned conditions shall be treated as prisoners of war for as long as they are detained.'[63] Such a provision would have codified the trend in State practice toward 'analogous treatment'. It also would have put no obligations on the liberation movement under Protocol I because the Article only obligated the recognized government to treat the captured members of the liberation movement as prisoners of war and did not require liberation movements to act similarly toward captured government prisoners.

This fairly conservative position developed in the pre-conference work

---

[59] See Res. 2 (I), CDDH/55, OR: vol. i. Part II, 5; discussions in plenary CDDH/SR.6 and SR.7, OR: vol. v. 55–72; and rules of procedure Rule 58 of CDDH/2/Rev.3, OR: vol. ii. 15.

[60] Bothe, 39.

[61] Article 1 of Draft Protocol I, OR: vol. i. Part III, 3. According to Article 2 common to the 1949 Geneva Conventions, the Conventions 'shall apply to all cases of declared war or of any other armed conflict which may arise between two or more of the High Contracting Parties, even if the state of war is not recognized by one of them'.

[62] Article 1(1), Draft Protocol II, OR: vol. i. Part III, 33.

[63] Note to Article 42, Draft Protocol I, OR: vol. i. Part III, 14.

by the ICRC did not, however, represent the views of a large number of government experts consulted on the matter. The ICRC noted in an extensive discussion on the subject in a report on the 1971 Conference of Government Experts that

Very many experts, by contrast, considered that since the UN General Assembly resolution No. 1514 of 14 December 1960, . . . such wars should be recognized as international and the movements fighting the colonial governments as subject to international law. The world community had clearly, on a number of occasions, made known its opinion on this subject and its wish that 'freedom fighters' be granted privileged treatment.[64]

Although the Western States expected a proposal of the kind envisioned in the ICRC footnote, or perhaps a strident resolution like those emerging from the General Assembly, the proposal tabled at the first session of the Diplomatic Conference took most of them by surprise.[65] Instead of amending the prisoner-of-war provisions, the Third World and Eastern European States proposed amendments to Article 1 of Protocol I which would apply the whole of the Geneva Conventions and the First Protocol to wars of national liberation. These proposals dominated the first session of the Conference and the continued participation of the Western States was in doubt.[66] Antonio Cassese, a member of the Italian delegation to the Conference, later described the positions of the delegations:

The Third World Countries (together with Australia, Norway, and Jugoslavia) proposed that the Protocol be applied to wars of national liberation whose aim is to achieve the principle of self-determination of peoples, as defined in certain United Nations instruments (mainly the Declaration on Friendly Relations of 1970). The Socialist countries proposed a more restrictive formula, indicating only three specific categories of wars of national liberation (those against colonial powers, racist regimes and foreign domination). The western powers reacted to this position with a rigid attitude, excluding *in toto* the applicability of the Protocol to any and all wars of national liberation.[67]

In fact, the opponents of the amendments did submit what was, in their minds, a counter-proposal which affirmed Article 1 of the 1949 Conventions and included an updated Martens Clause. The majority of States did

---

[64] *Protection of Victims of Non-international Armed Conflicts*, vol. v of the Report of the ICRC Conference of Government Experts, 24 May–12 June 1971 (Geneva: ICRC, 1971), 28.

[65] Charles Lysaght, 'The Attitude of Western Countries', in *The New Humanitarian Law of Armed Conflict*, vol. i, ed. Antonio Cassese (Naples: Editoriale Scientifica, 1979), 350; personal interview with Professor Georges Abi-Saab, 1 Apr. 1985.

[66] For a discussion of the various draft amendments and the process of compromise which led to Article 1(4) see Abi-Saab, *Recueil des cours*, 374–92; Salmon, 'La Conférence', *Revue Belge*, 12 (1976), 27–52; Bothe, 37–52.

[67] Antonio Cassese, 'A Tentative Appraisal of the Old and the New Humanitarian Law of Armed Conflict', in *The New Humanitarian Law of Armed Conflict*, vol. i, ed. Antonio Cassese (Naples: Editoriale Scientifica, 1979), 467.

not consider these amendments to be mutually exclusive nor did the Western amendment address the particular problems of liberation movements. Article 1 as adopted includes both the Western counter-proposal (CDDH/I/12) in paragraphs 1 and 2, the ICRC draft in paragraph 3, and the Communist and non-aligned proposal in paragraph 4.[68] Article 1 as amended was adopted overwhelmingly in the final session of the Conference by 87 votes in favour, one against (Israel), and 11 abstentions.[69] According to Article 1 concerning the General Principles and Scope of Application of Protocol I,

1. The High Contracting Parties undertake to respect and to ensure respect for this Protocol in all circumstances.

2. In cases not covered by this Protocol or by other international agreements, civilians and combatants remain under the protection and authority of the principles of international law derived from established custom, from the principles of humanity and from the dictates of public conscience.

3. This Protocol, which supplements the Geneva Conventions of 12 August 1949 for the Protection of War Victims, shall apply in the situations referred to in Article 2 common to those Conventions.

4. The situations referred to in the preceding paragraph include armed conflicts in which peoples are fighting against colonial domination and alien occupation and against racist regimes in the exercise of their right of self-determination, as enshrined in the Charter of the United Nations and the Declaration on Principles of International Law Concerning Friendly Relations and Cooperation among States in accordance with the Charter of the United Nations.

It is not necessary to dwell on the political motivations of the Article to examine its legal effects. There are several important points.

First, Article 1(4) refers to 'armed conflicts', which is not specifically defined in the Protocols or the Conventions. Article 1(2) of Protocol II states that 'internal disturbances and tensions, such as riots, isolated and sporadic acts of violence and other acts of a similar nature' are not armed conflicts. These situations can equally be excluded from the scope of Protocol I. The actual existence of an 'armed conflict' implies the use of force by both sides and, arguably, more than police forces by the High Contracting Party. Furthermore, although Article 1(4) refers to a 'people' which is fighting, according to Article 96(3), there must be an 'authority representing a people', which implies some form of organization. Beyond

---

[68] CDDH/I/11 (Non-aligned) and CDDH/I/5 (Socialist) were combined to form CDDH/I/41. CDDH/I/41 was slightly modified and combined with CDDH/I/12 (Western) by the Latin American countries to make CDDH/I/71. CDDH/I/71 was adopted by the First Committee 70:21:13. See CDDH/I/SR.2–SR.6 and SR.12–SR.14, OR: vol. viii. 7–50 and 87–114 for the debates on the drafts; CDDH/48/Rev. 1, Report of Committee I, OR: vol. x. 6.

[69] Those abstaining were Monaco, the United Kingdom, West Germany, Canada, Spain, the United States, France, Guatemala, Ireland, Italy, and Japan. CDDH/SR.36, para. 58, OR: vol. vi. 41.

this, there are no specific requirements as to the intensity of this 'armed conflict', as there are in Protocol II. In particular, the authority representing a people need not have control over a part of territory or the ability to conduct sustained and concerted military operations.

The British government declared on signing the Protocols that the intensity of an Article 1(4) conflict 'cannot be less than that required for the application of Protocol II'. This distinction tries to maintain the traditional law notion that the humanitarian law of war only applies when the rebel movement has a certain capacity analogous to that of a State. Although the intention of the British government was no doubt to ensure that the 'authority representing a people' was sufficiently well developed to be able to uphold its obligations under the Conventions and Protocols, thereby ensuring the equal application of the law to both belligerents, there is little support for their interpretation in the Protocols as written. The term 'armed conflict' is also used in Article 3 common to the 1949 Geneva Conventions which does not specifically require a similarly high threshold for its application. Likewise, the term 'armed conflict' is also used in Article 2 common to the 1949 Geneva Conventions to refer *inter alia* to undeclared war between two States. Here too, there appears to be no threshold below which the humanitarian law does not apply.

Article 43 of Protocol I, which defines combatants, does seem to restrict the field of application somewhat. According to it, armed forces of a party to a conflict must be 'under a command responsible to that Party' and 'subject to an internal disciplinary system which, *inter alia*, shall enforce compliance' with the law of war. This definition supports the idea that there must be an authority acting for this people which is responsible for the actions of its forces and suggests a certain degree of organization and development, but certainly not to the extent implied by the United Kingdom in its reservation.

The second important point relating to Article 1(4) is that the humanitarian protections apply when 'peoples' are fighting. Although Articles 44 and 96(3) suggest that there must be an authority capable of representing a 'people', the concept of 'people' is only defined indirectly by reference to the Declaration on Principles of International Law and the UN Charter. The Declaration on Principles of International Law limits the scope of Article 1(4) because it is concerned with bringing a 'speedy end to colonialism' and the separate status of 'a colony or other Non-Self-Governing Territory'. The Declaration excludes from the category of separate 'peoples' those living in sovereign and independent States 'possessed of a government representing the whole people belonging to the territory without distinction as to race, creed or color'. This limitation of the idea of peoples is both consistent with UN practice and much more restrictive in fact than the word 'peoples' would seem to imply. 'Peoples', as defined by the Declaration on Principles of International Law, are the restricted set of 'selves' discussed in Chapter 4: trust and mandated territories, non-self-governing territories, and possibly certain geographically distinct territories which are subordinate to the metropolitan State and non-self-governing with respect to the whole.[70] Thus, armed groups which seek to overthrow an established government which is representative of the whole people are still subject to Protocol II and/or Article 3 of the Geneva Conventions.

The scope of application is even further reduced by reference to three types of adversaries. The humanitarian law of war applies *in toto* when these peoples are fighting against 'colonial domination and alien occupation and against racist regimes'. This phrase was strongly criticized at the Conference for its subjectivity and political character. The term 'colonial domination' presents the least difficulty. Although there might be some doubt whether a particular case constitutes colonial domination or belligerent occupation, colonial domination is far less subjective and ambiguous than the idea of alien occupation or racist regimes.

'Racist regimes' is political in character and difficult to define. Bothe, Partsch, and Solf comment,

It certainly cannot be understood as meaning any State in which acts of racial discrimination committed by individuals may occur or where racial problems exist. The term means regimes in which racial discrimination is part of the official policy of the government.[71]

The key to such a distinction might be the election laws of the State concerned, if the State has elections. But racial discrimination can be far more subtle than South African apartheid—the State in mind when Article 1(4) was drafted. Objective definition remains elusive.

The third category, 'alien occupation', was the contribution of the Latin American States.[72] As originally proposed, the words 'colonial and alien domination' were used. Because the Latin American governments are often accused by their adversaries of being dominated by foreign powers, the phrase was changed to 'colonial domination and alien occupation'. A distinction should be made between 'alien occupation' and 'belligerent occupation'. The latter, when in the territory of a High Contracting Party, is already covered by the full Conventions even if there is no resistance to the occupation.[73] In contrast, the Declaration on Principles of International Law refers to 'alien subjugation, domination and exploitation' when encouraging a speedy end to colonialism, and alien occupation should be understood in this context. Furthermore, the idea of alien

---

[70] *Supra*, Sect. 4.6.
[71] Bothe, 50.
[72] CDDH/I/71, OR: vol. iii. 8–9.
[73] Article 2, para. 2 common to the 1949 Geneva Conventions.

occupation can be extended to 'peoples' in a territory which is *not* a High Contracting Party, occupied by a High Contracting Party and subsequently denied their right of self-determination. Examples would be South African occupation of Namibia and Moroccan control of the Western Sahara.

In actual fact, these contorted legal exercises are a way of discussing objectively that which was not objective. 'Colonial domination', 'alien occupation', and 'racist regimes' were words taken from United Nations resolutions and tailor-made for Portugal, Israel, and South Africa. If the conflicts in South Africa and Israel are resolved, Article 1(4) will not necessarily fade away, although many hope it will. Its subjective character makes it a prime target for flexible interpretation based on the exigencies of the moment.

A final point worth noting about the scope of Article 1(4) is that Protocol I and the Geneva Conventions do not apply between liberation movements. Thus, when two or more liberation movements are fighting each other as well as a High Contracting Party, as was the case in Angola, the full Conventions would presumably apply between the established government and each movement. Among themselves, however, the conflict would be of a non-international character and governed, if at all, by Protocol II, or Article 3.

This analysis shows that the scope of Article 1(4) is actually very limited. If it opens up a Pandora's box at all, it is an unexpectedly small one.

7.42 Provisions for Application: Article 96(3)

One of the main concerns of those opposed to the inclusion of Article 1(4) in the Protocols was that it would reintroduce discrimination into the humanitarian law of armed conflict. One of the fundamental principles of the law of war is that it applies equally to all parties irrespective of the cause of the conflict. The Western States feared that, in a war of national liberation, the State involved might assume obligations under humanitarian law which the liberation movements would not, thereby reintroducing discriminatory application which had gradually been eliminated since the Middle Ages.[74] Article 96(3) addresses these concerns.

Article 96(3) was contained in an amendment proposed by Norway in the last session of the Conference in 1977 and was adopted in a highly unusual fashion without reference to a working group and without discussion. The amendment was the result of informal negotiations which resulted in a delicately balanced compromise which the sponsors did not wish to jeopardize.[75] Article 96(3) provides that

---

[74] See statements of Mr Draper (UK), CDDH/I/SR.2, OR: vol. viii. 13; Mr Prugh (USA), CDDH/I/SR.2, OR: vol. vii. 14; Mr Kalshoven (Netherlands), CDDH/I/SR.4, OR: vol. viii. 31; Mr Girard (France), CDDH/I/SR.2, OR: vol. viii. 14.

[75] See Statements of Mr Freeland (UK), CDDH/I/SR.68, OR: vol. ix. 373; Mr Longva

The authority representing a people engaged against a High Contracting Party in an armed conflict of the type referred to in Article 1, paragraph 4, may undertake to apply the Conventions and this Protocol in relation to that conflict by means of a unilateral declaration addressed to the depository. Such declaration shall, upon its receipt by the depository, have in relation to that conflict the following effects:

(*a*) the Conventions and this Protocol are brought into force for the said authority as a Party to the conflict with immediate effect;

(*b*) the said authority assumes the same rights and obligations as those which have been assumed by a High Contracting Party to the Conventions and this Protocol; and

(*c*) the Conventions and this Protocol are equally binding upon all Parties to the conflict.

The Article has several important consequences for the application of the law of Geneva to wars of national liberation.

First, Article 96(3) makes clear that a liberation movement must declare its intention to apply the Conventions and Protocols by means of a unilateral declaration. Before such a declaration the Conventions and Protocol I would not apply.[76] Suggestions to the contrary made by Syria and Mexico in Committee I are inconsistent with the actual text, which is straightforward. The Conventions and Protocols 'are brought into force' by such a declaration. The question then becomes, what rules apply before such a declaration, or in the absence of it? The German delegation maintained that Article 3 would apply in such circumstances.[77] Dietrich Schindler and Michel Veuthey concur with this position.[78] To the extent that Article 3 embodies a minimum set of standards applicable in all armed conflicts this is no doubt the case. But, it would seem that even if a liberation movement fulfilling the qualifications of Article 1(4) did not make a declaration of intention to apply the Convention and Protocol I, the conflict would still be an international one, much as an armed conflict between two States when one or both are not High Contracting Parties and

---

(Norway), CDDH/I/SR.67, OR: vol. ix. 364. It is difficult to tell from the Official Records what elements were delicately balanced, and what positions were modified to form a compromise. According to Professor Draper of the UK delegation, most likely, there were some delegations who only wished to bind liberation movements as far as possible given the material conditions in which they found themselves. This, of course, would have opened a very large loophole for discriminatory application. Letter received from G. I. A. D. Draper, 21 Mar. 1985.

[76] This interpretation was supported by West Germany, Britain, and the US in CDDH/I/SR.67 and SR.68, OR: vol. ix. 364–76. Compare, however, the statements of Syria and Mexico CDDH/I/SR.67 and SR.68, OR: vol. ix. 366 and 372. See also explanations of vote in plenary, West Germany, CDDH/SR.46, Annex, OR: vol. vi. 372; Japan, CDDH/SR.46, Annex, OR: vol. vi. 379; United Kingdom, CDDH/SR.46, Annex, OR: vol. vi. 387.

[77] CDDH/SR.46, Annex, OR: vol. vi. 372 and CDDH/I/SR.68, OR: vol. ix. 369.

[78] Veuthey, 'Guerrilla Warfare and Humanitarian Law', 122; Dietrich Schindler, 'Different Types of Armed Conflicts', 116–63.

fail to observe the Conventions is still an international armed conflict.[79] . Furthermore, Article 96 makes quite clear that the declaration is necessary, unlike inter-State conflicts where a party to the Convention and Protocols is bound by it if their enemy 'accepts and applies the provisions thereof'.[80] A High Contracting Party is not bound to observe the Conventions and Protocols in an armed conflict against a liberation movement unless and until the liberation movement explicitly declares its intention to apply the humanitarian law of war. The unilateral obligation to respect the law of war when one's opponent accepts and applies its provisions even though not bound by accession to the treaty appears to be a rule for inter-State wars and not wars of national liberation.

Article 96 is also important because, unlike Article 1(4), it implies that the people fighting must have a certain capacity. A 'people' must have an 'authority' representing them in order to adhere to the Conventions, which implies a certain minimal level of organization. More important for the non-discriminatory application of the humanitarian law, Article 96 implies that this authority must have the capacity to uphold its obligations under the law of war. By its declaration to the depository, such an authority 'assumes the same rights and obligations as those which have been assumed by a High Contracting Party'. These two requirements—an authority representing the people and the capacity to uphold the law of war—are the curious offspring of both the traditional law requirements for recognition of belligerency, and the Hague and Geneva requirements for legitimate combatancy. This hybrid eliminates the control of territory and effect on the interests of the recognizing State from the list of requirements for recognition of belligerency, adds the need for a responsible authority capable of applying the law of war, and uses these modified criteria, combined with an explicit declaration of intent, to apply the whole of the humanitarian law of war.

A complicating factor introduced by Article 96(3) is that in order for the Conventions and Protocol to come into force, the people must be 'engaged against a High Contracting Party'. Article 1(4) ignores this point. This provision, though certainly justifiable and necessary as a matter of law, will greatly reduce the probability of the Protocol and Conventions ever being applied as one cannot expect that South Africa or Israel, the two 'target' States, will become High Contracting Parties. This provision created a unique problem in Zimbabwe. The British government declared upon signature that

[T]he provisions of the Protocol shall not apply to Southern Rhodesia unless and until the Government of the United Kingdom inform the depository that they are in

---

[79] See Article 96(2) of Protocol I.
[80] Article 96(2), Protocol I.

a position to ensure that the obligations imposed by the Protocol in respect of that territory can be fully implemented.[81]

Since the Smith regime was considered to be illegal and incapable of becoming a High Contracting Party even if it so desired, the liberation movements arrayed against it, which were recognized by the OAU and UN and probably met the qualifications of Article 1(4), had no possibility of issuing a declaration according to Article 96.[82]

It is quite likely that situations will arise where there has been no ratification of the Protocols by the State involved and there is no bilateral agreement as provided for in common Article 3. In such a case, national liberation movements must rely on 'triangular agreements' whereby the ICRC collects declarations from the parties to a conflict concerning compliance with the Geneva Conventions and Protocols or acceptance of the basic humanitarian principles therein. This procedure has a long history of use by the Red Cross. It has the advantage of securing humanitarian protection without the political consequences of recognizing a conflict as international or appearing to confer legitimacy on a liberation movement. Several liberation movements, though not all necessarily involved in wars falling within the scope of application of Protocol I, have made declarations of this kind.[83]

Article 96(3) also raises the question of whether the liberation movements involved must be recognized by the UN or the relevant regional intergovernmental organization. Neither Article 1(4) nor Article 96 requires recognition, but a number of States declared during the Conference that this was their interpretation of Article 96(3).[84] The United Kingdom was the only State to make a declaration to this effect upon signature.[85] This interpretation is consistent with UN practice and with the

---

[81] Reprinted in Bothe, 722.

[82] See Schindler, 'Different Types of Armed Conflicts', 141.

[83] The ANC on 28 Nov. 1980; SWAPO on 25 Aug. 1981; The Eritrean People's Liberation Front (EPLF) on 25 Feb. 1977; UNITA on 25 July 1980; Afghan National Liberation Front (ANLF) on 24 Dec. 1981; Hezbi Islami (Afghanistan) on 7 Nov. 1980; Islamic Society of Afghanistan (ISA) on 6 Jan. 1982; PLO by several declarations, most recently on 7 June 1982; Moro National Liberation Front (MNLF) of the Philippines, on 18 May 1981. South Africa, Ethiopia, Angola, Afghanistan, and Israel did not sign either Protocol. The Philippines signed Protocol I only. For an account of ICRC procedures for 'triangular agreements' see Michel Veuthey, 'Guerrilla Warfare and Humanitarian Law', 122–3; Michel Veuthey, 'Implementation and Enforcement', 83–96.

[84] Mauritania, CDDH/I/SR.67, OR: vol. ix. 366 and explanation of vote CDDH/SR.46, Annex, OR: vol. vi. 380 and CDDH/SR.58, Annex, OR: vol. vii. 324; Turkey, CDDH/I/SR.68, OR: vol. ix. 372, and explanation of vote CDDH/SR.46, Annex, OR: vol. vi. 386; Oman, CDDH/I/SR.68, OR: vol. ix. 375; Zaire, CDDH/I/SR.68, OR: vol. ix. 375; Indonesia, CDDH/SR.36, Annex, OR: vol. vi. 63.

[85] '. . . [I]n the light of the negotiating history, it is to be regarded as necessary also that the authority concerned be recognized as such by the appropriate regional intergovernmental organization.' Reprinted in Bothe, 722.

precedent set by the Conference itself, in which only recognized liberation movements participated. However, this requirement is not made explicit in the text of the Protocol.

When a liberation movement fighting against a High Contracting Party but not recognized by a regional intergovernmental organization makes a declaration in accordance with Article 96(3), the consequences are not entirely clear.[86] The depository might just circulate the declaration and States could make declarations in response as was the case with the Provisional Republic of Algeria. In a similar case, this seemed to be the sequence of events. The United Nations Council for Namibia acceded to the Geneva Conventions and the Two Protocols on 18 October 1983. The Swiss government includes this notification on its list of accessions. On 24 February 1984 South Africa deposited a statement with the Swiss government rejecting 'the so-called instruments of accession of the UN Council for Namibia . . . as having no legal effect'.[87]

Finally, there is the very important provision of Article 96(3)*c* which provides that the Conventions and Protocol I shall be 'equally binding upon all Parties'.

Fears that there would be an element of discrimination brought into the humanitarian law were not entirely unfounded. In the first session North Vietnam submitted a document which stated,

Where humanitarian treatment is concerned the spirit of the Geneva Conventions is essentially based on the outdated concept of the *equal rights* of the parties to a conflict. . . . *Equality or impartiality must be based on justice if it is to serve as the criterion for humanitarian treatment.*[88]

The Chinese delegate claimed in the first plenary session that 'a distinction between just and unjust wars, should be made in the new Protocols'.[89] Fortunately, these revisions, which would have returned humanitarian law to the medieval idea of *bellum justum*, received no support from any quarter including the liberation movements themselves and were quickly dropped.[90]

---

[86] The Swiss government does not list any declarations made in accordance with Article 96(3).

[87] Communication from the Republic of South Africa, reprinted in *IRRC* (Nov.–Dec. 1984), 363–4.

[88] Draft amendments submitted by the Democratic Republic of Vietnam, 12 Mar. 1974, CDDH/41, OR: vol. iv. 177–80.

[89] Mr PI Chi-Lung (China), CDDH/SR.12, OR: vol. v. 120.

[90] See Edward Kossoy, *Living with Guerrilla* (Geneva: Librairie Droz, 1976), 218–36 on the rebirth of the *bellum justum* doctrine and the Vietnam draft; David Forsythe, 'Support for a Humanitarian *Jus in bello*', *International Lawyer*, 11 (1977), 724; Nicolo Farina, 'The Attitude of the People's Republic of China', in *The New Humanitarian Law of Armed Conflict*, ed. Antonio Cassese (Naples: Editoriale Scientifica, 1979), 445–57.

7.43 Qualification of Combatants: Articles 43 and 44

Articles 1(4) and 96 provide the theoretical basis for the application of humanitarian law to wars of national liberation. Articles 43 and 44 are the concrete application of these principles. One of the most important protections under the law of war is immunity from punishment under municipal law for acts of violence not prohibited by international law. Articles 43 and 44 govern the conditions under which individuals shall be combatants and, if captured, entitled to prisoner-of-war status and therefore immune from prosecution under municipal law. As one might imagine, these provisions were some of the most controversial of the Diplomatic Conference, the result of which was a confusing and imprecise compromise.

Article 43 is a great improvement in clarifying the meaning of combatancy, its requirements, and its consequences. At least since the Brussels Conference of 1874, the issue of irregular forces has been a divisive one. Small States, threatened with or having experienced occupation, with small standing armies, have argued in favour of the inclusion of irregular forces as legitimate combatants. Large States with large standing armies have sought to restrict privileged treatment only to organized armed forces. The series of compromises which resulted in 1907 and again in 1949 have been partially revised by the 1977 Protocol.

The 1973 ICRC draft proposed keeping the distinction between regular and irregular combatants, the latter having to comply with more stringent criteria to gain the privileges of prisoner-of-war status.[91] During the initial stages of discussion most States concentrated on drafting changes. Then, late in the second session, Norway introduced an amendment which quickly formed the basis for discussion and eventually led to Article 43.[92] Article 43 changes the approach to the definition of armed forces. It makes no distinction between regular and irregular combatants, resistance movements and regular armies. Under Article 43 all armed forces are combatants; all combatants are entitled to participate in hostilities; and, if captured, all combatants are entitled to treatment as prisoners of war. The Article provides,

1. The armed forces of a Party to a conflict consist of all organized armed forces, groups and units which are under a command responsible to that Party for the conduct of its subordinates, even if that Party is represented by a government or an authority not recognized by an adverse Party. Such armed forces shall be subject to

---

[91] See Draft Article 42, OR: vol. i. Part III, 13; cf. Article 1, 1907 Hague Convention IV and Article 4A, 1949 Geneva Convention III.

[92] See CDDH/III/259, OR: vol. iii. 185; CDDH/III/SR.33, paras. 66–76, OR: vol. xiv. 332–4.

an internal disciplinary system which, *inter alia*, shall enforce compliance with the rules of international law applicable in armed conflict.

2. Members of the armed forces of a Party to a conflict (other than medical personnel and chaplains covered by Article 33 of the Third Convention) are combatants, that is to say, they have the right to participate directly in hostilities.

3. Whenever a Party to a conflict incorporates a paramilitary or armed law enforcement agency into its armed forces it shall so notify the other Parties to the conflict.

Some requirements of this Article are important for combatants in liberation wars.

Individuals fighting in a war of liberation may participate in hostilities and are entitled to prisoner-of-war status only if they are organized under a responsible command and subject to a disciplinary system capable of enforcing the law of war. These conditions suggest a degree of organization which is not implied in Article 1(4). They are consistent with the idea that only authorities capable of applying the law should receive its benefits.

A second development contained in Article 43 is that individuals who fulfil the requirements of the Article are combatants even if represented by a government or an *authority* not recognized by their enemy. Under the Geneva Conventions, irregular forces and resistance movements had to belong to a party to the conflict which was a State.[93] Only regular armed forces who belonged to an authority not recognized by their enemy were entitled to protection if captured. Irregular forces were not.[94] The result is that Article 43 extends the privileges of combatancy to irregular forces even when the authority commanding them is not recognized. This is particularly important in wars of national liberation.

Article 43 which defines armed forces and Article 44 concerning prisoner-of-war status are complementary. Article 44 was one of the most controversial of the Diplomatic Conference. On the one hand, there was a general desire to ease the requirements for prisoner-of-war status for irregular combatants. Geneva Convention III required that resistance movements wear a fixed distinctive sign recognizable at a distance and carry their arms openly in order to qualify for prisoner-of-war status. These conditions were considered to be increasingly anachronistic in modern guerrilla warfare. It was argued that unless an individual had a reasonable chance of gaining the benefits of a combatant, there was little reason for him to comply with the laws of war. On the other hand, there was a strong feeling that combatants should distinguish themselves from the civilian population in order to protect civilians from retaliation from an enemy who has been repeatedly attacked by individuals appearing to be peaceful

---

[93] Article 4A(2), 1949 Geneva Convention III.
[94] Article 4A(3), 1949 Geneva Convention III.

civilians. To blur the distinction in international law between a civilian and a combatant degrades the protection of civilians.

The debates on the Article were extensive and, because of the importance of the issue, some delegations requested a verbatim record of the thirty-third to thirty-sixth meetings of the Third Committee.[95] Some governments proposed that those fighting in wars of national liberation need not distinguish themselves from the civilian population.[96] At the other extreme were proposals to keep the Hague and Geneva requirements virtually intact.[97] The Spanish delegation even argued for tightening the requirements for prisoner-of-war status by proposing that resistance movements must 'exercise effective territorial jurisdiction'.[98] Between these extremes were proposals to extend prisoner-of-war status to resistance movements when they distinguish themselves in their military operations.[99] The American and British draft stated explicitly that failure to distinguish themselves from the civilian population in their military operations would result in denial of prisoner-of-war status. Those who failed to distinguish themselves in their military operations could be prosecuted under municipal law for any maiming or killing which would have been a legitimate act of war if they had distinguished themselves.

The questions of *when* an individual must distinguish himself and the consequences of failure to do so continued to divide the working group until the end of the third session in 1976, when a compromise text was developed by Mr Aldrich of the United States and Mr Van Luu of North Vietnam. Article 44 provides,

1. Any combatant, as defined in Article 43, who falls into the power of an adverse Party shall be a prisoner of war.

2. While all combatants are obliged to comply with the rules of international law applicable in armed conflict, violations of these rules shall not deprive a combatant of his right to be a combatant or, if he falls into the power of an adverse Party, of his right to be a prisoner of war, except as provided in paragraphs 3 and 4.

3. In order to promote the protection of the civilian population from the effects of hostilities, combatants are obliged to distinguish themselves from the civilian population while they are engaged in an attack or in a military operation preparatory to an attack. Recognizing, however, that there are situations in armed conflicts where, owing to the nature of the hostilities an armed combatant cannot so

---

[95] CDDH/III/SR.33 to 36, Annex, OR: vol. xiv. 445–556.

[96] See CDDH/III/73 and Add. 1, OR: vol. iii. 179, sponsored by Madagascar and SWAPO; also CDDH/III/253, OR: vol. iii. 183, sponsored by North Vietnam and later withdrawn. See CDDH/III/SR.33–SR.36, Annex, OR: vol. xiv. 451.

[97] CDDH/III/258 and Add. 1, sponsored by Argentina and Nicaragua, OR: vol. iii. 185.

[98] CDDH/III/209, OR: vol. iii. 182.

[99] CDDH/III/256, sponsored by the Netherlands, OR: vol. iii. 183–4; CDDH/III/257, sponsored by the UK and USA, OR: vol. iii. 184–5.

distinguish himself, he shall retain his status as a combatant, provided that, in such situations, he carries his arms openly:

    (*a*) during each military engagement, and

    (*b*) during such time as he is visible to the adversary while he is engaged in a military deployment preceding the launching of an attack in which he is to participate.

Acts which comply with the requirements of this paragraph shall not be considered as perfidious within the meaning of Article 37, paragraph 1(*c*).

4. A combatant who falls into the power of an adverse Party while failing to meet the requirements set forth in the second sentence of paragraph 3 shall forfeit his right to be a prisoner of war, but he shall, nevertheless, be given protections equivalent in all respects to those accorded to prisoners of war by the Third Convention and by this Protocol. This protection includes protections equivalent to those accorded to prisoners of war by the Third Convention in the case where such a person is tried and punished for any offenses he has committed.

This Article was a politically necessary compromise and is a model of vagueness—a dangerous condition for rules as fragile as those of the law of armed conflict. The substance of the Article is that combatants, as defined in Article 43, are entitled to prisoner-of-war status if captured. They are obliged to distinguish themselves from civilians, and if, in very exceptional cases, they cannot do so when they are engaged in an attack or in a military operation preparatory to an attack, they will not lose their prisoner-of-war status as long as they carry arms openly during each military engagement and during such time as they are visible to the enemy during deployment. If an individual fails to fulfil even these conditions, he does not get prisoner-of-war *status* but is entitled to prisoner-of-war *treatment*. There are several important points contained in this Article.

First, the distinction between prisoner-of-war status and prisoner-of-war treatment is more than cosmetic. An individual who fails to distinguish himself as provided can be tried and punished under municipal law for acts that would have been lawful if he was a combatant, e.g. killing, maiming, and attacking military targets. Since he has given up his status as a combatant, he is no longer entitled to participate in hostilities. However, such an individual must be treated as a prisoner of war and in particular the detaining power must comply with the judicial procedures applicable for prisoners of war. This does not prevent punishment, up to death, under municipal law.

Second, by this Article, failure to distinguish oneself from the civilian population is a breach of international law. Combatants are 'obliged' to distinguish themselves from the civilian population while they are engaged in an attack or in a military operation preparatory to an attack. Even when they find themselves in the exceptional case where they 'cannot so distinguish' themselves, this failure to distinguish themselves as combatants still remains a breach of international law for which they can be tried as war criminals, although they still retain prisoner-of-war status if they meet the conditions of the second sentence of paragraph 3.

Despite the clarification of combatancy defined in Article 43, Article 44 seems to suggest that the idea of unprivileged belligerency still has a place in the law of war. A combatant who fails to distinguish himself from the civilian population as provided in Article 44 loses his prisoner-of-war status. No other violation of the law of war deprives a combatant of the status of prisoner of war.[100]

Third, one cannot fail to note the controversy and differing interpretations which cloud the Article. Nowhere is it explained what 'operations preparatory to an attack' are and there are varying interpretations of what is meant by the phrase 'during such time as he is visible to the adversary while he is engaged in a military deployment preceding the launching of an attack'. Neither 'visibility' nor 'military deployment' is defined. The Article was passed in plenary by 73:1:21.[101] The different interpretations put forth in the explanations of vote illustrate the ambiguity of paragraphs 3 and 4.[102] The Egyptian government understood the phrase 'military deployment' meant 'the last step when the combatants were taking their firing positions just before the commencement of hostilities.'[103] Mr Freeland of the United Kingdom understood the same phrase to mean 'any movement towards a place from which an attack was to be launched.'[104]

The problem of varying interpretations was cogently summarized by the Swiss delegate explaining Switzerland's abstention:

[T]he explanations of vote by the delegations which had spoken on that article made it clearly apparent that no unity of view existed concerning it. Every one interpreted it as he thought fit. . . . The general principles of interpretation recognized in international law did not suffice; and even if that method were applied, it would not be possible to arrive at uniform interpretations. . . . Thus,

---

[100] According to Article 46, Protocol I, spies are denied the status of prisoner of war if captured, but they are not criminals under international law. Mercenaries have neither the right to be combatants nor the status of prisoners of war if captured. See Article 47, Protocol I.

[101] Israel opposed. Thailand, Uruguay, West Germany, Argentina, Australia, Brazil, Canada, Chile, Columbia, Spain, Guatemala, Honduras, Ireland, Italy, Japan, Nicaragua, New Zealand, the Philippines, Portugal, the UK, and Switzerland abstaining. See CDDH/SR.40, OR: vol. vi. 121.

[102] See explanations of vote CDDH/SR.40, OR: vol. vi. 121 *et seq.*, para. 23 (Italy); para. 31 (Argentina); para. 37 (Nigeria); para. 39 (Austria); para. 44 (Algeria); paras. 47 and 48 (Greece); paras. 52 and 53 (Australia); paras. 67 and 69 (Switzerland); para. 71 (Ireland); para. 74 (UK); para. 83 (Sweden); CDDH/SR.41, OR: vol. vi. 141 *et. seq.* para. 6 (Netherlands); para. 13 (Denmark); paras. 19 and 21 (Egypt); para. 22 (Chile); para. 24 (Canada); para. 31 (PLO); paras. 34 and 35 (Portugal); para. 45 (USA); para. 53 (Japan).

[103] Mr Al Ghunaimi (Egypt), CDDH/SR.41, para. 21, OR: vol. vi. 145.

[104] Mr Freeland (UK), CDDH/SR.40, para. 74, OR: vol. vi. 132.

Article [44] was not a rule of law, since it lacked the precision of a legal
standard . . . [105]

Both the United States and the United Kingdom declared upon signature
that their interpretation of 'military deployment' in Article 44 was 'any
movement towards a place from which an attack is to be launched'.[106]

Article 44 was a confusing if necessary compromise. There was
considerable disagreement about its true meaning. As a matter of law, the
Article requires State practice to clarify what the legislative history cannot.
To the extent that imprecision is a convenient doorway for abuse,
consistent State practice may never evolve.

Finally, it is important to note that the exceptions provided for in Article
44 apply not only in wars of national liberation as defined in Article 1(4),
but in all armed conflicts to which Protocol I applies, including belligerent
occupation. Paragraph 7 of the Article does reaffirm, however, that the
intention of the Article is 'not to change the generally accepted practice of
States with respect to the wearing of the uniform'.

7.44 The Process of Ratification

There were 126 States at the first session of the Diplomatic Conference,
121 at the second session, 106 at the third, and 109 at the fourth.[107] At the
conclusion of the Diplomatic Conference, on 10 June 1977, 102 States and
3 national liberation movements signed the Final Act.[108] Six months later
the Protocols were opened for signature and 62 States signed Protocol I.
As of 30 April 1987, 65 States, the Holy See, and the UN Council for
Namibia had ratified or acceded to the Protocol.[109] Thus far, China is the
only 'great power' to have ratified or acceded to the Protocol. There is a
general feeling that some Western States may be waiting for ratification by
the United States while many Eastern Bloc States are waiting for a Soviet
move. The absence of ratifications by these States is not as damning as a

---

[105] Mr Bindschedler (Switzerland), CDDH/SR.40, para. 69, OR: vol. vi. 131.

[106] Reprinted in Bothe, 721–3.

[107] China and South Africa did not participate after the first session.

[108] The liberation movements signed under a separate heading with the proviso that 'It is
understood that the signature by these movements is without prejudice to the positions of
participating States on the question of a precedent.' SWAPO, the PLO, and the PAC signed
the Act. The ANC and ANCZ (Rhodesia) did not.

[109] In chronological order they are Ghana, Libya, El Salvador, Ecuador, Jordan,
Botswana, Cyprus, Niger, Yugoslavia, Tunisia, Sweden, Mauritania, Gabon, Bahamas,
Finland, Bangladesh, Laos, Vietnam, Norway, South Korea, Switzerland, Mauritius, Zaire,
Denmark, Austria, St Lucia, Cuba, Tanzania, United Arab Emirates, Mexico, Mozambique,
St Vincent and the Grenadines, China, the UN Council for Namibia, Congo, Syria, Bolivia,
Costa Rica, Cameroon, Oman, Togo, Belize, Guinea, Central African Republic, Samoa,
Angola, Seychelles, Rwanda, Kuwait, Vanuatu, Senegal, Holy See, Comoros, Uruguay,
Suriname, St Christopher and Nevis, Italy, Belgium, Benin, Equatorial Guinea, Jamaica,
Antigua and Barbuda, Sierra Leone, Guinea-Bissau, Bahrain, Argentina, and Iceland.

ten-year delay might initially suggest. The Protocols will require changes in domestic law, as did the 1949 Geneva Conventions. In the case of the 1949 Geneva Conventions, for example, the United Kingdom ratified eight years after signature, the United States after six years and the USSR after five years.

No government involved in a conflict of the type described in Article 1(4) has signed, ratified, or acceded to the Protocol. In particular, South Africa and Israel are not signatories.[110] The only governments which have ratified Protocol I and which face some kind of internal armed opposition are El Salvador, Cyprus, Mozambique, and Angola. El Salvador has also ratified Protocol II. But in the areas of the world where these provisions are most applicable, the treaty is not in force.

7.5 Conclusions

The application of the international law of warfare to wars of national liberation could be described as a limited success. In light of the history of the last forty years and the development of treaty law, the following conclusions can be made.

1. The law of war has often been applied in wars of national liberation, usually following a period of repressive measures or special emergency legislation designed to crush the rebellion before it gains momentum. However, there are significant exceptions to this rule and it cannot be considered a customary rule of international law.

2. States have been more willing to apply the principles of international law and to *treat* detainees as prisoners of war rather than undertake obligations to apply the law or grant the *status* of prisoner of war primarily because the latter are still viewed as giving international legitimacy to the opponents of the established government.

3. National liberation movements have been less reluctant than States to apply the laws of war, to adhere to them openly, and to co-operate with the Red Cross. This is because they have an interest in internationalizing their conflict to gain legitimacy and because of the practical advantages gained for their detained members.

4. The 1977 Protocols Additional to the 1949 Geneva Conventions include wars against colonial domination, alien occupation, and racist regimes in the category of international armed conflicts to which the whole

---

[110] Although South Africa stopped participating in the Diplomatic Conference which developed the Protocols after the first session in 1974, the South African government did accede to 1899 Hague Declarations 2 and 3, and 1907 Hague Conventions IV, VII, VIII, IX, and XI on 10 Mar. 1978. It is possible that international interest encouraged the South African government to re-evaluate its position on the law of war.

of international humanitarian law applies. Sixty-five States have ratified or acceded to Protocol I. Sixty-two States have signed Protocol I. Of the States which have ratified the Protocol, none is involved in a conflict of the type described in Article 1(4).

5. The involvement of the International Committee of the Red Cross in wars of national liberation remains on the legal basis of their 'right of humanitarian intervention' rather than on the firmer basis of treaty law. It is likely to remain this way as long as States continue to be reluctant to undertake obligations in wars of national liberation even though they are sometimes willing to act in accordance with requirements of international law.

8

The Prospects for Application

The intent of this chapter is to withdraw from this microscopic examination of treaty provisions and recent State practice to take a broader view of trends and their importance for the progressive development of the law of armed conflict.

The law of war is divided into two branches, usually considered to be separate to ensure impartial humanitarian protection in warfare irrespective of the cause of the war. In the case of national liberation movements this separation is, in one way at least, artificial. The trend toward the application of the humanitarian law of war to internal wars and wars of national liberation in particular was caused by a number of factors, one of the most important of which was the idea that these peoples are a separate entity, and have an identity distinct from the government administering them. Thus, a war which may occur in the case where self-determination is denied is an international war even if it is not an inter-State war. Because it is international, the rules of international law concerning the conduct of operations in war should apply. In the case of wars of national liberation, we are witnessing the application of an entire body of law to an entity not previously considered to be subject to the law. Therefore, questions of legitimacy and international legal personality seep into the debate on the application of the humanitarian law of war.

During the 1974–7 Diplomatic Conference there was some confusion on the distinction between impartial application of the laws of war between belligerents—ensured by Article 96(3) of Protocol I—and the application of a body of law based on the justice or injustice of the cause for which a group is fighting. Discriminatory application of the law of war is definitely to be avoided. If one side in a conflict has more humanitarian protection because it is the 'just' side, then the law of armed conflict will quickly degenerate to the medieval practices of the victor dispensing God's justice. But the question of the type of conflict in which the law applies is a completely separate problem.

By the beginning of the twentieth century it was widely accepted that States were the only entities which could legitimately wage war. Therefore, the humanitarian protections of the law of war only applied as between States. The growth of the idea that identifiable peoples may wage war in order to become States led to the claim that in these conflicts, too, the humanitarian law should apply. The application of the body of humanitarian law to wars of national liberation is not based on the justice of the cause but on the nature of the conflict. Whereas the law of war used to apply in conflicts among States, there is now a growing consensus that it also applies or should apply between a State and a 'people'.

This is not the discriminatory application which is to be feared. On the contrary, the restrictions of the Geneva Conventions and Protocols are rigorous and apply equally to national liberation movements and governments alike. There are justifiable doubts about the ability of national liberation movements to fulfil these rigorous requirements in practice. However, the suggestion that the Protocols give the advantage to the 'terrorists' is not borne out by the text as agreed. Being a prisoner of war is more advantageous than being a convicted murderer, but there is no advantage given to one side over the other.

The logical extension of this argument is that the humanitarian law of war should be applied to all armed conflicts, non-international and international. Indeed, at the Diplomatic Conference Norway supported the idea of a single protocol to cover all types of armed conflicts. Although theoretically this may be a solution, in practice it is not politically possible for the same reasons it was not possible in 1949. States are not eager to give any advantages to their internal opponents. Since one of the fundamental duties of a State is the maintenance of public order and internal peace, one questions the advisability of extending the law of war to all internal disturbances, regardless of the intensity of the conflict, even if it were politically possible.

Of course, the extension of the law of armed conflict to wars of national liberation as defined in Article 1(4) was not caused solely by the growth of the idea of a right of self-determination and the decline of the perceived legitimacy of colonialism. In addition, in the last forty years there has been increasing concern for the rights of the individual against his own State. The growth of the idea that individuals may be subjects of international law and, in particular, the development of the law of human rights have also given impetus to the broader application of the humanitarian law of war. The protection of individuals in time of war can be seen as a subset of human rights law as well as a branch of international law on the use of force. As human rights law has developed, so too has human rights protection in war.

A further impetus behind this changing view of the situations in which the law of war applies is the need for law to adapt to life. The 1949 Geneva Conventions were drafted with World War II in mind. Since World War II, internal wars, guerrilla tactics, and internationalized internal wars have been more prevalent than conventional inter-State wars. If law fails to adapt to the environment it must regulate, it will quickly become anachronistic. An awareness of this fact also motivated the participants at the Diplomatic Conference.

Finally, one cannot ignore the tremendous change in the composition and nature of international society in the last forty years. The number of States has expanded nearly three-fold and the character of these States, their cultural history, economic development, and political foundations are often radically different from those of Europe. The European concept of a system of States has expanded to cover the whole world, and the law of armed conflict developed largely in a European context. The emergence to independence of so many non-European States inevitably affected the rules of international law developed by those States. On issues labelled 'anti-colonialist' this impact has been most significant.

All of these forces, as well as the self-interest of the parties involved, have led to the frequent if not universal application of the humanitarian law of war to wars of national liberation and to the inclusion of Article 1(4) in the 1977 Protocols.

The 1977 Protocols have changed the way we classify types of armed conflict for the purposes of applying humanitarian law. Before the 1949 Geneva Conventions were written, there were two legal situations. There were rules applicable in international wars, which also applied in civil wars when the seceding party was recognized as a belligerent. In all other cases conduct was governed by the municipal law of the State concerned.

With the adoption of the 1949 Geneva Conventions, there were three situations with different rules applying to each: international armed conflicts in which the whole of the Conventions applied; armed conflicts not of an international character in which the minimum provisions of Article 3 applied; and anything less than non-international armed conflict—tensions, disturbances, riots, or threats to public order—which remained a matter for municipal law.

With the conclusion of the 1977 Diplomatic Conference the types of situations in which some rules of humanitarian law apply have been further subdivided into five categories. There are traditional international armed conflicts. Second, there are Article 1(4) conflicts in which the authority representing a people has made a declaration of intention to apply the Conventions and Protocols. This type of conflict is characterized as international but differs from other international conflicts in that an explicit declaration is required for the law to apply. Third, there are conflicts as described in Protocol II between a State and 'organized armed groups which, under responsible command, exercise such control over a part of its territory as to enable them to carry out sustained and concerted military operations and to implement' Protocol II. In these situations of 'high threshold' internal armed conflict the protections of Protocol II apply. Fourth, there are Article 3 conflicts under the 1949 Conventions.[1] And finally, there are riots or internal disturbances which are regulated by municipal law. Thus, there is now a spectrum of situations in which different sets of rules apply. Whether this multiplication of categories enhances the quality of the law or eases its application is difficult to say. It certainly makes it more complex. In a situation like armed combat, this complexity may be a disadvantage.

The application of the law of armed conflict stretches the idea of law to its very limit. Its application is a difficult business and a dubious enterprise even in wars between States. Its observance depends on the will of governments when, in sober moments, they ratify treaties or incorporate the law of war into their own law. It depends even more heavily on the instantaneous decisions of young soldiers on the field of battle when their own lives are at risk. In guerrilla wars and in occupied territories the restraints imposed by the law of war appear to be particularly fragile. The parts of the law of war which have been most effective are often difficult to apply in guerrilla wars. Guerrillas depend on mobility; they often do not control a secure territory suitable for detention of prisoners; and they usually lack the administrative and judicial infrastructure which eases the law's application. That said, the observance of the law of war in wars of national liberation is not impossible, but one must not ignore the difficulties involved.

Even if there is widespread ratification of Protocol I, which is far from certain, Article 1(4) is not a panacea that will automatically strengthen the fragilities inherent in international humanitarian law. Certainly, the Article was a political statement when it was made, just as repeated condemnations of apartheid and colonialism emerging from the UN and elsewhere were political statements. In the final analysis, what matters is the effect of the Protocols on the actions of States. Here, Article 1(4) suffers from many of the same problems which have made Article 3 so difficult to apply. In the case of Article 3, States have been reluctant to admit that an armed conflict exists. It is difficult to imagine that Article 1(4) will affect this reluctance, especially when the State involved must not only admit that an armed conflict exists in its territory, but that it is a colonial, racist, or alien regime. Without this unlikely acknowledgement, the established government may still impede the application of humanitarian law and agencies like the ICRC will continue to operate based on their 'right of humanitarian initiative' rather than on the provisions of the Geneva Conventions and Protocols. In short, Article 1(4), like Inter-

---

[1] Presumably, a conflict such as that described in Article 1(4) in which the authority has not made a declaration to adhere to the full Conventions would be classified as a Protocol II or Article 3 conflict.

national Court of Justice opinions declaring South African occupation of Namibia illegal or General Assembly resolutions on self-determination for the Western Sahara, remains vulnerable to the shortcomings of international law generally. For this reason, it is likely that the application of the law of war to wars of national liberation will remain, as in Israel, a matter of humanitarian initiative and analogous application.

Finally, much of the rhetoric surrounding Article 1(4) is quite exaggerated. In its original form, as proposed by the non-aligned States, the Article would have been much broader. But because accommodation and compromise with the Western States was not possible, the non-aligned movement turned east and included the Soviet Bloc wording which restricts the field of application to those fighting against colonial domination, alien occupation, and racist regimes. As discussed in Chapter 7, there is tremendous difficulty defining these terms, but they are more limited than just the general idea of self-determination. It is also more difficult to envision the progressive application of the Article to other types of internal conflicts or wars of secession precisely because the wording of the Article was narrowed by the Soviet amendment. The sponsors of the non-aligned draft were dissatisfied with this outcome—particularly since the Western States ended up abstaining in the final vote anyway. Although some authors have since argued for the Article to be interpreted as broadly as possible, this plea will probably be no more effective than that made by Jean Pictet in the Red Cross Commentary on Article 3 of the 1949 Geneva Conventions. He too thought that 'the Article should be applied as widely as possible'. Of course, Jean Pictet also realized that 'A government has no worse foes than those who would overthrow it and it will wish to retain its liberty of action to crush or forestall any revolt, with no embarrassing witnesses to question the legitimacy of the means it uses.'[2]

---

[2] Jean Pictet (ed.), *The Geneva Conventions of 12 August 1949: Commentary* (Geneva: ICRC, 1952), i. 50; Jean Pictet, *Humanitarian Law and the Protection of War Victims* (Leiden: A. W. Sijthoff, 1975), 54.

Conclusion

It was stated at the outset that the purpose of this book was to explore how changes in ideas about self-determination of peoples have affected the use of force in international law. The conclusions at the end of sections and chapters provide specific answers to the questions posed. Here I shall state briefly what the direction of the argument has been.

The first three chapters of this book explained widely accepted ideas about the nature and rules of international law. It was argued that, in this traditional view, war was a relation between States and that States were the only actors in international society which could legitimately use force. All other uses of force were matters of municipal law in the State where the violence occurred. The rules of humanitarian law which have developed over the centuries to ameliorate the effects of warfare generally did not apply in armed conflicts not between States.

Part II traced the development of the idea that self-determination is a principle of international law. It was argued that since the end of World War II, and since 1960 in particular, there has been a growing consensus that identifiable 'peoples' have a status in international society and a personality in international law which is separate and distinct from that of the territory administering them. These 'peoples' have a right freely to choose their own political future.

To some extent, State practice has clarified who are the selves that have a right to self-determination. A 'people' is not an ethnic or religious group, but a territorial one. In practice, peoples who have a right to self-determination include trust and mandated territories, non-self-governing territories, and, in some cases, geographically distinct territories which are subordinate to the metropolitan State and non-self-governing with respect to the remainder of the State. Finally, it was argued that the right of peoples to self-determination is moderated by other legal principles including the principle of territorial integrity.

Part III explained the development of the idea that national liberation movements fighting to secure the right of their peoples to self-determination may legitimately use force as a matter of international law. Since the end of World War II, some States, particularly newly independent ones, have recognized governments prematurely and accepted liberation movements as representatives of their peoples as a way of enhancing the status of these movements. Despite the vehemence with which the anti-colonial States have argued their case, a powerful minority of States still do not accept that national liberation movements have the authority to use force in international law. Nevertheless, the acceptance of these movements by a large number of States as authorities capable of legitimately resorting to the use of force in world politics challenges traditional ideas about the nature of international society. It implies that 'the authority of the prince' is not synonymous with 'the authority of a sovereign State'. For the last four hundred years the sovereign State has consolidated its power and it remains the pre-eminent international actor. The acceptance of national liberation movements as authorities in their own right by a large number of States challenges this exclusive control of violence.

In the final section of this book it was argued that although States have been reluctant to undertake legal obligations to respect the humanitarian law of war in wars of national liberation, they often observe its rules. In this realm, State practice will probably remain ahead of codification of the law because States have no interest in appearing to acknowledge the legitimacy of their most bitter opponents. Although the 1977 Protocols Additional to the 1949 Geneva Conventions may appear to be a revolutionary development, they are, in fact, more evolutionary than revolutionary. Their practical effect is uncertain both because the 'target' States are unlikely to ratify the Protocols and because the fragilities inherent in international law may undermine the application of the Protocols as they have undermined the application of Article 3 of the 1949 Geneva Conventions.

The world in which there was nothing distasteful about empire is gone. In its place is a system of over 150 sovereign States in which the principle of self-determination is part of the body of rules governing the relationships among them. In this post-colonial world, the denial of self-determination is generally considered to be a evil of such magnitude that the use of force to secure it may be justified. Wars of national liberation are now widely considered to be international wars to which international law must apply.

Bibliography

'Aaland Islands Question: Report of the Committee of Jurists', *League of Nations Official Journal*, Special Supplement 3 (Oct. 1920), 3–14.

ABI-SAAB, GEORGES M., 'The Newly Independent States and the Rules of International Law: An Outline', *Howard Law Journal*, 8 (1962), 95–121.

—— 'Wars of National Liberation and the Laws of War', *Annales d'études internationales*, 3 (1972), 93–117.

—— 'Wars of National Liberation in the Geneva Conventions and Protocols', *Recueil des cours*, 165 (1979-IV), 353–445.

—— Personal interview, 1 Apr. 1985.

African Party for the Independence of Guinea-Portugal: Agreement Granting Independence of Portuguese Guinea, August 26, 1974, *International Legal Materials*, 13 (1974), 1244.

AKEHURST, MICHAEL, 'Humanitarian Intervention', in Hedley Bull (ed.), *Intervention in World Politics* (Oxford: Clarendon Press, 1984), 95–118.

ALDRICH, GEORGE H, 'Protocols to the Geneva Conventions on the Laws of War', *ASIL*, 74 (1980), 191–2.

—— 'New Life for the Laws of War', *AJIL*, 75 (1981), 764–83.

Amnesty International, *Report of an Amnesty International Mission to Northern Ireland, 28 November–6 December 1977* (London: Amnesty International, June 1978).

'The Angola Conflict and International Law', *South African YIL*, 1 (1975), 117–23.

ARANGIO-RUIZ, GAETANO, 'The Normative Role of the General Assembly of the United Nations and the Declaration of Principles of Friendly Relations', *Recueil des cours*, 137 (1972-III), 431–742.

Asian Regional Conference for Action Against Apartheid, *Manila Declaration for Action Against Apartheid*, 24–26 May 1982 (New York: United Nations Center Against Apartheid, 1982).

The Atlantic Charter and Africa from an American Standpoint, Study by the Committee on Africa, the War, and Peace Aims (New York: no pub., 1942).

AUSTIN, JOHN, *Lectures on Jurisprudence or The Philosophy of Positive Law*, 4th edn., ed. Robert Campbell (London: John Murray, 1873), vol. i.

AUTY, PHYLLIS and CLOGG RICHARD (eds.), *British Policy Towards Wartime Resistance in Yugoslavia and Greece* (London: Macmillan, 1975).

BAILEY, KENNETH, 'Making International Law in the UN', *ASIL*, 61 (1967), 233–39.

BAILEY, SYDNEY D., *Prohibitions and Restraints in War* (London: Oxford Univ. Press, 1972).

BAINS, J. S., 'Angola, the UN and International Law', *Indian JIL*, 3 (1963), 63–71.

BALLIS, WILLIAM, *The Legal Position of War: Changes in its Practice and Theory from Plato to Vattel* (London: Garland, 1973).

BASSIOUNI, M. CHERIF, ' "Self-determination" and the Palestinians', *ASIL*, 65 (1971), 31–40.

BAXTER, RICHARD R., 'So-called "Unprivileged Belligerency": Spies, Guerrillas, and Saboteurs', *BYIL*, 28 (1951), 323–45.

—— 'The Privy Council on the Qualifications of Belligerents', *AJIL*, 63 (1969), 290–6.

—— 'Perspective: The Evolving Laws of Armed Conflicts', *Military LR*, 60 (1973), 99–111.

—— 'The Geneva Conventions of 1949 and Wars of National Liberation', *Rivista di diritto internazionale*, 57 (1974), 193–203.

—— 'Ius in bello interno: The Present and Future Law', in *Law and Civil War in the Modern World*, ed. John Norton Moore (Baltimore: Johns Hopkins Univ. Press, 1974), 518–36.

—— 'Humanitarian Law or Humanitarian Politics? The 1974 Diplomatic Conference on Humanitarian Law', *Harvard ILJ*, 16 (1975), 1–26.

BEDJAOUI, MOHAMED, *Law and the Algerian Revolution* (Brussels: International Association of Democratic Lawyers, 1961).

BELKHERROUBI, ABDELMADJID, 'Essai sur une théorie juridique des mouvements de libération nationale', *Rev. égyptienne de droit international*, 28 (1972), 20–43.

BERTELSEN, JUDY, *The Palestinian Arabs: A Non-state Nation Systems Analysis* (London: Sage Publications, 1976).

BEST, GEOFFREY, *Humanity in Warfare: The Modern History of International Law of Armed Conflicts* (London: Weidenfeld and Nicolson, 1980).

BINDSCHEDLER-ROBERT, DENISE, *A Reconsideration of the Law of Armed Conflicts*, A Report prepared for the Conference on Contemporary Problems of the Law of Armed Conflicts, Geneva, 15–20 Dec. 1969 (New York: Carnegie Endowment for International Peace, 1971), 1–62.

BISHOP, WILLIAM W., 'General Course of Public International Law', *Recueil des cours*, 115 (1965-II), 150–470.

BLUM, YEHUDA, 'Reflections on the Changing Concept of Self-determination', *Israel LR*, 10 (1975), 509–14.

BOND, JAMES E., *The Rules of Riot: Internal Conflict and the Law of War* (Princeton: Princeton Univ. Press, 1974).

—— 'Amended Article 1 of Draft Protocol I to the 1949 Geneva Conventions: The Coming of Age of the Guerrilla', *Washington and Lee LR*, 32 (1975), 65–78.

BOTHE, MICHAEL, 'Article 3 and Protocol II: Case Studies of Nigeria and El Salvador', *Am. Univ. LR*, 31 (1982), 899–909.

—— PARTSCH, KARL JOSEF, and SOLF, WALDEMAR A., *New Rules for Victims of Armed Conflicts: Commentary on the Two 1977 Protocols Additional to the Geneva Conventions of 1949* (London: Martinus Nijhoff, 1982).

BOWEN, HERBERT W., *International Law: A Simple Statement of its Principles* (London: G. P. Putnam's Sons, 1896).

BOWETT, DEREK W., 'Self-determination and Political Rights in the Developing Countries', *ASIL*, 60 (1966), 129–35.

BRIERLY, J. L., *The Law of Nations: An Introduction to the International Law of Peace*, 1st edn. (Oxford: Clarendon Press, 1928).

—— *The Law of Nations: An Introduction to the International Law of Peace*, 6th edn., ed. Sir Humphrey Waldock (Oxford: Oxford Univ. Press, 1963).

BRIGGS, HERBERT W. (ed.), *The Law of Nations: Cases, Documents and Notes*, 2nd edn. (London: Stevens and Sons, 1953).

British Claims in the Spanish Zone of Morocco, Report III, 29 May 1923, in *Reports of International Arbitral Awards*, vol. ii. (New York: United Nations, n.d.), 615–742.

BROWNLIE, IAN, 'International Law and the Activities of Armed Bands', *ICLQ*, 7 (1958), 712–35.

—— *International Law and the Use of Force by States* (Oxford: Clarendon Press, 1963).

—— 'An Essay in the History of the Principle of Self-determination', in C. H. Alexandrowicz (ed.), in *Grotian Society Papers: Studies in the History of the Law of Nations, 1968* (The Hague: Nijhoff, 1970), 90–9.

—— (ed.), *Basic Documents in International Law*, 2nd edn. (Oxford: Oxford Univ. Press, 1972).

—— 'Humanitarian Intervention', in John Norton Moore (ed.), *Law and Civil War in the Modern World* (London: Johns Hopkins Press, 1974), 217–28.

—— *Principles of Public International Law*, 3rd edn. (Oxford: Clarendon Press, 1979).

—— *African Boundaries* (London: C. Hurst, 1979).

—— (ed।)., *Basic Documents on Human Rights*, 2nd edn. (Oxford: Clarendon Press, 1981).

—— 'Recognition in Theory and Practice', *BYIL*, 53 (1982), 197–211.

BRUCE, NEIL, 'Portugal's African Wars', *Conflict Studies*, 34 (London: Institute for the Study of Conflict, 1973).

BUCHHEIT, LEE C., *Secession: The Legitimacy of Self-determination* (New Haven: Yale Univ. Press, 1978).

BULL, HEDLEY, *The Anarchical Society: A Study of Order in World Politics*, (London: Macmillan, 1977).

BURKE, CATHERINE, 'International Recognition of a Non-state Nation: The Palestine Liberation Organization and the United Nations' (M.Phil. Thesis, Oxford, 1979).

CALOGEROPOULOS-STRATIS, ARISTIDIS S., *Droit humanitaire et droits de l'homme: La Protection de la personne en période de conflit armé* (Geneva: Institut Universitaire de Hautes Études Internationales, 1980).

CASSESE, ANTONIO, 'The Spanish Civil War and the Development of Customary Law Concerning Internal Armed Conflicts', in Antonio Cassese (ed.), *Current Problems of International Law* (Milan: Dott. A. Giuffre, 1975), 287–318.

—— 'A Tentative Appraisal of the Old and the New Humanitarian Law of Armed Conflict', in vol. i of Antonio Cassese (ed.), *The New Humanitarian Law of Armed Conflict* (Naples: Editoriale Scientifica, 1979), 461–501.

CASTEL, J. G., *International Law: Chiefly as Interpreted and Applied in Canada*, 3rd edn. (Toronto: Butterworth, 1976).

CASTREN, ERIK, *The Present Law of War and Neutrality* (Helsinki: Suomalainen Tiedeakatemia, 1954).

—— *Civil War* (Helsinki: Suomalainen Tiedeakatemia, 1966).

CHALIAND, G., *Armed Struggle in Africa*, trans. David Rathray and Robert Leonhardt (London: Monthly Review Press, 1969).

—— *The Palestinian Resistance*, trans. Michael Perl (Harmondsworth: Penguin, 1972).

—— *The Struggle for Africa: Conflict of the Great Powers*, trans. A. M. Berrett (London: Macmillan, 1982).

CHARPENTIER, JEAN, 'La Reconnaissance du G.P.R.A.' *AFDI*, 5 (1959), 799–816.

—— 'La France et le G.P.R.A.', *AFDI*, 7 (1961), 855–70.

CHEN, TI-CHIANG, *The International Law of Recognition: With Special Reference to Practice in Great Britain and the United States* (London: Stevens and Sons, 1951).

CIOBANU, DAN, 'The Attitude of the Socialist Countries', in vol. i of Antonio Cassese (ed.), *The New Humanitarian Law of Armed Conflict* (Naples: Editoriale Scientifica, 1979), 399–444.

CLARKE, ROGER S., 'The "Decolonization" of East Timor and the United Nations Norms on Self-determination and Aggression', *Yale Journal of World Public Order*, 7 (1980), 2–44.

CLAUDE, INIS L., 'Collective Legitimization as a Political Function of the United Nations', *International Organization*, 20 (1966), 367–79.

CLAUSEWITZ, CARL VON., *On War*, ed. and trans. Michael Howard and Peter Paret (Princeton: Princeton Univ. Press, 1976).

CLISSOLD, STEPHEN (ed.), *A Short History of Yugoslavia: from Early Times to 1966* (Cambridge: Cambridge Univ. Press, 1966).

COBBAN, ALFRED, *The Nation State and National Self-determination* (London: Collins, 1969).

CONDORELLI, LUIGI. 'Les Pays afro-asiatiques', in vol. i of Antonio Cassese (ed.), *The New Humanitarian Law of Armed Conflict*, (Naples: Editoriale Scientifica, 1979), 386–98.

Conference of Heads of State or Government of Non-aligned Countries, 'Programme for Peace and International Co-operation: Declaration as Adopted by the Conference, Cairo—October 1964', *Indian JIL*, 4 (1964), 599–621.

CRAWFORD, JAMES, *The Creation of States in International Law* (Oxford: Clarendon Press, 1979).

CRISTESCU, AURELIU, 'The Historical and Current Development of the Right to Self-determination on the Basis of the Charter of the United Nations and Other Instruments Adopted by the United Nations Organs, with Particular Reference to the Promotion and Protection of Human Rights and Fundamental Freedoms', 3 vols., study for the United Nations Commission on Human Rights, Sub-commission on Prevention of Discrimination and Protection of Minorities, UN Doc. E/CN.4/Sub. 2/404. (New York: United Nations, 1978).

DAMIS, JOHN, *Conflict in Northwest Africa: The Western Sahara Dispute* (Stanford, Calif.: Hoover Institution Press, 1983).

DAVIDSON, BASIL, *Growing From Grass Roots: The State of Guinea-Bissau* (London: Committee for Freedom, 1974).

—— *No Fist is Big Enough to Hide the Sky: The Liberation of Guiné and Cape Verde* (London: Zed Press, 1981).

DAVIES, NORMAN, *God's Playground: A History of Poland* (Oxford: Clarendon Press, 1981), vol. ii.

DE ST JORRE, JOHN, *The Nigerian Civil War* (London: Hodder and Stoughton, 1972).

DINSTEIN, YORHAM, 'Terrorism and Wars of Liberation Applied to the Arab–Israeli Conflict: An Israeli Perspective', *Israel Yearbook on Human Rights*, 3 (1973), 78–92.

—— 'The New Geneva Protocols: A Step Forward or Backward?' *Yearbook of World Affairs*, 33 (1979), 265–83.

DJONOVICH, DUSAN J., *United Nations Resolutions* (Dobbs Ferry, NY: Oceana).

DOOSE, JEFFREY A., 'The UN Definition of Aggression: A Preliminary Analysis', *Denver J. of IL and Policy*, 5 (1975), 171–99.

DRAPER, G.I.A.D., *The Red Cross Conventions* (London: Stevens and Sons, 1958).

—— 'The Implementation of the Modern Law of Armed Conflicts', The Hebrew University of Jerusalem Lionel Cohen Lectures, 1972 (Jerusalem: Magnes Press, 1973).

—— 'The Relationship Between the Human Rights Regime and the Law of Armed Conflicts', *Israel Yearbook on Human Rights*, 1 (1971), 191–207.

—— 'The Ethical and Juridical Status of Constraints in War', *Military Law Review*, 55 (1972), 169–85.

—— 'Wars of National Liberation and War Criminality', in Michael Howard (ed.), *Restraints on War* (Oxford: Oxford Univ. Press, 1979), 135–62.

—— 'The Implementation and Enforcement of the Geneva Conventions of 1949 and of the Two Additional Protocols of 1978', *Recueil des cours*, 164 (1979-III), 1–54.

—— Letter to author, 21 Mar. 1985.

DUGARD, C. J. R., 'The Organization of African Unity and Colonialism: An Inquiry into the Plea of Self-defence as a Justification for the Use of Force in the Eradication of Colonialism', *ICLQ*, 16 (1967), 157–90.

—— 'South West Africa and the "Terrorist Trial" ', *AJIL*, 64 (1970), 19–41.

—— 'SWAPO: The *Jus ad bellum* and the *Jus in bello*', *South African Law Journal*, 93 (1976), 144–58.

—— *Human Rights and the South African Legal Order* (Princeton, NJ: Princeton Univ. Press, 1978).

EDGELL, ALVIN G., 'Nigeria/Biafra', in Morris Davis (ed.), *Civil Wars and the Politics of International Relief: Africa, South Asia and the Caribbean* (London: Praeger, 1975), 50–73.

EGZIABHER, DAWIT G., Director, Political Department, Organization of African Unity, Letter to author, 29 Nov. 1984.

—— Head of Decolonization and Sanctions Division, Organization of African Unity, Letter to author, 11 Mar. 1985.

EIDE, ASBIORN, 'The New Humanitarian Law in Non-international Armed Conflict', in vol. i of Antonio Cassese (ed.), *The New Humanitarian Law of Armed Conflict* (Naples: Editoriale Scientifica, 1979), 277–309.

—— 'Sovereign Equality Versus the Global Military Structure: Two Competing Approaches to World Order', in vol. i of Antonio Cassese (ed.), *The New Humanitarian Law of Armed Conflict* (Naples: Editoriale Scientifica, 1979), 21–40.

ELDER, DAVID A., 'The Historical Background of Common Article 3 of the Geneva Conventions of 1949', *Case Western Reserve JIL*, 2 (1979), 37–70.

EMERSON, RUPERT, *From Empire to Nation: The Rise to Self-assertion of Asian and African Peoples* (Cambridge, Mass.: Harvard Univ. Press, 1960).

—— 'Self-determination', *ASIL*, 60 (1966), 35–41.

—— 'Self-determination', *AJIL*, 65 (1971), 459–75.

EPPSTEIN, JOHN, *The Catholic Tradition of the Law of Nations* (London: Burns, Oates and Washbourne, 1935).

The Estate of Jean-Baptiste Caire (France) v. *United Mexican States*, decision No. 33 of the French–Mexican Claims Commission, 7 June 1929, in vol. v of *Reports of International Arbitral Awards* (New York: UN, n.d.), 516–34.

Ex parte Quirin, 317 US 1 1942, *AJIL*, 37 (1943), 152–71.

FALK, RICHARD A., 'Janus Tormented: The International Law of Internal War', in James N. Rosenau (ed.), *International Aspects of Civil Strife* (Princeton, NJ: Princeton Univ. Press, 1964), 185–248.

—— 'On the Quasi-legislative Competence of the General Assembly', Editorial Comment, *AJIL*, 60 (1966), 782–91.

—— 'The International Regulation of Internal Violence in the Developing Countries', *ASIL*, 60 (1966), 58–67.

—— *Legal Order in a Violent World* (Princeton, NJ: Princeton Univ. Press, 1968).

—— (ed.), *The International Law of Civil War* (London: Johns Hopkins Press, 1971).

—— 'Intervention and National Liberation', in Hedley Bull (ed.), *Intervention in World Politics* (Oxford: Clarendon Press, 1984), 119–34.

FARER, TOM J., 'Humanitarian Law and Armed Conflicts: Toward the Definition of "International Armed Conflict" ', *Columbia LR*, 71 (1971), 37–72.

—— 'The Laws of War 25 Years After Nuremberg', *International Conciliation*, 583 (May 1971).

FARINA, NICOLO, 'The Attitude of the People's Republic of China', in Antonio Cassese (ed.), *The New Humanitarian Law of Armed Conflict* (Naples: Editoriale Scientifica, 1979), 445–57.

FAWCETT, J. E. S., 'Security Council Resolutions on Rhodesia', *BYIL*, 41 (1965–6), 103–21.

—— *The Law of Nations*, 2nd edn. (Harmondsworth: Penguin, 1971).

FEINBERG, NATHAN, *The Arab–Israel Conflict in International Law* (Jerusalem: Hebrew University, 1970).

FENWICK, CHARLES G., 'Can Civil Wars be Brought Under the Control of International Law?', *AJIL*, 32 (1938), 538–42.

FINGER, SEYMOUR M., 'A New Approach to Colonial Problems at the United Nations', *International Organization*, 26 (1972), 143–53.

FIRMAGE, EDWIN BROWN, 'National Liberation and the Third World', in John Norton Moore (ed.), *Law and Civil War in the Modern World* (London: Johns Hopkins Univ. Press, 1974), 304–47.

FLORY, MAURICE, 'Algérie et droit international', *AFDI*, 5 (1959), 817–44.

—— 'Négotiation ou dégagement en Algérie', *AFDI*, 7 (1961), 836–55.

FONTEYNE, JEAN-PIERRE, 'Forcible Self-help by States to Protect Human Rights: Recent Views from the UN', in Richard B. Lillich (ed.), *Humanitarian Intervention and the UN* (Charlottesville: Univ. Press of Virginia, 1973), 197–221.

FORD, W. J., 'Resistance Movements and International Law', 3 parts, *IRRC*, 79–81 (1967).

—— 'Members of Resistance Movements', *Netherlands International LR*, 24 (1977), 92–108.

FORSYTHE, DAVID P., 'The 1974 Diplomatic Conference on Humanitarian Law: Some Observations', *AJIL*, 69 (1975), 77–91.

—— 'Support for a Humanitarian *Jus in bello*', *International Lawyer*, 11 (1977), 723–8.

FRALEIGH, ARNOLD, 'The Algerian Revolution as a Case Study in International Law', in Richard Falk (ed.), *The International Law of Civil War* (London: Johns Hopkins Univ. Press, 1971), 179–243.

FRANCK, THOMAS M., 'The Stealing of the Sahara', *AJIL*, 70 (1976), 694–721.

—— and RODLEY, NIGEL S., 'After Bangladesh: The Law of Humanitarian Intervention by Military Force', *AJIL*, 67 (1973), 275–305.

FREY-WOUTERS, ELLEN, 'The Relevance of Regional Arrangements to Internal Conflicts in the Developing World', in John Norton Moore (ed.), *Law and Civil War in the Modern World* (London: Johns Hopkins Press, 1974), 458–96.

FRIEDLANDER, ROBERT A., 'Sowing the Wind: Rebellion and Violence in Theory and Practice', *Denver JIL and Policy*, 6 (1976–7), 83–93.

FRIEDMANN, WOLFGANG, *The Changing Structure of International Law* (London: Stevens and Sons, 1964).

—— 'Intervention, Civil War and the Role of International Law', *ASIL*, 59 (1965), 67–75.

—— 'General Course in Public International Law', *Recueil des cours*, 127 (1969-II), 41–246.

GALLOWAY, L. THOMAS, *Recognizing Foreign Governments: The Practice of the United Nations* (Washington: Am. Enterprise Institute, 1978).

GANN, LEWIS H., *Guerrillas in History* (Stanford: Hoover Institution Press, 1971).

GARDINER, Lord, *Minority Report of the Committee of Privy Councilors Appointed to Consider Authorized Procedures for the Interrogation of Persons Suspected of Terrorism*, originally published by HMSO Cmnd. 4901, Mar. 1972 (Dublin: Amnesty International, 1972).

GARNER, JAMES W., 'Questions of International Law in the Spanish Civil War', Editorial Comment, *AJIL*, 31 (1937), 66–73.

—— 'Recognition of Belligerency', *AJIL*, 32 (1938), 106–13.

GASSER, HANS-PETER, 'International Non-international Armed Conflicts: Case Studies of Afghanistan, Kampuchea and Lebanon', *Am. Univ. LR*, 31 (1982), 911–33.

GIBSON, RICHARD, *African Liberation Movements: Contemporary Struggles Against White Minority Rule* (London: Oxford Univ. Press, 1972).

GILLESPIE, JOAN, *Algeria: Rebellion and Revolution* (London: Ernest Benn, 1960).

GINSBURGS, GEORGE G. ' "Wars of National Liberation" and the Modern Law of Nations: The Soviet Thesis', *Law and Contemporary Problems*, 29 (1964), 910–42.

GOODRICH, LELAND, HAMBRO, EDVARD, and SIMONS, ANNE, *Charter of the United Nations: Commentary and Documents*, 3rd rev. edn. (London: Columbia Univ. Press, 1969).

GORELICK, ROBERT E., 'Wars of National Liberation: Jus ad bellum', *Case Western Reserve JIL*, 11 (1979), 71–93.

GRAHAM, DAVID E., 'The 1974 Diplomatic Conference on the Law of War: A Victory for Political Causes and a Return to the "Just War" Concept of the Eleventh Century', *Washington and Lee LR*, 32 (1975), 25–63.

GRAHL-MADSEN, ATLE, 'Decolonization: The Modern Version of a "Just War" ', *German Yearbook of IL*, 22 (1979), 255–73.

GREEN, L. C., 'Self-determination and Settlement of the Arab–Israeli Conflict', *ASIL*, 65 (1971), 40–8.

GREENSPAN, MORRIS, *The Modern Law of Land Warfare* (Los Angeles: Univ. of California Press, 1959).

GREIG, D. W., *International Law*, 2nd edn. (London: Butterworth, 1976).

GROS ESPIELL, HECTOR, *Implementation of UN Resolutions Relating to the Right of Peoples Under Colonial and Alien Domination to Self-determination*, A Study for the Sub-commission on Prevention of Discrimination and Protection of Minorities of the Commission on Human Rights, UN Doc. E/CN.4/Sub. 2/390/ and Corr. 1 and Add. 1, 22 June 1977.

GROTIUS, HUGO, *De jure belli ac pacis libri tres*, ed. James Brown Scott, trans. Francis W. Kelsey, vol. ii (Oxford: Clarendon Press, 1925).

GUTTERIDGE, J. A. C., *The United Nations in a Changing World* (Manchester: Manchester Univ. Press, 1969).

HACKWORTH, GREEN H., *Digest of International Law*, vol. i (Washington: GPO, 1940).

HALL, WILLIAM EDWARD, *A Treatise on International Law*, 5th edn., ed. Atlay (Oxford: Clarendon Press, 1904); 8th edn., ed. A. Pearce Higgins (Oxford: Clarendon Press, 1924).

HANNAI, JACOB, SWAPO Chief Representative in Western Europe, personal interview, 15 Mar. 1985.

HATSCHEK, JULIUS, *An Outline of International Law* (London: Bell and Sons, 1930).

HENRIKSEN, THOMAS H., 'People's War in Angola, Mozambique and Guinea-Bissau', *Journal of Modern African Studies*, 14 (Sept. 1976), 377–99.

HIGGINS, ROSALYN, 'The Legal Limits to the Use of Force by Sovereign States: United Nations Practice', *BYIL*, 37 (1961), 269–319.

—— *The Development of International Law Through the Political Organs of the United Nations* (London: Oxford Univ. Press, 1963).

—— 'Internal War and International Law', in vol. iii of C. E. Black and R. A. Falk (eds.), *The Future of the International Legal Order* (Princeton, NJ: Princeton Univ. Press, 1971), 81–121.

—— 'International Law and Civil Conflict', in Evan Luard (ed.), *The International Regulation of Civil Wars* (London: Thames and Hudson, 1972), 160–86.

HORNE, ALISTAIR, *A Savage War of Peace: Algeria 1954–1962* (London: Macmillan, 1977).

HOUBEN, PIET-HEIN, 'Principles of International Law Concerning Friendly Relations and Co-operation Among States', *AJIL*, 61 (1967), 703–36.

HOWARD, MICHAEL, 'Tempermenta belli: Can War Be Controlled?', in Michael Howard (ed.), *Restraints on War* (Oxford: Oxford Univ. Press, 1979).

HYDE, CHARLES CHENEY, *International Law Chiefly as Interpreted and Applied by the United States*, 2nd rev. edn., vol. i (Boston: Little, Brown and Co., 1947).

International Commission of Jurists, 'The Western Sahara', *ICJ Review*, 32 (June 1984), 25–32.

—— 'South Africa', *ICJ Review*, 20 (June 1978), 15–18.

—— 'Eritrea's Claim to Self-determination', *ICJ Review*, 26 (June 1981), 8–14.

—— 'Lebanon', *ICJ Review*, 31 (Dec. 1983), 9–16.

—— 'East Timor and Self-determination', *ICJ Review*, 32 (June 1984), 1–6.

—— 'South Africa', *ICJ Review*, 33 (Dec. 1984), 24–7.

International Commission to Enquire into Reported Violations of International

Law by Israel During its Invasion of the Lebanon, 28 Aug.–29 Nov. 1982, *Israel in Lebanon* (London: Ithaca Press, 1983).

International Committee of the Red Cross, *The ICRC and the Algerian Conflict* (Geneva: ICRC, 1962).

—— *ICRC Activities in the Middle-east, 1967–1979: Extracts from ICRC Annual Reports* (Geneva: ICRC, 1979).

—— 'Protection and Assistance in Situations not Covered by International Humanitarian Law', Comments by the ICRC, *IRRC*, 205 (July–Aug. 1978), 210–14.

—— *Summary of the Activities of the International Committee of the Red Cross: 1983* (Geneva: ICRC. 1983).

—— *Survey of Current Activities* (Geneva: ICRC, Oct. 1984).

JASTER, ROBERT S., 'A Regional Security Role for Africa's Front-line States: Experience and Prospects', *Adelphi Papers*, No. 188 (London: IISS, Spring 1983).

JENKS, C. W., 'The Legal Personality of International Organizations', *BYIL*, 22 (1945), 267–75.

JENNINGS, R. Y., *The Acquisition of Territory in International Law* (Manchester: Manchester Univ. Press, 1963).

JENNINGS, WILLIAM IVOR, *The Approach to Self-government* (Cambridge: Cambridge Univ. Press, 1956).

JESSUP, PHILIP C., *A Modern Law of Nations* (n.p.: Archon Books, 1968).

JOHNSON, D. N. H., 'The Effect of Resolutions of the General Assembly of the United Nations', *BYIL*, 32 (1955–6), 97–122.

JOHNSON, HAROLD S., *Self-determination Within the Community of Nations* (Leiden: A. W. Sijthoff, 1967).

JOHNSON, JAMES TURNER, *Ideology, Reason, and the Limitation of War: Religious and Secular Concepts 1200–1740* (Princeton: Princeton Univ. Press, 1975).

—— *Just War Tradition and the Restraint of War* (Princeton, NJ: Princeton Univ. Press, 1981).

KAHIN, GEORGE M., *Nationalism and Revolution in Indonesia* (Ithaca, NY: Cornell Univ. Press, 1952).

KALSHOVEN, FRITS, 'Human Rights, the Law of Armed Conflicts and Reprisals', *IRRC*, 11 (Apr. 1971), 183–92.

—— 'Reaffirmation and Development of International Humanitarian Law Applicable in Armed Conflicts: The First Session of the Diplomatic Conference, Geneva, 20 Feb.–29 Mar. 1974', *NYIL*, 5 (1974), 3–34.

—— 'Reaffirmation and Development of International Humanitarian Law Applicable in Armed Conflicts: The Diplomatic Conference, Geneva, 1974–1977', *NYIL*, 8 (1977), 107–35.

KAMANU, ONYEONORO S., 'Secession and the Right of Self-determination: An OAU Dilemma', *Journal of Modern African Studies*, 12 (1974), 355–76.

KAPUNGU, LEONARD T., 'The OAU's Support for the Liberation of Southern Africa', in Yassin El-Ayouty (ed.), *The Organization of African Unity After Ten Years: Comparative Perspectives* (London: Praeger, 1975), 135–51.

KAY, DAVID A., 'The Politics of Decolonization: The New Nations and the UN Political Process', *International Organization*, 21 (1967), 786–811.

KEEN, M. H., *The Laws of War in the Late Middle Ages* (London: Routledge and Son, 1965).

KELLEY, JOSEPH B. and PELLETIER, GEORGE A., 'Theories of Emergency Government', *South Dakota Law Review*, 2 (1966), 42–69.

—— 'Legal Control of Populations in Subversive Warfare', *Virginia JIL*, 5 (1965), 174–200.

KELSEN, HANS, *Principles of International Law*, 2nd edn., ed. Robert W. Tucker (London: Holt, Rinehart and Winston, 1966).

KHAIRALLAH, DAOUD L., *Insurrection Under International Law: With Emphasis on the Rights and Duties of Insurgents* (Beirut: Lebanese Univ., 1973).

KOSIRNIK, RENE, Head of Legal Division, ICRC, personal interview, 9 Apr. 1985.

KOSSOY, EDWARD, *Living With Guerrilla: Guerrilla as a Legal Problem and a Political Fact* (Geneva: Librairie Droz, 1976).

—— personal interview, 3 Apr. 1985.

LANDE, GABRIELLA ROSNER, 'The Changing Effectiveness of General Assembly Resolutions', in Richard A. Falk and Saul H. Mendlovitz (eds.), *The United Nations*, vol. iii of *The Strategy of World Order* (New York: World Law Fund, 1966), 227–35.

LANGER, ROBERT, *Seizure of Territory: The Stimson Doctrine and Related Principles in Legal Theory and Diplomatic Practice* (Princeton: Princeton Univ. Press, 1947).

LAUTERPACHT, HERSCH, *Recognition in International Law* (Cambridge: Cambridge Univ. Press, 1947).

—— 'The Subjects of the Law of Nations', *LQR*, 63 (1947), 438–60.

—— 'Voting Procedure on Questions Relating to Reports and Petitions Concerning the Territory of South-west Africa', Separate Opinion, ICJ Rep. (1955), 90–123.

—— *International Law and Human Rights* (n.p.: Archon Books, 1968).

Lawless v. *Republic of Ireland*, Doc. A63.550, 1 July 1961, *Yearbook on the European Convention of Human Rights* (1961), 438–89.

LAWRENCE, T. J., *The Principles of International Law*, 7th edn., rev. Percy H. Winfield (London: Macmillan, 1923).

LAZARUS, CLAUDE, 'Le Statut des mouvements de libération nationale à l'organisation des Nations Unies', *AFDI*, 20 (1974), 173–200.

Leah Zemel v. *Ministry of Defense and Commander of Ansar Prison (Israel)*, Israeli High Court Case 593/82, May 1983.

Legal Consequences for States of the Continued Presence of South Africa in Namibia (South West Africa) Notwithstanding Security Council Resolution 276 (1970), Advisory Opinion, ICJ Rep. (1971), 15–345.

LEIFER, MICHAEL, *Indonesia's Foreign Policy* (London: George Allen and Unwin, 1983).

LEVI, WERNER, *Contemporary International Law: A Concise Introduction* (Boulder, Col: Westview Press, 1979).

LEVIE, HOWARD S., *Protection of War Victims: Protocol I to the 1949 Geneva Conventions*, 4 vols. (Dobbs Ferry, NY: Oceana Publications, 1979).

LIEBER, FRANCIS, *Instructions for the Government of Armies of the United States in the Field* (New York: D. Van Nostrand, 1863).

LILLICH, RICHARD B., 'Humanitarian Intervention: A Reply to Ian Brownlie and a Plea for Constructive Alternatives', in John Norton Moore (ed.), *Law and Civil War in the Modern World* (London: Johns Hopkins Univ. Press, 1974), 229–51.

The S. S. Lotus, *Publications of the Permanent Court of International Justice*, Ser. A. No. 10, judgment 9, 1927.

LUARD, EVAN, 'Civil Conflicts in Modern International Relations', in Evan Luard (ed.), *The International Regulation of Civil Wars*, (London: Thames and Hudson, 1972), 7–25.

LYSAGHT, CHARLES, 'The Attitude of Western Countries', in vol. i of Antonio Cassese (ed.), *The New Humanitarian Law of Armed Conflict* (Naples: Editoriale Scientifica, 1979), 349–85.

McDOUGAL, MYERS S. and REISMAN, W. MICHAEL, 'Rhodesia and the United Nations: The Lawfulness of International Concern', *AJIL*, 62 (1968), 1–19.

MacFARLANE, S. N., 'The Idea of National Liberation' (D.Phil. Thesis, Oxford, 1982).

McNEMAR, DONALD W., 'The Post-independence War in the Congo', in Richard A. Falk (ed.), *The International Law of Civil War*, (London: Johns Hopkins Univ. Press, 1971), 244–302.

MALLISON, W. T. and MALLISON, S. V., 'An International Law Appraisal of the Juridical Characteristics of the Resistance of the People of Palestine: The Struggle for Human Rights', *Revue Égyptienne de droit international*, 28 (1972), 1–19.

—— 'The Juridical Status of Privileged Combatants Under the Geneva Protocol of 1977 Concerning International Conflicts', *Law and Contemporary Problems*, 42 (1978), 4–31.

—— *Armed Conflict in Lebanon, 1982: Humanitarian Law in a Real World Setting* (Washington: Am. Ed. Trust, 1983).

MANI, V. S., 'The 1971 War on the Indian Sub-continent and International Law', *Indian JIL*, 12 (1972), 83–99.

MAREK, KRYSTYNA, *Identity and Continuity of States in Public International Law* (Geneva: Librairie E. Droz, 1954).

Military Prosecutor v. *Omar Muhamed Kassem* et al., 1 S J M C 402, 13 Apr. 1969, in *Israel Yearbook on Human Rights*, 1 (1971), 456–60.

MILLER, LINDA B., *World Order and Local Disorder* (Princeton, NJ: Princeton Univ. Press, 1967).

MIYAZAKI, SHIGEKI, 'The Application of the New Humanitarian Law', *IRRC*, 217 (July-Aug. 1980), 184–92.

Mohamed Ali and another v. *Public Prosecutor*, 3 All ER 499 (P C) 1968.

MONDLANE, EDUARDO. *The Struggle for Mozambique* (Harmondsworth: Penguin, 1969).

MOORE, JOHN BASSETT, *A Digest of International Law*, vol. i (Washington: GPO, 1906).

—— *International Law and Some Current Illusions and Other Essays* (New York: Macmillan, 1924).

MOORE, JOHN NORTON, 'The Control of Foreign Intervention in Internal Conflict', *Virginia JIL*, 9 (1969), 209–342.

—— 'A Theoretical Overview of the Laws of War in a Post-Charter World, with Emphasis on the Challenge of Civil Wars, "Wars of National Liberation", Mixed Civil-international Wars, and Terrorism', *Am. Univ. LR*, 31 (1982), 841–7.

MOREILLON, JACQUES, 'The International Committee of the Red Cross and the Protection of Political Detainees', *IRRC*, 169 (Apr. 1975), 171–83.

MOWER, A. GLENN, 'Observer Countries: Quasi Members of the United Nations', *International Organization*, 20 (1966), 267–83.

NALDI, J., 'The Organization of African Unity and the Saharan Arab Democratic Republic', *Journal of African Law*, 26 (1982), 152–62.

NANDA, VED P., 'Self-determination in International Law: The Tragic Tale of Two Cities—Islamabad (West Pakistan) and Dacca (East Pakistan)', *AJIL*, 66 (1972), 321–36.

NAWAZ, M. K., 'Editorial Comment: Bangla Desh and International Law', *Indian JIL*, 11 (1971), 251–66.

NURICK, L., and BARRETT, R. W., 'Legality of Guerrilla Forces Under the Laws of War', *AJIL*, 40 (1946), 563–83.

O'BRIEN, WILLIAM V.,'The *Jus in bello* in Revolutionary War and Counter-insurgency', *Virginia JIL*, 18 (1978), 193–242.

Official Records of the Diplomatic Conference on the Reaffirmation and Development of International Humanitarian Law Applicable in Armed Conflicts, Geneva (1974–1977), 17 vols. (Berne: Federal Political Department, 1978).

OKEKE, CHRIS N., *Controversial Subjects of Contemporary International Law* (Rotterdam: Rotterdam Univ. Press, 1974).

OPPENHEIM, L., *International Law: A Treatise*, 6th edn., 2 vols., ed. H. Lauterpacht (London: Longman, Green and Co., 1940).

—— *International Law: A Treatise*, 7th edn., 2 vols., ed. H. Lauterpacht (London: Longman, 1963).

O'ROURKE, VERNON A., 'Recognition of Belligerency and the Spanish War', *AJIL*, 31 (1937), 398–413.

PADELFORD, NORMAN, 'International Law and the Spanish Civil War', *AJIL*, 31 (1937), 226–43.

PETREN, S., *Fisheries Jurisdiction Case*, Dissenting Opinion, ICJ Rep. (1974), 151–63.

PICTET, JEAN S. (ed.), *The Geneva Conventions of 12 August 1949: Commentary*, 4 vols. (Geneva: ICRC, 1952).

—— *Humanitarian Law and the Protection of War Victims* (Leiden: A. W. Sijthoff, 1975).

PINTO, ROGER, 'Les Règles du droit international concernant la guerre civile', *Recueil des cours*, 114 (1965-I), 455–553.

POMERANCE, MICHLA, *Self-determination in Law and Practice: The New Doctrine in the United Nations* (London: Martinus Nijhoff, 1982).

Prize Cases, 2 Black 635, US Sup. Ct. 1862.

Reparation for Injuries Suffered in the Service of the United Nations, ICJ Rep. (1949), 173–220.

RIESMAN, MICHAEL, 'Humanitarian Intervention to Protect the Ibos', in Richard Lillich (ed.), *Humanitarian Intervention and the United Nations* (Charlottesville: Univ. Press of Virginia, 1973), 167–95.

Right of Passage Over Indian Territory, ICJ Rep. (1960), 6–144.

ROBERTS, ADAM, and GUELFF, RICHARD (eds.), *Documents on the Laws of War* (Oxford: Clarendon Press, 1982).

ROLING, BERT V. A., 'Criminal Responsibility for Violations of the Laws of War', *Revue belge de droit international*, 12 (1976), 8–26.

RONZITTI, N., 'Resort to Force in Wars of National Liberation', in Antonio Cassese (ed.), *Current Problems of International Law: Essays on UN Law and on the*

Law of Armed Conflict (Milan: Dott. A. Guiffre, 1975), 319–55.

—— 'Wars of National Liberation: A Legal Definition', *Italian Yearbook of International Law*, 1 (1975), 192–205.

ROSAS, ALLAN, *The Legal Status of Prisoners of War: A Study in International Humanitarian Law Applicable in Armed Conflicts* (Helsinki: Suomalainen Tiedeakatemia, 1976).

ROSENBLAD, ESBJORN, *International Humanitarian Law of Armed Conflict: Some Aspects of the Principle of Distinction and Related Problems* (Geneva: Institut Henry-Dunant, 1979).

ROUSSEAU, CHARLES, 'Chronique des faits internationaux: Guinée-Bissau', *Revue générale de droit international public*, 78 (Oct.–Dec. 1974), 1166–71.

ROVINE, ARTHUR W., *Digest of United States Practice in International Law* (Washington: GPO, 1975).

RUBIN, ALFRED P., 'Terrorism, "Grave Breaches" and the 1977 Geneva Protocols', *ASIL*, 74 (1980), 192–6.

RUSSELL, FREDERICK H., *The Just War in the Middle Ages* (Cambridge: Cambridge Univ. Press, 1975).

SAGAY, I., 'The Legal Status of Freedom Fighters in Africa', *Eastern Africa LR*, 6 (1973), 15–29.

SALMON, J. A., 'La Conférence diplomatique sur la réaffirmation et le développment du droit international humanitaire et les guerres de libération nationale', *Revue belge de droit international*, 12 (1976), 27–52, and Part II, 13 (1977), 353–78.

—— and VINCINEAU, MICHEL, 'La Pratique du pouvoir exécutif et le contrôle des chambres législatives en matière de droit international (1973–1974): Guinée Bissau', *Revue belge de droit international*, 12 (1976), 334–6.

SCHACHTER, OSCAR, 'The United Nations and Internal Conflict', in John Norton Moore (ed.), *Law and Civil War in the Modern World* (London: Johns Hopkins Press, 1974), 401–45.

SCHINDLER, DIETRICH, 'State of War, Belligerency, Armed Conflict', in vol. i of Antonio Cassese (ed.), *The New Humanitarian Law of Armed Conflict* (Naples: Editoriale Scientifica, 1979), 3–20.

—— 'The Different Types of Armed Conflicts According to the Geneva Conventions and Protocols', *Recueil des cours*, 163 (1979-II), 116–63.

—— 'Human Rights and Humanitarian Law: Interrelationship of the Laws', *Am. Univ. LR*, 31 (1982), 935–43.

—— 'International Humanitarian Law and Internationalized Internal Armed Conflicts', *IRRC*, 230 (Sept.–Oct. 1982), 255–64.

SCHUTTE, J. E., 'The Applicability of the Geneva Conventions on the Protection of War Victims and Protocol I to the Relation Between a Contracting Party and its own Nationals', International Institute of Humanitarian Law, VIIth Round Table on Current Problems, San Remo, 8–12 Sept. 1981.

SCHWARZENBERGER, GEORG, *A Manual of International Law*, 1st edn. (London: Stevens and Sons, 1947).

—— 'The Protection of Human Rights in British State Practice', in George W. Keeton and Georg Schwarzenberger (eds.), *Current Legal Problems*, vol. i (London: Stevens and Sons, 1948), 152–69.

—— 'International Jus cogens?' *Texas LR*, 43 (1965), 445–78.

—— *International Law as Applied by International Courts and Tribunals*, vol. i of *International Law* (London: Stevens and Sons, 1968).

—— 'Human Rights and Guerrilla Warfare', *Israel Yearbook on Human Rights*, 1 (1971), 246–57.

—— and ABROWN, E.D., *A Manual of International Law*, 6th edn. (Abingdon: Professional Books, 1976).

SCOTT, JAMES BROWN (ed.), *The Reports to the Hague Conferences of 1899 and 1907* (Oxford: Clarendon Press, 1917).

SETON-WATSON, HUGH, *Nations and States* (London: Methuen, 1977).

SHAMGAR, MEIR, 'Legal Concepts and Problems of the Israeli Military Government: The Initial Stage', in vol. i of Meir Shamgar (ed.), *Military Government in the Territories Administered by Israel: 1967–1980* (Jerusalem: Hebrew Univ. Press, 1982), 13–60.

SILVERBURG, SANFORD R., 'The Palestine Liberation Organization in the United Nations: Implications for International Law and Relations', *Israel Law Review*, 12 (1977), 365–92.

SIM, RICHARD, 'Kurdistan: The Search for Recognition', *Conflict Studies*, 224 (London: Institute for the Study of Conflict, 1980).

SINHA, S. PRAKESH, 'Perspective of the Newly Independent States on the Binding Quality of International Law', *ICLQ*, 14 (1965), 121–31.

—— 'Has Self-determination become a Principle of International Law Today?', *Indian JIL*, 14 (1974), 332–61.

SIOTIS, JEAN, *Le Droit de la guerre et les conflits armés d'un caractère non-international* (Paris: Librairie Générale de Droit et de Jurisprudence, 1958).

SLOAN, F. B., 'The Binding Force of a "Recommendation" of the General Assembly of the United Nations', *BYIL*, 25 (1948), 1–33.

SMITH, H. A., *Great Britain and the Law of Nations*, vol. i (London: P. S. King and Son, 1932).

SOHN, LOUIS B., *United Nations Law*, 2nd rev. edn. (Brooklyn: The Foundation Press, 1967).

STARKE, J. G., *An Introduction to International Law*, 5th edn. (London: Butterworth, 1963).

STASSEN, J. C., 'Intervention in Internal Wars: Traditional Norms and Contemporary Trends', *South African YIL*, 3 (1977), 65–84.

STONE, JULIUS, *The Legal Controls of International Conflict*, rev. edn. (Sydney: Maitland, 1959).

SUREDA, A. RIGO, *The Evolution of the Right of Self-determination: A Study of UN Practice* (Leiden: A. W. Sijthoff, 1973).

SUTER, KIETH, *An International Law of Guerrilla Warfare: The Global Politics of Law-making* (London: Frances Pinter, 1984).

SWINORSKI, CHRISTOPHE (ed.), *Studies and Essays on International Humanitarian Law and Red Cross Principles in Honor of Jean Pictet* (The Hague: Martinus Nijhoff, 1984).

Swiss Federal Department of Foreign Affairs, Letter to author, 30 Apr. 1985.

—— Letter to author, 10 Feb. 1987.

TAUBENFELD, HOWARD J., 'The Applicability of the Laws of War in Civil Wars', in John Norton Moore (ed.), *Law and Civil War in the Modern World* (Baltimore: Johns Hopkins Univ. Press, 1974).

TOMAN, JÏRI, 'La Conception soviétique des guerres de libération nationale', in Antonio Cassese (ed.), *Current Problems of International Law* (Milan: A. Giuffre, 1975), 355–75.

TRAININ, I. P., 'Questions of Guerrille Warfare in the Law of War', *AJIL*, 40 (1946), 534–62.

TRAVERS, PATRICK J., 'The Legal Effect of UN Action in Support of the Palestine Liberation Organization and the National Liberation Movements of Africa', *Harvard ILJ*, 17 (1976), 561–80.

TUCKER, ROBERT W., *The Just War: A Study in Contemporary American Doctrine* (Westport, Conn.: Greenwood Press, 1960).

UDECHUKU, E. C., *Liberation of Dependent Peoples in International Law*, 2nd edn. (London: African Publications Bureau, 1978).

UMOZURIKE, U. O., 'Self-determination in International Law' (D.Phil. Thesis, Oxford, 1969).

United Nations, Center Against Apartheid, *International Year of Mobilization for Sanctions Against South Africa 1982: Programme of Action* (New York: United Nations, 1982).

—— *The United Nations and Decolonization: Highlights of United Nations Action in Support of Independence for Colonial Countries and Peoples*, UN Doc. O: UN/I. 1980 (20) (New York: UN, 1980).

VALLAT, FRANCIS A., 'The Competence of the UN General Assembly', *Recueil des cours*, 97 (1959-II), 209–92.

VATTEL, EMMERICH DE, *The Law of Nations*, trans. Joseph Chitty (Philadelphia: T. & J. W. Johnson, 1863).

VERHOEVEN, JOE, *La Reconnaissance internationale dans la pratique contemporaine*, (Paris: Éditions A. Pedone, 1975).

VERRIER, ANTHONY, *International Peacekeeping: United Nations Forces in a Troubled World* (New York: Penguin, 1981).

VERWEY, WIL D., 'Decolonization and Ius ad bellum: A Case Study on the Impact of the United Nations General Assembly on International Law', in Robert J. Akkerman (ed.), *Declarations on Principles: A Quest for Universal Peace* (Leiden: A. W. Sijthoff, 1977), 121–40.

—— 'The International Hostages Convention and National Liberation Movements', *AJIL*, 75 (1981), 69–92.

VERZIJL, J. H. W., *International Law in Historical Perspective*, vol. i (Leiden: A. W. Sijthoff, 1968).

VEUTHEY, MICHEL, 'The Red Cross and Non-international Conflicts', *IRRC*, 10 (Aug. 1970), 411–23.

—— 'La Guérilla: Le Problème du traitement des prisonniers', *Annales d'études internationales*, 3 (1972), 119–36.

—— *Guérilla et droit humanitaire* (Geneva: Institut Henry-Dunant, 1976).

—— 'Implementation and Enforcement of Humanitarian Law and Human Rights Law in Non-international Armed Conflicts: The Role of the International Committee of the Red Cross', *Am. Univ. LR*, 33 (1983), 83–97.

—— 'Guerrilla Warfare and Humanitarian Law', *IRRC*, 234 (May–June 1983), 115–37.

WALDOCK, HUMPHREY, 'General Course on Public International Law', *Recueil des cours*, 106 (1962-II), 1–251.

WAMBAUGH, SARAH, *A Monograph on Plebiscites: With a Collection of Official Documents* (London: Oxford Univ. Press, 1920).
—— *Plebiscites Since the World War*, 2 vols. (Washington: Carnegie Endowment for International Peace, 1933).
WEISBERG, HOWARD L., 'The Congo Crisis 1964: A Case Study in Humanitarian Intervention', *Virginia JIL*, 12 (1972), 261–76.
Western Sahara Advisory Opinion, ICJ Rep. (1975).
WHEATON, HENRY, *Elements of International Law*, the literal reproduction of the edn. of 1866 by Richard Henry Dana, ed. George G. Wilson (Oxford: Clarendon Press, 1936).
WIGHT, MARTIN, *Systems of States*, ed. Hedley Bull (Leicester: Leicester Univ. Press, 1977).
WILSON, DUNCAN, *Tito's Yugoslavia* (Cambridge: Cambridge Univ. Press, 1979).
WILSON, GEORGE G., 'The Guerrilla and the Lawful Combatant', *AJIL*, 37 (1943), 494–5.
WOLF, UDO, 'Prisoner-of-war Status and the National Liberation Struggles', *Intl. Rev. of Contemporary Law*, 1 (1984), 31–46.
WORTLEY, B. A., 'Observations on the Revision of the 1949 Geneva "Red Cross" Conventions', *BYIL*, 54 (1983), 143–66.
WRIGHT, QUINCY, *A Study of War*, 2 vols. (Chicago: Univ. of Chicago Press, 1942).
—— 'Recognition and Self-determination', *ASIL*, 48 (1954), 23–37.
—— 'The Legality of Intervention Under the United Nations Charter', *ASIL*, 51 (1957), 79–90.
—— 'US Intervention in the Lebanon', *AJIL*, 53 (1959), 112–25.
—— 'The Goa Incident', *AJIL*, 56 (1962), 617–32.

Index